普通高等教育"十二五"规划教材

通信工程专业英语

（第 2 版）

马丽华　李瑞欣　郑光威
徐志燕　李勇军　王豆豆　编著

北京邮电大学出版社
·北京·

内 容 提 要

本教材旨在拓展学生专业词汇量，熟悉本领域内的专业术语及专业英语的特殊语法，掌握专业英语翻译技巧。本教材不仅从理论上概括了英语翻译的主要技巧及写作的基本技巧，而且配合以大量的例句及实践性练习，通过"熟能生巧"的训练，培养学生对这些技巧和方法的灵活运用的能力。

全书共分五个部分。第一部分为专业英语基础知识，介绍了科技英语的特点、相关翻译理论、翻译方法以及写作。第二部分精心选择了20篇通信技术领域的文章进行通信工程专业英语的学习。第三部分为10篇相关文献阅读，可供有兴趣的学生自学。第四部分给出了全部课文的参考译文。第五部分的附录补充了常用数学名词和公式的英文表达方法。

本教材的内容由浅入深、选材广泛，适合作为大学通信工程专业三、四年级本科生的专业英语教材，教学中可根据具体教学要求进行内容的取舍。也可供研究生及广大工程技术人员使用。

图书在版编目(CIP)数据

通信工程专业英语/马丽华等编著．--2版．--北京：北京邮电大学出版社，2014.8(2018.1重印)
ISBN 978-7-5635-4034-1

Ⅰ.①通… Ⅱ.①马… Ⅲ.①通信工程—英语 Ⅳ.①H31

中国版本图书馆 CIP 数据核字(2014)第 138071 号

书　　　　名	通信工程专业英语(第2版)
著作责任者	马丽华　李瑞欣　郑光威　徐志燕　李勇军　王豆豆　编著
责 任 编 辑	陈岚岚
出 版 发 行	北京邮电大学出版社
社　　　　址	北京市海淀区西土城路 10 号(邮编:100876)
发 　行　 部	电话:010-62282185　传真:010-62283578
E-mail	publish@bupt.edu.cn
经　　　　销	各地新华书店
印　　　　刷	北京鑫丰华彩印有限公司
开　　　　本	787 mm×1 092 mm　1/16
印　　　　张	17
字　　　　数	420 千字
印　　　　数	4 001—5 000 册
版　　　　次	2009 年 8 月第 1 版　2014 年 8 月第 2 版　2018 年 1 月第 3 次印刷

ISBN 978-7-5635-4034-1　　　　　　　　　　　　　　　　　定　价:34.00 元

· 如有印装质量问题,请与北京邮电大学出版社发行部联系 ·

第2版前言

通信工程专业英语作为通信工程类专业的专业课程之一，是一门文理兼顾，语言应用与通信专业知识紧密结合的课程。本教材旨在拓展通信工程及相关专业学生的专业词汇量，使学生熟悉本领域内的专业术语及专业英语的特殊语法，掌握专业英语翻译技巧，用英文按要求写出专业应用文，初步具备用英文进行专业沟通的能力，为学生阅读外语文献资料和以后进一步从事本专业及相近专业的研究打下基础。本教材不仅从理论上概括了英语翻译的主要技巧及写作的基本技巧，而且配合以大量的例句及实践性练习，通过"熟能生巧"的训练，培养学生对这些技巧和方法的灵活运用的能力。

本教材在课文与文献的选材上一是注重基础理论，突出通信工程最本质的概念和主流技术，这些基本点是这门学科的基石，已经应用了多年并且还将应用下去；二是敏锐地捕捉前沿技术，这些技术还有长久的发展空间，其他新技术将在其基础之上成长。同时，兼顾了语言的规范性与纯正性，以及专业知识的广泛性与先进性、全面性与扩展性。

自2009年《通信工程专业英语》第一版出版后，已将近五年时间。承蒙出版社和读者的青睐，要求修改再版。按照技术的最新发展和读者的建议，再版时替换了1篇课文，去掉了2篇阅读文献，并给出所有课文的参考译文。全书共分五个部分。第一部分为专业英语基础知识，介绍了专业英语的特点、相关翻译理论、翻译方法以及写作等，有助于后续其他课程的学习和教学。第二部分精心选择了20篇通信技术领域的文章进行通信工程专业英语的学习。书中课文精选自国外知名大学近年编著的通信工程教科书或最新科技文献。所选课文行文流畅，概念准确，深入浅出，生僻词少，同时其内容又紧跟科学技术的发展，适于专业英语的学习。所选内容包含通信的基本理论与概念以及当前的主流通信技术，有助于把专业英语的学习与专业知识的学习结合起来，也有助于提高学生学习专业英语的兴趣，并学以致用。每篇课文之后列出了该课生词及词意，同时对课文中的难句、长句以及难以理解的词组进行了注释。单词和注释以专业词汇和专业性较强的句子为主，主要是让学生能正确理解书中所叙述的科技问题和阐述的观点。适量、形式多样的练习题利于教与学的组织与开展，也便于读者自我检查。第三部分为与本专业相关的英文科技文献阅读,可供有兴趣及学有余力的学生自学。第四部分给出了全部课文的参考译文。第五部分的附录补充了常用数学名词和公式的英文表达方法。

本书的再版由马丽华、李瑞欣、郑光威、徐志燕、王豆豆和李勇军共同编著,主编是马丽华和李瑞欣。本书引用了一些文献中发表的内容,它们使得本书能够反映通信技术发展的当前水平和专业英语的基础知识。在此,对这些成果的作者表示深深的感谢。同时感谢北京邮电大学出版社对本书再版付出的辛勤劳动。

由于经验不足,加之编者水平有限和时间仓促,书中的疏漏之处在所难免,敬请读者批评指正。

编 者

目 录

第一部分 专业英语基础知识

1.1 专业英语的特点 ·· 1
1.2 专业英语基础 ·· 2
   1.2.1 词汇 ··· 2
   1.2.2 翻译的准则与方法 ·· 4
   1.2.3 翻译中的变换 ··· 8
   1.2.4 长句的译法 ··· 11
   1.2.5 篇章的翻译 ··· 15
   1.2.6 数量和数学符号 ·· 17
1.3 科技论文写作指导 ··· 18
   1.3.1 科技论文的构成 ·· 18
   1.3.2 科技论文摘要的写作方法 ·· 19
   1.3.3 科技论文中总结的写法 ··· 21
1.4 文献检索简介 ·· 23
   1.4.1 文献检索的意义 ·· 23
   1.4.2 文献检索方法简介 ·· 23
   1.4.3 国内检索系统 ··· 25
   1.4.4 国际著名的六大检索系统 ·· 25

第二部分 通信技术

Unit 1: The Evolution of Communication Theories ··· 26
Unit 2: Digital Communication System ·· 32
Unit 3: Pulse Code Modulation ··· 40
Unit 4: Common-Channel Signaling ··· 49
Unit 5: The Sampling Theorem ·· 59
Unit 6: Evolution of Lightwave Systems ·· 63
Unit 7: Fiber Optic ·· 68

Unit 8: Synchronous Digital Hierarchy ································· 76
Unit 9: WDM ·· 81
Unit 10: Introduction to Computer Networks ······················· 88
Unit 11: Share the Internet Wealth ···································· 93
Unit 12: Introduction to 3G ··· 98
Unit 13: Comparison between GSM and CDMA ···················· 102
Unit 14: Packet Switching ··· 107
Unit 15: Residential Broadband ·· 113
Unit 16: Frame Relay and ATM ·· 119
Unit 17: Introduction to SPC Digital Telephone Exchanges ····· 125
Unit 18: Bluetooth ··· 132
Unit 19: Integrating RFID on Event-based Hemispheric Imaging for Internet of Things Assistive Applications ··· 139
Unit 20: Image & Video ·· 146

第三部分 英文文献阅读

READING 1: Lightwave System Components ······················· 153
READING 2: Fiber to the Home ·· 157
READING 3: Technologies on Fourth-Generation Mobile Communication ········ 160
READING 4: Polarization Mode Dispersion of Installed Fibers ··· 163
READING 5: High-Bandwidth Plastic Optical Fiber ··············· 167
READING 6: Asynchronous Transfer Mode (ATM) ················ 172
READING 7: Embedded Systems and Applications ················· 180
READING 8: The Added Advantages of Digital Technology ····· 186
READING 9: Open Systems Interconnection Reference Model ··· 190
READING 10: Computer Security ······································ 196

第四部分 参考译文

第 1 单元 通信理论的进化 ··· 202
第 2 单元 数字通信系统 ·· 204
第 3 单元 脉冲编码调制 ·· 207
第 4 单元 公共信道信令 ·· 212
第 5 单元 抽样定理 ··· 217
第 6 单元 光波系统的发展变革 ··· 219
第 7 单元 光纤 ··· 221

第 8 单元　同步数字系列 …………………………………………………… 224
第 9 单元　波分复用 ………………………………………………………… 226
第 10 单元　计算机网络简介 ………………………………………………… 227
第 11 单元　分享互联网财富 ………………………………………………… 230
第 12 单元　3G 简介 ………………………………………………………… 232
第 13 单元　GSM 与 CDMA 之比较 ………………………………………… 234
第 14 单元　分组交换 ………………………………………………………… 236
第 15 单元　居民宽带 ………………………………………………………… 239
第 16 单元　帧中继和异步传递模式 ………………………………………… 243
第 17 单元　程控数字电话交换机介绍 ……………………………………… 246
第 18 单元　蓝牙 ……………………………………………………………… 248
第 19 单元　基于事件的半球形成像 RFID 一体化物联网辅助应用 ……… 251
第 20 单元　图像和视频 ……………………………………………………… 254

第五部分　附　录

Ⅰ　数学公式的英语读法 ……………………………………………………… 258
Ⅱ　数的表示与读法 …………………………………………………………… 260

参考文献 …………………………………………………………………… 262

第一部分

专业英语基础知识

1.1 专业英语的特点

随着科学技术的飞速发展,各国之间在科技领域的交流也日趋广泛,外文专业文献大量涌现,各种国际学术会议也不断举行。目前,英语是世界上最通用的语言,通信方面的许多专业论文、书刊都用英文写作。所以,掌握好专业英语的阅读、翻译和书写的方法对我们了解最新的技术动态、吸收先进的科技成果是至关重要的。

为了在较短的时间内掌握好专业英语,首先要了解通信工程专业英语的三大特点。

1. 专业性

专业英语的专业性体现为它的特殊专业内容和特殊专业词汇。词汇是构成句子的基本元素,对词汇含义不能确定,就很难理解句子内容,甚至会出现可笑的、相反的结果。很多公共英语在专业领域内被赋予了专业含义,这就要求我们熟悉所学专业的知识,如 FTTC(光纤到路边)、Spontaneous Emission(自发辐射)、Bit-error Rate(误码率)。

新词汇也层出不穷,有的是随着本专业发展应运而生的,有的是借用公共英语中的词汇,有的是借用外来词汇,有的则是人为构成的词汇。有些专业词汇是需要对专业知识有相当的了解之后才会明白其意思的,例如:

Active optical network (AON) 有源光网络

Dispersion shifted fiber (DSF) 色散位移光纤

Add and drop multiplexer (ADM) 分插复用器

Erbium-doped fiber amplifier (EDFA) 掺铒光纤放大器

Multiplexer (MUX) 复用器

Pulse-code modulation (PCM) 脉冲编码调制

2. 灵活性

专业英语一般讲述的是通信系统的工作原理、设备、性能以及使用方法。这就决定了专业英语的客观性和灵活性。在学习过程中,尤其是在阅读专业文章时,必须尊重客观内容,不能主观想象。为了表示一种公允性和客观性,往往在句子结构和词性的使用上比较灵活。

如英语动词中有的表示动作,有的表示相对静止的状态。

(1) TV differs from radio in that it sends and receives pictures.

电视与无线电的区别在于电视能够发送和接收图像。(表示状态)

(2) These two RF signals are arranged to differ by a constant frequency by suitable

design of the RF amplifier and oscillator tuning circuit constants.

通过合理设计射频放大器及振荡调谐电路常数,这两个射频信号用于找出一个固定频率。(表示动作)

3. 简明性

为求简练,专业英语中常希望能够用尽可能少的单词来清晰地表达原意。这就导致了非限定动词、动词化单词及词组或其他简化形式的广泛使用。与普通英语相比,专业英语很注重客观事实和真理,并且要求逻辑性强,条理规范,表达准确、精练、正式。

1.2 专业英语基础

1.2.1 词汇

词汇是语言的基础,是英文句子的基本构成元素。词义的准确把握是英汉互译的最基本要求。专业英语中的词汇可分为四类:普通词汇、专业词汇、专业缩写词汇和转意词汇。

1. 普通词汇

科技英语作为英语的一个分支,当然要大量使用普通词汇,尤其是普通词汇中的冠词、动词、副词、形容词、介词、数词、连接词,也部分地使用普通词汇中的名词、代词,但很少使用感叹词。下面是一些例子。

冠词:a, an, the

动词:be, do, take, have, get, give, find, form, increase, obtain, show, work, operate, perform, carry, account

副词:all, more, ago, already, before, finally, immediately, nearly, usually, never, frequently, actually, so, slowly

形容词:all, great, high, large, more, small, good, big, round, square, hard, little, simple, complex, basic, common, internal, external, usual

介词:about, above, after, among, at, behind, beside, between, beyond, by, except, for, from, in, into, of, off, on, over, up, upon, to, by means of, toward

数词:naught, one, two, ten, twenty-three, hundred, thousand, million, billion, trillion, first, second, third, one half, two third, a quarter, seven percent

连接词:and, as, as if, as well as, both…and, either…or, but, not only…but also, for, if, even if, or, yet, while

名词:energy, form, material, line, process, time, result, unit, value, area, field, method, effect, distance, limit, period, direction

代词:other, such, that, this, their, these, which, it, its, itself

这些词汇在科技英语中的意义和用法与在普通英语中基本是一致的,因此读者一般不会有多大困难。

2. 专业词汇

在科学技术的各个领域都有大量各自特有的专业词汇。下面列举一些在通信技术中常用的专业词汇。

amplifier, electromagnetic wave, phase-shift keying, Nyquist rate, Rayleigh fading, transceiver, serial data transmission

专业词汇数量庞大,常令初涉专业英语的读者胆寒。但是稍加仔细观察就会发现,专业词汇绝大部分是名词或名词词组,以及少量形容词。且词意单一,罕有歧义,用法简单。只要注意积累,掌握一定数量的专业词汇(例如1 000个以上)并不是太困难的事。

3. 专业缩写词汇

在专业英语文献中,还常出现一些专业缩写词汇。尤其是通信技术和电子信息技术中的专业缩写词汇很多,且新的缩写词汇仍不断涌现。更有一些缩写词汇是从不同的原文缩写而成,故有多义。掌握一定数量的专业缩写词汇(如200~500个)是顺利阅读专业文献所必需的。专业缩写词汇一般采用首字母组合法来构成,从其书写形式和读音方法来分可分为如下三类。

(1) 整个词整体发音,每一个字母都大写且无句点分隔,例如:

DOS (Disk Operation System)
ROM (Read-Only Memory)
RAM (Random Access Memory)
MOS (Metal-Oxide Semi-conductor)

这类词书写时每一个字母一定都要大写。它们的一般特点是:在某一专业领域内使用率较高;一般首字母数较多(三个以上);其字母组合较易整体发音。这类缩写词汇在书写时每个首字母都要大写,且当作一个单词来读。

需要指出的是,还有一类词符合上述三个条件,但已在专业领域被当成一个普通术语而将长期存在下去,这时其规则一般为:书写时每个字都小写(即已视为一个普通单词),而发音上仍视为一个整体来读,如 radar (radio detecting and ranging)、laser (light amplification by stimulated emission of radiation),因为"雷达"、"激光"已成为专业领域中的普通术语。

(2) 整个词的读音是依次读出每一个字母,每个字母都大写,且无句点分开,例如:

PCM (Pulse Code Modulation)
SSB (Single Side Band)
IEEE (Institute of Electrical and Electronic Engineers)
ITU (International Telecommunications Union)
CATV (Cable Television; Community Antenna Television)
LAN (Local Area Network)
WWW (World Wide Web)
ISDN (Integrated Services Digital Network)
ATM (Asynchronous Transfer Mode)
FDDI (Fiber Distributed Data Interface)
DSP (Digital Signal Processing; Digital Signal Processor)

这类词的一般特点是:在某一专业领域内知名度、使用频率较高;其首字母组合不便于作为一个整体发音。这类词无论是否有长久使用的可能,因其不便作为一个单词发音,所以只以全部字母大写的形式出现而不将其列入普通单词行列。发音时,重音一般放在最后一个字母上。

需要指出的是,这类词前面有无冠词完全视其原来的完全表达方式中有无冠词而定,有冠词的则应保留,否则无冠词。

(3) 顺序读出每一个字母代表的原单词。书写上大小写皆可,但必须一致(即要大写都要大写,要小写都要小写),每个首字母后跟一个句点,如:

  e. m. f. 读作 electro-motive force
  i. f. 读作 intermediate frequency
  e. g. 读作 exempli gratia 或 for example
  i. e. 读作 id est 或 that is to say
  d. c. 读作 direct current
  a. c. 读作 alternating current

需要指出的是,这类词在现代科技英语中有一些新的倾向,在读音上多已改为(2)中的读音规则,即顺序读出每一个字母,且重音在最后一个字母上。拼写上除一些较传统的词外,如 i. e. ,e. g. ,其他一般都改为大写每一字母且去掉句点的形式,如 a. c. 改为 AC,i. f. 改为 IF 等。

4. 转意词汇

科技英语中还有不少词汇是从普通词汇中借用、移植过来的,并赋予它们不同于普通应用时的专门含义。但它们也可能以普通词汇的意义出现在专业英语文献中,这就是所谓的转意词汇。它们的数量虽不及前几类词汇多,但因其多义性和转意性,是较难掌握的,尤其令对专业不很熟悉的读者更感困惑。下面列举一些在通信技术中常见的转意词。

转意词	普通含义	专业含义
relay	接转,接力	继电器,中继器,中转站
admittance	准入,接纳	导纳
coherent	一致的,连贯的	相干的,相关的
filter	过滤器,漏斗	滤波器
burst	爆炸,胀裂	脉冲
network	网,网状组织	网络
spectrum	范围,光谱	频谱
rectifier	修正者	整流器
regulator	调整者	稳压器
modulator	调节者	调制器
flip-flop	翻跟斗	触发器
potential	潜在的,潜力	电位
carrier	运载工具	载波,载流子

1.2.2 翻译的准则与方法

翻译是一种语言表达法,是译者根据原作者的思想,用本国语言表达出来的过程。这就要求译者必须确切理解和掌握原著的内容和意思,丝毫不可以离开它而主观地发挥译者个人的想法和推测。在确切理解的基础上,译者必须很好地运用本国语言把原文通顺而流畅地表达出来。随着国际学术交流的日益广泛,专业英语已经受到普遍的重视,掌握一些专业英语的翻译技巧是非常必要的。专业英语作为一种重要的英语文体,与非专业英语文体相比,具有词义多、长句多、被动句多、词性转换多、非谓语动词多、专业性强等特点,这些特点都是由专业文献的内容所决定的。因此,专业英语的翻译也有别于其他英语文体的翻译。在专业翻译中,要达到融会贯通,必须了解相关的专业,熟练掌握同一事物的中英文表达方式。单纯靠对语言的把握也能传达双方的语言信息,但运用语言的灵活性特别是选词的准确性会受到很大的限制。要解决这个问题,翻译人员就要积极主动地熟悉这个专业领域的相关翻译知识。了解了专业领域,在翻译过程中对语言的理解能力和翻译质量就会大幅度提高。

1. 翻译的准则

关于翻译的标准,历来提法很多。有的主张"信、达、雅",有的主张"信、顺",有的主张"等值"等,并曾多次展开广泛的争论和探讨。但是,从他们的争论中可以看出,有一点是共同的,即一切译文都应该包括原文思想内容和译文语言形式这两个方面;简单地说,符合规范的译文语言,确切忠实地表达原著的风格,这就是英语翻译的共同标准。

- 信(true):译文须忠实于原文的含义,并尽可能保留原文的风格。
- 达(smooth):译文须通顺流畅,符合汉语规范习惯。
- 雅(refined):在保证前两项准则的基础上,译文应优美、雅致、简明。

译文首先必须满足"信"的准则,译文应忠实原文,准确、完整、科学地表达原文的内容,包括思想、精神与风格。译者不得任意对原文内容加以歪曲、增删、遗漏和篡改。这就要求正确理解原文的含义。为此,不但要解决前一节所说的三个关键问题,还要注意英语词汇相对于汉语的不同用法。其次,译文语言必须通顺,符合规范,用词造句应符合本民族语言的习惯,要用民族、科学、大众的语言,以求通顺易懂。不应有文理不通、逐词死译和生硬晦涩等现象。

以上为英语翻译的共同标准。专业英语大部分都是科技文献和情报技术资料,其主要功能是论述科学事实、探讨科学问题、传授科学知识、记录科学实验、总结科学经验等,其翻译标准应略区别于一般翻译。通常的专业英语翻译标准应该是:准确规范、通顺易懂、简洁明晰。

所谓准确,就是忠实地、不折不扣地传达原文的全部信息内容,所谓规范,就是译文要符合所涉及的科学技术或某个专业领域的专业语言表达规范。通顺易懂指译文明白晓畅、文理通顺、结构合理、逻辑关系清楚。简洁明晰就是译文要简短精练、一目了然,要尽量避免烦琐、冗赘和不必要的重复。在这三个标准中,准确的译文必须是通顺的,而译文的通顺必须以准确为基础和前提。在做到准确和通顺的基础上,如能做到简洁,则是科技英语翻译的理想境界。

以下给出几个具体实例以供参考。

(1) The importance of the laser can not be overestimated in that it can provide extremely high capacity for communications.

译文 1:在提供极大的通信容量方面,对激光的重要性不能估计过高。

译文 2:在提供极大的通信容量方面,对激光的重要性不可能估计过高。

译文 1 不准确,因为 can not 表示 overestimated 在逻辑上是不会出现的,而不是对 overestimated 的否定。

(2) In the AND circuit, "1" signals on all inputs give an "1" output; output is "0", if all inputs are not "1".

译文 1:在"与"电路中,若所有输入端为"1"信号,则输出"1";若所有输入不是"1",则输出"0"。

译文 2:在"与"电路中,若所有输入端为"1"信号,则输出"1";若输入不全为"1",则输出"0"。

译文 1 不准确,因为 all…not 是部分否定。

(3) Velocity change if either the speed or the direction changes.

译文 1:假如力的大小或方向改变了,速度跟着要变化。

译文 2:如果(物体运动的)速率和方向有一个发生变化,则(物体的)运动速度也随之发生变化。

译文 1 与原文差距较大。原文采用"either…or"(两者居其一)这种着重点没有译出;物理学中,速度和速率是两个不同的概念,速度(velocity)是矢量,而速率(speed)是标量,在译文 1 中没有体现出来。

(4) A material object cannot have a speed greater than the speed of light.

译文 1:一个物体不会有一个大于光速的速度。

译文 2:一个物体的速度绝不会超过光速。

译文 2 明显比译文 1 更通顺,更符合汉语的表达方式和习惯。

(5) It is forbidden to dismantle it without permission so as to avoid any damage to its parts.

译文 1:为了避免损坏设备的零件,未经许可不得拆卸该设备。

译文 2:严禁乱拆,以免损害设备部件。

尽管译文 1 比较准确、规范,但译文 2 在做到这两点的基础上更简洁。

2. 翻译的一般方法

要把一种语言文字所表达的意义用另一种语言文字表达出来,必须掌握一些常见的翻译方法。

(1) 直译与意译

直译:就是基本保持原文表达形式及内容,不做大的改动,同时要求语言通顺易懂,表达清楚明白。例如:

Physics studies force, motion, heat, light, sound, electricity, magnetism, radiation, and atomic structure.

物理学研究力、运动、热、光、声、电、磁、辐射和原子结构。

The outcome of a test is not always predictable.

试验的结果并不总是可以预料的。

意译:是将原文所表达的内容以一种释义性的方式表达出来,强调的是"神似",即不拘泥于原文在词序、语序、语法结构等方面的形式,用译语的习惯表达方式将原文的本意翻译出来。例如:

We can get more current from cells connected in parallel.

电池并联时提供的电流更大。

The law of reflection holds good for all surface.

反射定律对一切表面都适用。

直译和意译不是两种完全孤立的翻译方法,在翻译实践中,应学会将两者有机结合起来,要以完整、准确、通顺地表达出原文的意义为翻译的最终目的。

(2) 合译与分译

翻译英语句子时,有时我们可以把原文句子的结构保留下来,并在译文中体现出来。但在不少情况下,我们则必须对原句子的结构做较大的改变,合译法和分译法就是改变原文句子结构的两种常用的方法。

合译:就是把原文两个或两个以上的简单句或复合句,在译文中用一个简单句来表达。例如:

Leaves are to the plant what lungs are to the animal.

植物叶子的作用好比动物的肺一样。

There are some metals which posses the power to conduct electricity and ability to be magnetized.

某些金属具有导电和被磁化的能力。

分译:就是把原文的一个简单句中的一个词、词组或短语译成汉语的一个句子,这样原文的一个简单句就被译成了汉语的两个或两个以上的句子。例如:

With the same number of protons, all nuclei of a given element may have different numbers of neutrons.

虽然某个元素的所有原子核都含有相同数目的质子,但它们含有的中子数可以不同。

A brief summary of the gas generation schemes facilitates the DR process descriptions.

为了更清楚地阐述直接还原工艺过程,我们对气体产生的工艺流程进行了简单介绍。

汉语习惯于用短句表达,而英语使用长句较多,由于英汉两种语言的句型结构的这种差异,在科技英语翻译过程中,要把原文句子中复杂的逻辑关系表达清楚,经常采用分译法。

(3) 增译与省译

英语与汉语在表达上有很大的差异。在翻译过程中,如果按原文英语句子一对一地翻译,译文则很难符合汉语的表达习惯,会显得生搬硬套、牵强附会。在翻译过程中,译者应遵循汉语的习惯表达方式,在忠实原文的基础上,适当地进行增译或省译。

增译:就是在译文中增加原文省略或原文中无词而有其义的词语,使译文既能准确地表达原文的含义,又更符合汉语的表达习惯和修辞需要。例如:

High technology is providing visually and hearing impaired people with increased self-sufficiency.

高科技**设备**在**不断**增强视力和听力损伤者的生活自理能力。(增译了名词"设备",副词"不断")

省译:严格地来说,翻译时不允许对原文的内容有任何删略,但由于英汉两种语言表达方式的不同,英语句子中有些词语如果硬是要译成汉语,反而会使得译文晦涩难懂。为使译文通顺、准确地表达出原文的思想内容,有时需将一些词语省略不译。例如:

For the **purpose** of our discussion, let us neglect the friction.

为了便于讨论，我们将摩擦力忽略不计。(省译了名词 purpose)

In solids the force of attraction between the molecules is so great that the arrangement of the molecules becomes rigid.

固体分子间的吸引力很大，使得分子排列得很坚固。(省译了介词 in)

Little information **is given** about the origin of life.

关于生命起源方面的资料很少。(省译了谓语动词 is given)

(4) 顺译与倒译

顺译：就是按照与原文相同或相似的语序进行翻译。顺译可以是完全顺译，也可以是基本顺译。基本顺译是指为了表达准确和通顺而进行个别语序的调整。例如：

Space programs demand tremendous quantities of liquid hydrogen and oxygen as rocket fuel.

航天计划需要大量的液氢和液氧作为火箭的燃料。

倒译：有时完全按照原文的词序来翻译是很困难的，为了使译文更加通顺，更符合汉语的表达习惯，需采用完全不同于原文词序的方法来翻译，称之为倒译。例如：

Too large a current must be used.

不得使用过大的电流。

The converse effect is the cooling of a gas when it expends.

气体在膨胀时对其冷却是一种逆效应。

Thus the bending stress is very easily computed.

因此，极容易计算出其弯曲应力。

3. 翻译的过程

翻译的过程一般分为三个阶段：理解阶段、表达阶段和校对阶段。

(1) 理解阶段

透彻理解原著是确切表达的前提。理解原文必须从整体出发，不能孤立地看待一词一句。每种语言几乎都存在着一词多义的现象。因此，同样一个词或词组，在不同的上下文搭配中、在不同的句法结构中就可能有不同的意义。一个词、一个词组脱离上下文是不能正确理解的。因此，译者首先应该结合上下文，通过对词义的选择、语法的分析，彻底弄清楚原文的内容和逻辑关系。

(2) 表达阶段

表达就是要寻找和选择恰当的归宿语言材料，把已经理解了的原作内容重新叙述出来。表达的好坏一般取决于理解原著的深度和对归宿语言的掌握程度。故理解正确并不意味着表达一定正确。

(3) 校对阶段

校对阶段是理解和表达的进一步深化，是使译文符合标准的一个必不可少的阶段，是对原文内容的进一步核实，对译文语言的进一步推敲。校对对于科技文献的译文来说尤为重要，因为科技文章要求高度精确，公式、数据较多，稍一疏忽就会给工作造成严重的损失。

1.2.3 翻译中的变换

不同的语言有一定的共性，更有不同的语法规则和习惯，因此忌讳逐字逐句式的硬译。

而须在正确理解原文的基础上,做适当的变换以符合汉语的规范和习惯,才能使译文满足"达"的要求。

1. 词类的变换

汉语中动词的使用远比英语多,用法也更为灵活。英语有冠词,而汉语则没有。英语中大量地使用介词,而汉语中却用得不多。两种语言之间的这些区别就需要在翻译中适当变换词类。下面举例说明。

(1) Digital computers are essentially machines for **recording** numbers, **operating** with numbers and **giving** the result in numerical forms.

数字计算机本质上是**记录**数字、**运算**数字和**给出**数字形式的结果的机器。(译文把原文中的动名词变换成了动词)

(2) A continuous **increase** in temperature of a gas in a container will lead to a continuous increase in the internal pressure within the gas.

不断**提高**密闭容器内的气体温度,会使气体的内部压力不断增大。(译文把原文中的名词变换成了动词)

(3) Noise-figure is minimized **by** a parametric amplifier.

利用参量放大器把噪声系数降到最小。(译文把原文中的介词变换成了动词)

(4) The miniature receiving antenna was developed as an **alternative** to that larger one.

这种小型天线是为**取代**那种大型天线而研制的。(译文把原文中的名词变换成了动词)

(5) Gas **differ from** solids in that the former have greater compressibility than the latter.

气体与固体的**区别**在于前者较后者有更大的可压缩性。(有些时候,英语中的一些动词不便于译成汉语动词,而宜改译成名词或其他词类。本句译文把原文动词 differ 变换成了名词)

2. 词序的变换(Changes in World Order)

汉语主要用词序来表示句中各词间的逻辑关系,而英语除用词序外,还常用介词、分词、副词等表示各词的逻辑关系。故在翻译时常需要做适当的词序变换,否则译文不流畅,甚至错误。

(1) The main device failure mode is secondary breakdown.

译文1:主要器件的失效模式是二次击穿。

译文2:器件的主要失效模式是二次击穿。

译文1按原序直译,意思却错了。译文2变换了词序,意思却对了。main 不是用来说明 device,而是说明 mode。

(2) The word transistor is coined by using parts of "transfer" and "resistor".

译文:晶体管这个词是由"变换"和"电阻器"的某些部分组成的。

此句中 transistor 是 word 的同位语。同位语的翻译常需要换序。

(3) Integrated circuits were successfully developed in America in 1958.

译文:集成电路于1958年在美国研制成功。

谓语与状语的词序在英语和汉语中是不一样的。英语词序中,谓语—方式状语—地点状语—时间状语。汉语词序中,时间状语—地点状语—方式状语—谓语。

(4) An electric field can be produced by any charges present in space.

译文1:电场可由空间存在的任何电荷所产生。

译文2:空间存在的任何电荷均会产生电场。

科技英语中大量使用被动语态,而汉语则更喜欢用主动语态。译文2是按主动语态翻译的,其词序当然要做相应的变换。英语常用分词和介词短语进行修饰,它们总是位于被修饰的事物之后。译成汉语时,常需换成前置的词序。

3. 省略(Ellipsis)

冠词在英语中的使用频率极高,但汉语中却根本没有冠词。英语广泛使用介词、代词表示词语间的逻辑关系,而汉语更多的是借助于词序来表达逻辑关系。因此在翻译中,常需做适当的省略以符合汉语的习惯。

(1) Any substance is made of atoms, whether it is a gas, a liquid or a solid.

任何物质,无论气体、液体或固体,都是由原子组成的。(译文中省去了冠词 a)

(2) The intensity of sound is inversely proportional to the square of the distance measured from the source of the sound.

声强与到声源的距离的平方成反比。(译文中省略了冠词 the)

(3) Intel Pentium is a new type of microprocessor.

Intel 奔腾是一种新型微处理器。(译文中省略了介词 of,但未略去冠词 a)

(4) It is 30 cubic meters in volume.

体积是 30 立方米。(译文中省略了代词 it 和介词 in)

4. 补充(Supplements)

科技英语行文简练,且常用省略。因此在译成汉语时,有时需根据汉语的习惯做适当的补充。

(1) Radar astronomy is the radar investigation of celestial objects.

译文1:雷达天文学是天体的雷达研究。

译文2:雷达天文学是用雷达研究天体的科学。

译文1是直译,显得生硬。译文2做了一些补充,显得流畅。

(2) The attenuation of the filter is nearly constant to within 0.5 dB over the entire frequency band.

译文1:该滤波器的衰减在整个频带内接近恒定在 0.1 dB 以内。

译文2:该滤波器的衰减近于恒定,整个频带内的变化在 0.5 dB 以内。

译文2做了一点补充,显得更符合汉语习惯。

(3) The first term of Fourier series is called the fundamental, the others the harmonics.

译文1:傅里叶级数的第一项称为基波,其他的谐波。

译文2:傅里叶级数的第一项称为基波,其他各项称为谐波。

原文中的第二分句是不完整的省略句,译文2中做了补充才符合汉语习惯。

(4) The power transistors are generally encased in metal for protection.

译文1:功率晶体管通常封装在金属中加以保护。

译文 2：功率晶体管通常封装在金属外壳中加以保护。

原文省略了"外壳"，译文 2 将其补充进去，这样才符合汉语习惯。

5．引申（Extensions）

直译常常让人感到生硬、拗口，而在正确理解原意的基础上进行适当引申，常可使译文流畅、明了。

（1）As rubber prevents electricity from passing through it, it is used as insulating material.

直译：因为橡胶阻止电通过，所以用作绝缘材料。

引申：因为橡胶不导电，所以用作绝缘材料。

（2）The product yield is a sensitive function of process control.

直译：产品成品率是工艺管理的灵敏函数。

引申：产品成品率与工艺管理密切相关。

（3）Integrated circuits are more of a science, than of a technology.

直译：集成电路中的科学比技术多。

引申：集成电路与其说是技术，不如说是科学。

（4）At present, the state of most semiconductor device technology is such that the device design and process technology must be supplemented by screening and inspection procedures, if ultimate device reliability is to be obtained and controlled.

译文：目前，大多数半导体器件的技术尚未十分完善，以致若要获得并控制器件最终的可靠性，就必须辅以筛选和检验，以弥补设计和工艺技术之不足。

可以看出，译文中不但作了词类、词序、省略、补充等方面的变换，还把原句隐含的意义引申出来，使译文明确流畅。

1.2.4 长句的译法

科技英语中长句占有很大的比例，它能体现科技英语的严密性、逻辑性和复杂性。长句的结构特点是后置定语、非谓语动词、同位语、宾语从句、定语从句、状语从句等成分多，有时一个句子中能包含所有这些成分。

英语的句式特点是结构严谨，用一句话表达好几层意思，而且习惯将重要信息前置，后面接一些含有次要信息的补充说明性的句子；然而汉语习惯一层含义就用一个简单短句来表达，并且通常重点内容放在句子后面。因此在翻译时要根据汉语的习惯将复杂的长句分切成多个成分，翻译成多个短句。

翻译长句时需要注意的是：

① 弄清句子的逻辑关系；

② 根据上下文和全句内容领会句子的要义；

③ 辨别该长句的主从结构，分切句子的内容；

④ 分清上下层次及前后联系，然后根据汉语的特点、习惯和表达方式翻译。

翻译长句常用的方法有顺译法、倒译法、分译法以及综合译法。

1．顺译法

如果英语长句所叙述的事件是按照时间顺序或按照逻辑关系安排的，并与汉语表达方法基本一致时,便可采用顺译法,也就是基本按照英语的语序,把英语长句拆分为汉语中的短句,不必打乱原文的顺序。

(1) If such alloys possess other properties which make them suitable for die casting①, they are obvious choices for the process②, because their lower melting point will lead to longer die lives③ than would be obtained with alloys of higher melting points④.

分析：如上所示,本句由一个主句和四个从句组成。其句法结构依次如下：①是 if 引导的条件状语从句,其中包含 which 引导的定语从句修饰名词 properties；②是主句；③是 because 引导的原因状语从句；④是 more…than 结构的比较状语从句。翻译时采用顺译法先翻译第①部分,**如果这类合金具有使它们适于压铸的其他性能**,其中的定语从句译为"的"字结构的定语,即"使它们适于压铸的"；再翻译第②部分,**它们显然可以被选来用于压铸**；然后翻译第③部分,即原因从句,**因为它们熔点较低。所以……可以延长压铸模寿命**,注意翻译原因状语从句时采用了分译法,即将其主语部分译成一个分句；最后翻译第④部分,**比起高熔点合金来**,并将此插在原因状语从句中。

参考译文：如果这类合金具有使它们适于压铸的其他性能,它们显然可以被选来用于压铸,因为它们熔点较低,比起高熔点合金来,可以延长压铸模寿命。

(2) However, even if prediction becomes possible①, people who live in areas② where earthquakes are a common occurrence③ will still have to do their best to prevent disasters by building structures④ that are resistant to ground movement⑤ and by being personally prepared. ⑥.

分析：本句是由一个主句、三个定语从句和一个让步状语从句组成。其具体句法结构依次如下：①是 even if 引导的让步状语从句；②是定语从句修饰主句的主语 people；③是 where 引导的定语从句修饰 areas；④是主句(其中主句的主语 people 被两个定语从句隔开)；⑤是第三个定语从句修饰 building structures；需要注意的是主句中的两个 by 引导的状语短语被 that 引导的定语从句隔开了。翻译时采用顺译法,这一点可以从以上例句所表明的序号清楚地看到。汉译时,先翻译①,**即使可以预测**；再翻译②和③,**居住在地震频发区的人们还是应尽力预防灾难**,其中包含两个定语从句,who 引导的定语从句译为"的"字结构,where 引导的定语从句采用短语法被译为"地震频发"；然后翻译④,**办法是建造……的房屋**,其中⑤为定语从句被融合到④,译为"的"字结构的短语即**能够抗震的**；最后翻译⑥,**同时做好个人准备**。

参考译文：然而,即使可以预测,居住在地震频发区的人们还是应尽力预防灾难,办法是建造能够抗震的房屋,同时做好个人准备。

翻译练习：

① Now, a team of astronomers has discovered evidence that the object, whatever it may be, is spewing vast quantities of energetic particles that collide with a surrounding irregular ring of cold hydrogen gas.

② However, in cases that had episodes of increased PAP/AOP ratio, the mean duration of function was increased to five days, and this was almost certainly related to the use of continuous tolazoline infusion through the catheter.

2. 倒译法

有些英语长句子的表达顺序可能与汉语的表达顺序正好相反，这种长句子在翻译时就得用倒译法。

(1) "This rotating, lumpy doughnut provides strong evidence⑤that something exotic is going on deep in the heart of the Milky Way⑥," said Terry Jones④, an astronomer at the University of Minnesota③ who, as a member of an international team ①, has been studying the phenomenon②.

分析：这是一个主从复合句，由一个主句、一个宾语从句和两个定语从句构成。其具体结构为：④是主句；⑤和⑥是直接引语作谓语动词 said 的宾语从句，该宾语从句中又含有 that 引导的定语从句修饰名词 evidence；③是主语 Terry Jones 的同位语；①和②是 who 引导的定语从句修饰名词 astronomer，其中①是定语从句中由 as 引导的短语作方式状语。整个句子主要结构的翻译采用倒译法，翻译的顺序从例句中所标明的序号可一目了然。即先译①as 引导的方式状语，**作为国际考察小组的一名成员**，再译②定语从句，**一直在对这个现象进行研究的**(定语从句译为"的"字结构的定语)，然后将同位语短语③和主句的主语与谓语④全译为**明尼苏达大学天文学家特里·琼斯说**，最后翻译位于句首的宾语从句⑤和定语从句⑥**这个不断旋转的像炸面饼圈样的凹凸不平的氢气环提供了有力的证据，说明在银河系中心深处有一种奇异的东西在活动**。

参考译文：作为国际考察小组的一名成员一直在对这个现象进行研究的明尼苏达大学天文学家特里·琼斯说"这个不断旋转的像炸面饼圈样的凹凸不平的氢气环提供了有力的证据，说明在银河系中心深处有一种奇异的东西在活动。"

(2) Scientists are learning a great deal about⑦how the large plates in the earth's crust move ②, the stresses between plates③, how earthquakes work ④, and the general probability⑥that given place will have an earthquake⑤, although they still cannot predict earthquakes ①.

分析：本句由一个主句、四个并列宾语(其中两个宾语从句、两个短语)、一个定语从句和一个让步状语从句组成。其具体句法结构依次是：①是 although 引导的让步状语从句；②是宾语从句；③是名词短语作宾语；④是宾语从句；⑤是定语从句修饰宾语 probability；⑥是名词短语作宾语；⑦是主句。整个句子主要结构的翻译采用倒译法，翻译的顺序从例句中所标明的序号可一目了然。汉译时，先翻译①，**尽管科学家仍无法预测地震**；再翻译四个并列宾语中的前三个，即②、③和④，**地壳中的大板块如何运动，板块间的压力如何，地震如何发生**；然后翻译带有定语从句的第四个宾语，即⑤和⑥，**某地区发生地震的一般概率为多少**，最后翻译⑦，即主句，**他们了解得越来越多**。

参考译文：尽管科学家仍无法预测地震，但对地壳中的大板块如何运动、板块间的压力如何、地震如何发生、某地区发生地震的一般概率为多少，他们了解得越来越多。

从上面的例句我们可以看出，即使是倒译法，也只是指整个结构上的句子倒译，不必也不可能要求句子的每个局部成分都采用倒译。

翻译练习：

① Just as a pace satellite, once it has got away from the pull of the earth's atmosphere, continues to circle round and round the earth for ever, so an electric current circling a frozen ring of mercury should continue to flow forever, if the temperature is kept below the essential four degrees above absolute zero.

② It is very interesting to note the differently chosen operating mechanism by the different manufacturers, in spite of fact that the operating mechanism has a major influence on the reliability of the circuit-breakers.

3. 分译法

在英语长句子中,有时主句与从句或短语之间关系并非十分紧密,且翻译时为使译文更符合汉语的表达习惯,使行文方便,往往可以将繁杂的长句子拆分开翻译。分译时,为了使译文语义连贯,常常可以适当地增译或者省译某些词语。

The classical metallurgical processes of smelting the oxides with carbon in the presence of a fusible slag①, such as are used for the production of many of the commoner metals②, are not applicable to the range of rather rare elements about which this section is written③, if the metals are required in pure condition④.

分析:该句由一个主句、一个方式状语从句和一个条件状语从句组成。其中主句的主语与谓语被 such as 引导的方式状语从句隔开,主句后又有 about which 引导的定语从句修饰 rare elements,最后是 if 引导的条件状语从句。该句由于主句太长,适合采用分译法,即将主句分译成两个分句。具体的译法为:先翻译①,即主句的主语,把它译成一个分句,**传统的冶金过程是用碳将易熔渣中的氧化物熔化**;然后翻译②,**许多普通金属都是这样生产的**;再翻译③,即主句的谓语部分,将该部分译为另一个分句,**但这种方法并不适用于生产本文所提到的这些稀有金属元素**;最后翻译④,**尤其是需要获得纯净金属时更是如此**。

参考译文:传统的冶金过程是用碳将易熔渣中的氧化物熔化,许多普通金属都是这样生产的,但这种方法并不适用于生产本文所提到的这些稀有金属元素,尤其是需要获得纯净金属时更是如此。

翻译练习:

① This development is in part a result of experimental studies indicating that favorable alterations in the determinants of myocardial oxygen consumption may reduce ischemic injury and that reduction in afterload may be associated with improved cardiac performance.

② In order to understand what happens during sintering of compacts, the changes in density, in dimensions, in metallographic structure and in mechanical properties during sintering must be studied from an experimental point of view, beginning with those in compacts from a single metal powder or from homogeneous solid solution alloy powders.

4. 综合译法

有些长句单纯采用以上所说的三种译法都感到不妥,这时就应仔细分析与推敲,有顺译、有倒译又有拆分地对全句进行综合处理。

As the science of gene grows①, we may be able to create genes② that can turn themselves off⑤after they have gone through a certain number of cell divisions③or after the gene has produced a certain amount of the desired product④.

分析：该句由一个主句、三个时间状语从句和一个定语从句组成，其中两个 after 引导的时间状语从句是修饰定语从句的谓语 turn off 的。该句总体采用分译法，即将主句②和⑤分译为两个分句，具体的翻译方法是：先采用顺译法翻译①，即 as 引导的时间状语从句，**随着基因表现科学的发展**；然后翻译②，即主句，**我们也许能够创造这样一些基因**，再采用倒译法翻译③和④，即两个 after 引导的时间状语从句，**当它们经过了一定次数的细胞分裂后，和或者当它们产生了一定数量的合乎需要的产品之后**；然后再将定语从句⑤译为一个独立的分句，**这种基因能够自行衰亡**。

参考译文：随着基因表现科学的发展我们也许能够创造这样一些基因：当它们经过了一定次数的细胞分裂后或者当它们产生了一定数量的合乎需要的产品之后这种基因能够自行衰亡。

翻译练习：

① The first long distance communication must have arisen shortly after conversation, with the discovery that it was possible to make oneself heard from a distance by shouting, or banging objects together to make a sound that travels far.

② By 1996, not only transmission over 11 300 km at a bit rate of 5 Gbit/s had been demonstrated by using actual submarine cables, but commercial transatlantic and transpacific cable systems also became available.

1.2.5 篇章的翻译

科技语篇与文学语篇不同，具有自身鲜明的特点。在行文方面：科技英语以客观陈述为主，语体正式，语篇组织严谨，观点明确、逻辑性强、结构紧凑，没有插叙倒叙。语法方面：科技篇章中句子结构完整，且句式复杂长句多。常用的语法结构有被动语态、非谓语动词、条件句、虚拟语气、后置定语、定语从句等。词汇方面：科技文章中专业术语多，复合词多，名词多且为长词，很少使用口语词汇。总之，由于科技英语的主要目的是表达科学发展、科学事实、实验报告等，所以其语篇特点为正式、准确、严密、精练、清晰。

（1）忠实原文格式

科技文章的格式较为固定，其结构严谨、层次分明、逻辑性强，翻译时，不得随意改变其特有的固定格式与风格，如实准确地将原文再现是科技篇章翻译的基本要求。

（2）遣词准确，保持一贯

科技语篇的用词特点是专业术语多，且同一词语在不同专业领域中的意义不尽相同。我们在翻译时要特别注意一个词在某一特定的专业领域中的特有词义，不能将科技词语误认为不具有特殊专业含义的普通词语，并应严格遵循某一专业技术领域的用语习惯，某一词语一经译出，即应保持一贯性(consistency)，不应在上下文中随意改动，引起概念上的混乱。在科技翻译中，特别需要恪守严谨的作风，不容丝毫的主观随意性。

（3）熟练掌握常用结构

科技英语篇章在语法结构上有较强的倾向性，有许多句式出现的频率很高，熟练地掌握这些句式的翻译规律,就能既保证译文的准确性和可读性,又可以提高翻译的效率。如:It has been generally believed that/It is widely acknowledged that(人们普遍认为),It was incorrectly believed that(人们错误地认为),It can be concluded that(可以断定),It can be defined as(其定义为),It was not until 1897 that(直到 1897 年),There has been so much emphasis on(人们一直过于强调),Attempts are being made to do(人们还在努力),No case has ever been found(尚未发现),It has been discovered that(业已发现),It has been proved that(业已证明),It should be noted that(应该注意到),It should be paid attention(应予以重视),It is suggested that(有人建议),It is quite remarkable that(更不可思议的是),It goes without saying that(不言而喻),We have already observed that(我们注意到),we shall limit our discussion to(我们只讨论),As the name implies(如其名所示),it has become very hard to do sth.(很难),supposing that(假定,假设),provided that(倘若,只要),seeing that(由于,鉴于),in simple terms(简单地说)等。熟悉这些常用结构的翻译无疑是十分必要的。掌握尽可能多的科技英语常用结构,也是科技翻译的基本功之一。

(4) 注重逻辑性、科学性、专业性

准确翻译科技英语的关键,在于透彻地理解原文,注重科技语篇的逻辑性、科学性及专业性。因此仅仅掌握了单个词的词义和常用结构的翻译还是很不够的。事实证明,应用中的科技英语句式常常远比一些常用结构复杂而多变。这就要求我们翻译时,要避免将原文进行字面意义的串联、拼凑或主观臆断,要透彻地分析句子的深层结构,积极了解相关的专业知识,使译文既要有逻辑性与科学性,又要符合专业要求,力求做到文理通顺,准确、有效地表达出原文的内容。

翻译示例:

A memory is a medium or device capable of storing one or more bits of information in binary systems, a bit is stored as one of two possible states, representing either a 1 or a 0. A flip-flop is an example of a 1-bit memory, and a magnetic tape, along with the appropriate transport mechanism and read/write circuitry, represents the other extreme of a large memory with an over-billion-bit capacity.

Computer memory can be divided into two sections. The section common to all computers is the main memory. A second section, called the file or secondary memory, is often present to store large amounts of information if needed.

The main memory is composed of semiconductor devices and operates at much higher speeds than does the file memory. Typically a word or set of data can be stored or retrieved in a fraction of a microsecond from the main memory.

We shall limit our discussion to semiconductor main memory. There are two broad classifications within semiconductor memories, the read-only memory (ROM) and the read-write memory (RWM). The latter is also called a RAM to indicate that this is a random-access memory. Random access simply means that…

存储器是能够存储一位或多位信息的媒体或装置。在二进制系统中一位以两种可能状态之一进行存储,分别代表 1 或 0。触发器就是一位存储器的例子。配有合适的传送装置和读写电路的磁带是大存储器的另一个极端的例子,存储能力在 10 亿位以上。

计算机的存储器可以分成两部分。所有计算机都有的部分是主存储器。第二部分称为文件存储器或辅助存储器,在需要的时候常用以存储大量的信息。

主存储器是由半导体器件组成的,其运行速度比文件存储器快得多。一般来说,以零点几微秒的时间即可对主存储器存或取一个字或一组数据。

我们只讨论半导体型主存储器。半导体型存储器分为两大类:只读存储器(ROM)和读写存储器(RWM)。后者也称为 RAM——随机存取存储器。随机存储的意思只是说……

在这段文章的译文中,译者将普通词汇 memory,按照专业术语的要求译成"存储器",并坚持一贯性原则,在翻译 main memory, file memory, and secondary memory, the read-only memory (ROM), the read-write memory (RWM), random-access memory 等词时,将其中的 memory 始终保持一致地译为"存储器"。

1.2.6 数量和数学符号

1. 关于数量

数量及数量间大小关系的表示在科技专业文章中是非常普遍也是非常重要的,对英文中出现的数量及其关系的表示方法的理解与掌握对读者准确理解或撰写英文文章是十分重要的。

数量及数学公式的表示和读法参见附录Ⅰ和附录Ⅱ。关于数量增减(about increase and decrease)的表示通过下面几个例子来加以说明。

(1) The production of various ICs has been increased four times as against 1995.

译文 1:各种集成电路的产量增加到 1995 年的四倍。

译文 2:各种集成电路的产量较 1995 年增加了三倍。

在翻译增加倍数的时候,若按增加净量(不含基数,如译文 2),则应遵循($n-1$)的规则。若按增加后的总量(包含基数,如译文 1),则按原句的倍数翻译。

(2) The switching time of the new type transistor is shortened by a factor of three.

译文 1:新型晶体管的开关时间缩短了三分之二。

译文 2:新型晶体管的开关时间缩短为三分之一。

为避免引起歧义,关于减小的翻译最好不译成减小多少倍,而译成分数或百分数。若按减小净量来翻译,则遵循($n-1$)/n 的规则(如译文 1)。若按减小后的余量翻译,则为 $1/M$(如译文 2)。

(3) The cost of TV set was reduced by 70%.

电视机的成本降低了 70%。

(4) We have radio experiments every three weeks.

我们每三周(每隔二周)做一次无线电实验。

every 按"每隔"来翻译时,须遵循($n-1$)规则。

2. 数学符号和希腊字母

(1) 常用数学符号(Mathematic Symbols)

符号	意义或读法	符号	意义或读法
∵	because	//	is parallel to
∴	therefore	⊥	is perpendicular to
=	equal, is equal to	≈	is approximately equal to
>	greater than	( )	round brackets, parentheses
<	less than	[ ]	square (angular) brackets
&	and	{ }	braces
→	leads to, tends	Σ	sigma, summation of

(2) 常用希腊字母(Grecian Letters)

希腊字母目前在各种国际语言中都被采用为专业技术中的物理量等代表符号。在专业英语中，希腊字母出现频率很高，望读者正确掌握希腊字母的大小写符号及其名称和读音。下面列出了一些常用希腊字母的大小写符号及其名称。

字母	读音	字母	读音	字母	读音	字母	读音
α	Alpha	Δ, δ	Delta	Λ, λ	Lambda	ρ	Rho
β	beta	ε	Epsilon	μ	Mu	Σ, σ	Sigma
Γ, γ	gama	ζ	Zeta	ν	Nu	τ	Tao
ξ	xi	Φ, φ	Phi	η	eta	π	pi
Ψ, ψ	psi	Ω, ω	omega				

1.3 科技论文写作指导

科技论文的定义有很多。简单地说，科技论文是对创造性的科研成果进行理论分析和总结的科技写作文体，它是通过运用概念、判断、推理、证明或反驳等逻辑思维手段，来分析表达自然科学理论和技术开发研究成果的。

1.3.1 科技论文的构成

一篇完整的论文一般由以下几个部分组成。

1. 标题(Title)

科技论文必须有一个简明、确切的标题。标题必须简短精练，概括性强，一般应控制在 12 个单词以内。标题应该鲜明地概括论文的主题。为了简明，标题一般不是一个完整的句子，而只是一个词组，甚至不必强求语法上的严格性或完整性而进行适当省略。

(1) 表示法

通常可以采用不含从句的名词短语、动名词短语或"on 短语"，如 Optical Networking Beyond WDM；Analysis of Nonlinearities on Coherent Ultradense WDM-PONs Using Volterra Series；Study of the stability of an array cathode；On fault-tolerant routing in hypercubes。

(2) 字母大写的规则

标题中字母的大小写通常有两种规则,一种是标题的第一个单词的首字母大写;另一种是标题的首字母以及标题中每个实词的首字母大写。例如:

(A) Detailed Analysis of the Effect of Equalizer Parameters on Equalization Performance

2. 作者(Author)

作者姓名的3种写法是:

(1) 姓氏字母全部大写,如 QIAO Weidong;

(2) 姓氏下面划一横线,如 QIAO Weidong;

(3) 姓氏后面加逗号,如 Qiao, Weidong。

3. 摘要(Abstract 或 Summary)

摘要是论文的一个重要组成部分,有利于读者概要地了解论文的主要内容,有利于编目检索。联合国教科文组织建议:"全世界公开发表的科技论文,不管由什么文字写成,都应附有一篇短小精悍的英文摘要。"由此可见撰写英文摘要的重要性。论文摘要的质量好坏,直接影响论文本身的科学价值和对外学术交流的效果。摘要虽然一般放在正文的前面,但却应在整篇论文完成以后再进行写作,以便如实摘取论文的要点。

论文摘要一般包括如下内容:

(1) 研究的目的与意义;

(2) 研究的方法与途径;

(3) 研究的成果与结论;

4. 目录(Contents)

5. 正文(Text)

6. 致谢(Acknowledgements)

在论文结束后,作者通常会以简短的文字对给予支持与帮助的人表示感谢,可用如下方式:

I am thankful (grateful, deeply indebted) to sb. for sth.

I would like to thank sb. for sth.

Thanks are due to sb. for sth.

The author wishes to express his sincere appreciation to sb. for sth.

The author wishes to acknowledge sb.

The author wishes to express his gratitude for sth.

7. 参考文献(References or Bibliography)

8. 作者简介(Biography)

1.3.2 科技论文摘要的写作方法

1. 英文摘要的时态

英文摘要时态的运用也以简练为佳,常用一般现在时、一般过去时,少用现在完成时、过去完成时,进行时态和其他复合时态基本不用。

(1) 一般现在时。用于说明研究目的、叙述研究内容、描述结果、得出结论、提出建议或讨论等,或涉及公认事实、自然规律、永恒真理等,都要用一般现在时。

(2) 一般过去时。用于叙述过去某一时刻(时段)的发现、某一研究过程(实验、观察、调查、医疗等过程)。需要指出的是,用一般过去时描述的发现、现象,往往是尚不能确认为自然规律、永恒真理的,而只是当时如何如何;所描述的研究过程也明显带有过去时间的痕迹。

(3) 现在完成时和过去完成时。完成时少用,但不是不用。现在完成时把过去发生的或过去已完成的事情与现在联系起来,而过去完成时可用来表示过去某一时间以前已经完成的事情,或在一个过去事情完成之前就已完成的另一过去行为。例如:Concrete has been studied for many years. Man has not yet learned to store the solar energy.

2. 英文摘要的语态

采用何种语态,既要考虑摘要的特点,又要满足表达的需要。一篇摘要很短,尽量不要随便混用,更不要在一个句子里混用。

(1) 主动语态。现在主张摘要中谓语动词尽量采用主动语态的越来越多,因其有助于文字清晰、简洁及表达有力。The author systematically introduces the history and development of the tissue culture of poplar 比 The history and development of the tissue culture of poplar are introduced systematically 语感要强。必要时,The author systematically 都可以去掉,而直接以 Introduces 开头。

(2) 被动语态。以前强调多用被动语态,理由是科技论文主要是说明事实经过,至于那件事是谁做的,无须一一证明。事实上,在指示性摘要中,为强调动作承受者,还是采用被动语态为好。即使在报道性摘要中,有些情况下被动者无关紧要,也必须用强调的事物做主语。例如:In this case, a greater accuracy in measuring distance might be obtained.

3. 英文摘要的人称

原来摘要的首句多用第三人称 This paper 等开头,现在倾向于采用更简洁的被动语态或原形动词开头。例如:To describe…, To study…, To investigate…, To assess…, To determine…, The torrent classification model and the hazard zone mapping model are developed based on the geography information system. 行文时最好不用第一人称,以方便文摘刊物的编辑刊用。

4. 几个容易出错的地方

冠词的用法。主要是定冠词 the 易被漏用。the 用于表示整个群体、分类、时间、地名以外的独一无二的事物、形容词最高级等,较易掌握,用于特指时常被漏用。这里有个原则,即当我们用 the 时,听者或读者已经确知我们所指的是什么。例如:The author designed a new machine. The machine is operated with solar energy. 由于现在缩略语越来越多,要注意区分 a 和 an,如 an X ray。

(2) 数词的用法。避免用阿拉伯数字作首词,如:Three hundred Dendrolimus tabulaeformis larvae are collected…中的 Three hundred 不要写成 300。

(3) 单复数。一些名词单复数形式不易辨认,从而造成谓语形式出错。

5. 论文摘要的常用句型(Some Useful Patterns Used in the Abstract)

(1) In this papers,… is (are) presented (described, discussed, investigated, studied)

(2) This paper (article, thesis) focuses on (presents, describes, discusses)…

(3) The purpose (aim, objective, attempt) of this paper is to…

(4) The approach is based on…

(5) Conditions are considered for…

(6) The requirement for…

(7) The simulation is performed by using…

(8) This method is confirmed experimentally with…

(9) The result of this study can be summarized for…

(10) Results for …are found to be close to the experimental data.

(11) This paper demonstrates…

(12) The analysis of this study illustrates…

6. 例子(Examples)

(1) Title: A General Purpose VLSI Frequency Synthesis System

Abstract: A design for a general purpose VLSI frequency synthesizer is presented. It is shown that a simple basic design can have a fully professional performance. Some of the special requirements placed on the VLSI technology are discussed.

(2) Title: Extraction of Frequency Modulation Laws in Sound Synthesis

Abstract: The general scope of this study is computer music, especially the digital synthesis of music sounds. The paper presents a method of estimating modulation laws, using the "skeleton" associated with the wavelet transform and its application to signals generated by the frequency modulation synthesis technique.

(3) Title: Very Fast Discrete Fourier Transform Using Number Theoretic Transform

Abstract: It is shown that number theoretic transform (NTT) can be used to compute discrete Fourier transform (DFT) very efficiently. By noting some simple properties of number theory and the DFT, the total number of real multiplications for a length$-p$ DFT is reduced to $(p-1)$. For a proper choice of transform length, the number of adds per point is approximately the same as the number for FFT algorithms.

1.3.3 科技论文中总结的写法

结论(conclusion)是整篇文章的最后总结。尽管多数科技论文的著者都采用结论的方式作为结束,并通过它传达自己欲向作者表述的主要意向,但它不是论文的必要组成部分。

1. 内容

结论不应该是正文各段小结的简单重复,而是回答"研究出什么(what)"。它应该以正文中的实验或考察中得到的现象、数据和阐述分析作为依据,由此完整、准确、简洁地指出以下内容:

(1) 对研究对象进行考察或实验得到的结果所揭示的原理及其普遍性;

(2) 研究中有无发现例外或本论文尚难以解释和解决的问题;

(3) 与先前已经发表过的研究工作的异同;

(4) 本论文在理论上与实用上的意义与价值；

(5) 对进一步深入研究本课题的建议。

2. 注意事项

(1) 总结很重要，但要注意总结应该是简洁的；

(2) 对分析性论文，可以提到结论的不足，这也表明论文主题的复杂性；

(3) 不要仅仅是引言的重复，试着用另外一种方式叙述主题。

3. 常用表达形式

(1) The following conclusions can be drawn from…由……可得出如下结论……

(2) It can be concluded that…可得出结论……

(3) It is generally accepted(believed, held, acknowledged) that…一般认为……(用于表示肯定的结论)

(4) It is suggested(proposed, recommended, desired) that…建议……

4. 总结示例

(1) 示例1：

In this paper we have presented a positioning system for Bluetooth enabled devices. Bluetooth is an inexpensive and small size solution and will probably be integrated in a range of different devices. With a positioning system based on Bluetooth we are able to make these devices location aware. This will open up for new applications and services that can be developed on these devices.

We have showed that the current implementation is fast enough for the task at least for one device. We have also showed that future changes will probably make it even faster and by that make it suitable for more devices and in that higher accuracy.

With the use of our location server, even the devices that cannot run any third party software can be used as position sources.

(2) 示例2：

As can be seen from earlier discussions, the process model of Shannon has some deficiencies. Nevertheless, it has not been forgotten and indeed the basic process model appears in recent books on organizational behaviour, for example, the 1994 edition of Organizations: *Behaviour*, *Structure*, *Processes*. Components from the process model have been included in later models such as the Berb model and the Generalized communication model.

It is clear, however, that the "softer" components such as human behaviour must be added to any process of communication analysis. It is also clear that "hard" mathematical and technological are still extremely important. In summarizing effective communication to be analyzed and designed, a pluralist approach is necessary through using theories and perspectives from multiple disciplines.

1.4 文献检索简介

文献信息检索是指从任何文献信息集合中查出所需信息的活动、过程和方法。广义的文献信息检索还包括文献信息存储，两者又往往合并称为"文献信息存储与检索"。对于信息用户来说，信息检索仅指信息的查找过程。

1.4.1 文献检索的意义

1. 充分利用已有的文献信息资源，避免重复劳动

科学研究具有继承和创造两重性，科学研究的两重性要求科研人员在探索未知或从事研究工作之前，应该尽可能地收集与之相关的资料、情报。研究人员在开始研究某一课题前，必须利用科学的文献检索方法来了解课题的进展情况，在前人的研究基础上进行研究。可以说一项科研成果中95%是别人的，5%是个人创造的。科研人员只有通过查找文献信息，才能做到心中有数，防止重复研究，将有限的时间和精力用于创造性的研究中。

2. 缩短查找文献信息的时间，提高科研效率

目前文献信息的数量和类型增加十分迅速，而科研人员不可能将世界上所有的文献都阅读完。根据美国科学基金会统计，一个科研人员花费在查找和消化科技资料上的时间占全部科研时间的51%，计划思考占32%，实验研究占9%。由上述统计数字可以看出，科研人员花费在科技出版物上的时间为全部科研时间的60%左右。如果科研人员掌握好科学的文献信息检索方法，就可以缩短查阅文献的时间，获取更多的文献信息，从而提高科研效率。

3. 促进专业学习，实现终生学习

掌握了科学的文献信息检索方法，可以把学生引导到超越教学大纲的更广的知识领域中去，促进学生的专业学习。在当代社会，人们需要终生学习，不断更新知识，才能适应社会发展的需要，掌握了科学的文献信息检索方法，在研究实践和生产实践中根据需要查找文献信息，就可以无师自通，很快找到一条吸取和利用大量新知识的捷径。

1.4.2 文献检索方法简介

文献检索是科学研究工作中的一个重要步骤，它贯穿研究的全过程。文献不仅仅是选题依据，选题确定以后，必须围绕选题广泛地查阅文献资料，能否正确地掌握文献检索方法，关系到研究的过程、质量，以及能否出成果，因此必须掌握文献检索的技能。了解和掌握文献的分类及其特点，是迅速有效地查找所需信息的必要前提。

1. 文献的类型

一级文献，即原始文献，是由亲自经历事件的人所提供的各种形式的材料和各种原著。这种文献是搞好研究的第一手资料，对研究工作有很大的价值。

二级文献，指对一级文献加工整理而成的系统化、条理化的文献资料。如索引、书目、文摘，以及类似内容的各种数据库等。

三级文献，指在二级文献的基础上对一级文献进行分类后，经过加工、整理而成的带有个人观点的文献资料。如数据手册、年鉴、动态综述、述评等。

2. 检索文献的步骤

（1）分析研究课题。在检索之前先要分析检索的课题，一要分析主题内容，弄清课题的关键问题所在，确定检索的学科范围；二要分析文献类型，不同类型的文献各具特色，根据自己的检索需要确定检索文献类型范围；三要确定检索的时间范围；四要分析已知的检索线索，逐步扩大。

（2）确定检索工具。正确地确定检索工具，能使我们在浩瀚的文献海洋中畅游无阻，从而以最简捷的方法，迅速、准确地获得研究所需的文献信息。几种检索工具如下。

① 索引：把文献的一些特征，如书目、篇名、作者，以及文献中出现的人名、地名、概念、词语等组织起来，按一定的顺序（字母或笔画）排列，供人检索。

② 文摘：它概括地介绍原文献的内容，简短的摘要使人们不必看全文就可以大致了解文章的内容，是一种使用广泛的检索工具，如《新华文摘》、《教育文摘》等。

③ 书目：它将各种图书按内容或不同学科分类所编制的目录，如《全国总书目》。

④ 参考性与资料性工具书：它的范围很广，如辞典、百科全书、年鉴等。

⑤ 计算机和互联网：可以通过搜索引擎等对文献进行查询。

（3）确定检索方法。常用的检索方法如下。

① 顺序查找法：从课题研究的起始年代开始往后顺序查找，直到近期为止，这种方法查全率高，但费时。

② 回溯查找法：这是利用某一篇论文（或专著）后面所附的参考资料为线索，跟踪追查的方法。这种查找方法针对性更强、直接、效率高。

③ 计算机检索：计算机以其强大的数据处理和存储能力成为当今最为理想的信息检索工具。计算机检索有以下优点：检索速度快，检索范围大（它可以同时对跨越几年甚至几十年的数据做检索）；检索途径多（计算机的数据库能提供十几种甚至几十种的检索工具，还可以使用逻辑的方法把它们组合起来使用），非常灵活；可以同时检索多个数据库（计算机可以把几个数据库同时打开供检索，并且可以去掉其中重复的数据）；可以立刻得到原文（由于早期的检索系统大多提供索引、文摘等二级文献，有时我们不得不再去寻找原文即一级文献），现在使用计算机全文检索系统，当场就能看到全文，并且根据需要还可以打印出来。

3. 计算机的检索方式

当前广泛使用的计算机检索包括：联机检索、光盘检索和国际互联网检索。

联机检索（online retrieval）是指用户利用计算机终端设备，通过通信线路，从信息中心的计算机（主机）数据库中检索出所需要的信息的过程。它允许用户以人机对话、联机会话这样交互的方式（interactive）直接访问系统及数据库，检索是实时（real time）、在线（online）进行的。用户的提问一旦传到主机被接收后，机器便立刻执行检索运算，很快将检索结果传送到用户终端，用户可反复修改检索方式，最后获得较满意的检索结果。联机检索能远程登录到国内外检索系统。大型检索系统不仅数据库多，而且数据库的文献报道量大，高达数以百万条记录，数据更新及时，系统检索点多，组合方式多样，输出形式、输出方式多样。用户容易得到最新、最准确和最完全的检索效果。

基于 Web 方式的联机检索使用 WWW 浏览器在 Windows 界面下交互作业，给用户揭示到一篇篇文章的信息，有很强的直观性，也可以检索多媒体信息。Web 版数据库检索大量采用超文本。超文本(hypertext)的内容排列是非线性的,它按知识(信息)单元及其关系建立起知识结构网络,如具有图形、画面的信息又称为超媒体(hypermedia),超文本(媒体)的检索是通过超文本链接(hyperlink)来实现的。其形式有的在网页的文字处有下划线,或以图标方式标志,用户点击(point-and click)这些标志便能进入到与此信息相关的下一页,在该页面上通过超文本链接进入下一个页面,超文本起信息导向作用。这样,用户从一个页面转向另一个页面的控制过程中获取自己所需要的信息。

Web版文献数据库检索在采用超文本的基础上又将命令检索、菜单检索方式融合其内交互使用,集各种检索机制为一体。许多大型国际联机检索系统在互联网上开设了自己的站点,提供用户检索服务。

1.4.3 国内检索系统

目前我国高校和科研机构一般根据自己的专业设置和科研需要购置不同的数据库,下面是常见和常用的一些数据库。

《中国期刊网全文数据库》(http://www.cnki.edu.cn);
《万方数据资源系统》(http://www.wfdata.com.cn);
《重庆维普中文科技期刊数据库》(http://www.cqvip.com.cn);
《中国专利数据库》(http://www.sipo.gov.cn);
《中国生物医学文献数据库》(http://www.cbm.imicams.ac.cn);
《中国科技论文在线》(http://www.paper.edu.cn);
《国家科技成果网》(http://www.nast.org.cn);
《国家科技图书文献中心》(http://www.nstl.gov.cn)。

1.4.4 国际著名的六大检索系统

(1) 美国《科学引文索引》(Science Citation Index,SCI)。
(2) 美国《工程索引》(Engineering Index,EI)。
(3) 美国《化学文摘》(Chemical Abstracts,CA)。CA报道的化学工业文献量占全世界化学化工文献总量的98%左右,是当今世界上最负盛名、收录最全、应用最为广泛的查找化学化工文献大型检索工具。
(4) 英国《科学文摘》(Science Abstract,SA;或INSPEC)。
(5) 俄罗斯《文摘杂志》(Abstract Journals,AJ)。
(6) 日本《科学技术文献速报》,现扩充为大型数据库"日本科学技术情报中心"(Japan Information Center Science and Technology,JICST)。

第二部分

通信技术

Unit 1

The Evolution of Communication Theories

TEXT

For many years communications in organizations have been examined in terms of transmission and efficiency in a variety of ways. However the work of Shannon and Weaver with their communication transmission model provided a basis for much of subsequent thinking in the way communications were analyzed [1]. The model, however, has been used and continues to be used for purposes for which it was never designed. In essence it is a data transmission model and does not purport to be a communication theory in which wider considerations, such as language, semiotics, sociometric and culture aspects must be included in order to analyze organizational communications [2]. In addition, the proliferation of available transmission channels has made communication analysis more complex and made it an essential task for organizational planning.

The process model of Shannon and further developed with Weaver, see Fig. 1, is essentially a model of data transmission. It is based on an information theory, which was developed by Hartley and Nyquist and incorporated into Shannon's channel capacity theorem.

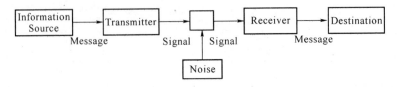

Fig.1 General communication system

Information theory is based on the predictability of messages, resulting in the information content of a message monotonically decreasing with increasing probability of its occurrence. Equation (1) shows how the information content of a message I, can be quantified in terms of binary bits according to its probability of occurrence p_m.

$$I_m = -\log_2 p_m \tag{1}$$

The information content of a message is therefore a measure of its scarcity. Hence, with a message that is a certainty, it carries no information and has an information content of zero. A most important aspect of the theory is that it does not measure the meaning or semantics of the message. The average information content of a binary sender is known as its entropy H, and is related to the information content of each message as defined by Equation 1 and their related probabilities. This is expressed in Equation (2).

$$H = -\sum p_i \log_2 p_i \tag{2}$$

The channel capacity theorem relates the maximum rate of transmission C, expressed in terms of binary bits per second for a digital communication channel, to those resources used to transport the signals and the environment for the transmission[3]. In the model, signals are used to represent messages and they take a form that is the most suitable for the transmission medium. The entities used to model the resources are the signal power S, the time taken to transmit the signal T, and finally the bandwidth or capacity of the channel B. The aspects of the environment that are considered are those that distort or interfere with the signals. These aberrations are modeled as the noise power spectral density of the channel C, and the resulting noise power N, is the product of the noise spectral density and the bandwidth of the channel. The channel capacity as advocated by Shannon is shown in Equation (3).

$$C = B\log_2(1 + S/N) \tag{3}$$

The time T required to transmit a message is shown by Equation (4).

$$T = IC \tag{4}$$

In order to decrease the time to transmit message it is therefore necessary to make the channel capacity C as large as possible. From Equation (3) the channel capacity can be maximized by increasing the bandwidth B, this may not be possible for wireless systems where bandwidth is a premium. In the UK auction for third generation licence's, five mobile communication operators paid E22.5bn for the bandwidth required for the provision of their services. For cable systems, as are used by wire-line operators to provide telephony, Internet access and broadcast radio and television, distance and cost of technology determines the bandwidth. But, there is also an engineering trade off between bandwidth and noise, by increasing the bandwidth, noise is also increased. The increase in noise, can in principle, be compensated for by increasing the signal power S, but again this has the disadvantage that a channel's increase in signal power is another channel's increase in interference and hence noise [4]. In addition, for mobile devices, an increase in transmission power has healthy consequences, and also reduces the time between battery recharging which is a big inconvenience to users.

From examining Shannon's channel capacity theorem it can be seen that it only addressed the various factors that contribute to the actual transmission of data between the sender and recipient, and that it does not consider the information value of the message to the recipient [5].

Therefore in order to bring in other aspects that need to be considered, and to broaden the perspective on communication, developments in the area of meaning transmission and attribution must be added to the basic model. For example, before considering the entities of a communication system it is necessary to distinguish between data and information. Data can be considered to be received messages that have no meaning attached to them, whilst information requires some active processing to be performed by the receiving party [6]. This information is then linked into the person's mental models to add to their knowledge. Fiske argues that the conceptual models used to describe and design communication systems can be categorized as either process or as semiotic models. The process model advocated by Shannon in 1948 takes an engineering perspective whilst semiotic models are based on human perception.

The development of communication modes based on cognition, perception and meaning attribution can now be seen as complementary to an engineering perspective on communication. The following communication models illustrate the different perspectives that have been taken to extend the understanding of communication.

Berlo in his examination of the elements involved in communication said, "One must understand human's behaviors in order to understand communication". He constructed a model of interpersonal communication that contains four components that affect the fidelity of communication.

Source —The transmitter of a communication would be used as moderators of the message: communicative skills; attitudes; knowledge; social understanding; the culture in which the communication takes place.

Message —the message would have the following elements: content, structure, code.

Channel —the channel by which the message is encoded and decoded. For example, speech, vision or other sensory channels.

Receiver —the recipient of the communication would use their own moderators as the source.

However, these would not necessarily be the same.

Berlo had therefore introduced human factors that contribute towards intended and perceived meaning into the communication process. The fidelity of the communication is the degree to which these meanings are the same.

Ross produced a model which had many of the features of Berlo's model, but included an emotion factor for both sender and receiver. This could affect the meaning attributed by the receiver. For example anger or depression can cause a distortion of the communication.

The combination of factors in the communicative event he called the "climate situation".

Hellriegal et al observe that in order to achieve an "ideal state" whereby the sender's intended meanings and the receiver's interpretation of them are the same, so the language must be the same. This has implications in that it is not only the language, e.g. English, French, Russian etc, which must be the same, but also the use of the language, in terms of situation specificity, jargon, acronyms and so on, must be very similar.

The notion of a successful communication was examined by Myer who introduced the concept of a "persuasive communication". That is to say, the more persuasive a communication is, the more likely it is to succeed. He identified a number of variables that could affect the persuasiveness of a communication, such as the credibility of the communicator and activeness or passiveness of the transmission channel. With regards to the message content he found that it could be affected by recency (last message) and primacy (first message) effects. Myers had introduced a sociological dimension into the analysis of communication.

NEW WORDS AND PHRASES

purport	v.	声称
semiotics	n.	记号语言学
sociometric	n.	社会测量
proliferation	n.	繁殖,增殖
theorem	n.	定理,法则
predictability	n.	可预言
monotonically	adv.	单调地,无变化地
occurrence	n.	事件,发生
semantics	n.	语义学
channel	n.	信道,频道
aberration	n.	失常
noise	n.	杂音,干扰,噪声
premium	n.	额外
auction	n.	拍卖
recipient	n.	接收者
fidelity	n.	保真度,精度
moderator	n.	缓和剂
jargon	n.	行话
acronyms	n.	缩写词(只取首字母)
recency	n.	崭新

NOTES

[1] For many years communications in organizations have been examined in terms of

transmission and efficiency in a variety of ways. However the work of Shannon and Weaver with their communication transmission model provided a basis for much of subsequent thinking in the way communications were analyzed.

本句可译为：多年以来，从传输和有效性的角度来说，已经用多种方式调查过各种组织机构中的通信，然而 Shannon 和 Weaver 的通信模型为后来分析通信方式的许多见解提供了基础。

[2] In essence it is a data transmission model and does not purport to be a communication theory in which wider considerations, such as language, semiotics, sociometric and culture aspects must be included in order to analyze organizational communications.

本句可译为：本质上，它是一个数据传输模型，而不是宣称一个通信理论：在该理论中，为了分析组织通信，它一定要包括更广泛的考虑因素，诸如语言、记号语言、社会测量和文化等。

其中，in which…organizational communications 是一个定语从句，修饰 theory。

[3] The channel capacity theorem relates the maximum rate of transmission C, expressed in terms of binary bits per second for a digital communication channel, to those resources used to transport the signals and the environment for the transmission.

本句可译为：信道容量准则显示出传输容量的最大率与传送信号的资源及传输环境之间的关系，以数字通信信道每秒的二进制位表示。

其中，relate…to 表示"与……有关"，译为"显示出……与……的关系"。expressed in terms of binary bits per second for a digital communication channel 是过去分词短语作后置修饰语。

[4] The increase in noise, can in principle, be compensated for by increasing the signal power S, but again this has the disadvantage **that** a channel's increase in signal power is another channel's increase in interference and hence noise.

本句可译为：原则上，噪声的增加能够通过增加信号功率 S 来补偿，但是有一个缺点：一个信道的信号功率的增加意味着另一个信道干扰（噪声）的增加。

其中，that 引导的从句是同位语从句，用来解释 disadvantage。

[5] From examining Shannon's channel capacity theorem it can be seen that it only addressed the various factors that contribute to the actual transmission of data between the sender and recipient, and that it does not consider the information value of the message to the recipient.

本句可译为：从对 Shannon 信道容量准则的检验可以看出，它仅仅陈述了影响发送者与接收者之间实际数据传输的各种原因，没有考虑接收者接收到的信息的信息量。

其中，it 是形式主语，真正的主语是 that it only addressed … and that it does not consider …。

[6] Data can be considered to be received messages that have no meaning attached to them, whilst information requires some active processing to be performed by the receiving party.

本句可译为：数据被认为是接收到的没有相关意思的信息，而信息要求接收者把意思和消息联系起来，因此接收方需要做一些积极的加工。

其中，whilst 是连词，意思等同 while，表示"同时"。

EXERCISES

一、根据课文内容回答以下问题

1. What is the relationship between the information content of a message and the probability of its occurrence?

2. How can we increase the channel capacity according to the channel capacity theorem?

3. What are the advantages and disadvantages of the increase in signal power?

4. What is the difference between data and information?

二、将下述词组译成中文

channel capacity　　　information content　　　signal power　　　noise power
noise spectral density　　fidelity of communication

三、将以下短文译成中文

1. For cable systems, as are used by wire-line operators to provide telephony, Internet access and broadcast radio and television, distance and cost of technology determines the bandwidth. But, there is also an engineering trade off between bandwidth and noise, by increasing the bandwidth, noise is also increased.

2. Therefore in order to bring in other aspects that need to be considered, and to broaden the perspective on communication, developments in the area of meaning transmission and attribution must be added to the basic model. For example, before considering the entities of a communication system it is necessary to distinguish between data and information. Data can be considered to be received messages that have no meaning attached to them, whilst information requires some active processing to be performed by the receiving party.

3. The development of communication modes based on cognition, perception and meaning attribution can now be seen as complementary to an engineering perspective on communication. The following communication models illustrate the different perspectives that have been taken to extend the understanding of communication.

Unit 2

Digital Communication System[1]

TEXT

The use of digital methods for the transmission of analog signals is becoming increasingly common in telecommunication systems. There are two major reasons for this. First, if digital rather than analog signals are transmitted, then the system remains nearly immune to noise as long as it is below a threshold level[2]. This is due to the fact that for long-distance transmission the digital signal can be regenerated at each repeater, creating a new, noise-free signal[3]. Thus, noise does not accumulate as it would in a comparable analog system. Second, the components of a digital system lend themselves well to integrated implementation using large-scale-integrated (LSI) circuits.

Even in such a digital transmission system, however, many signals which are being processed are usually analog in nature. There analog signals need therefore to be converted into digital format. These are various modulation schemes to accomplish this, including pulse-width modulation (PWM), pulse amplitude modulation (PAM), and pulse code modulation (PCM)[4]. PCM is currently the most commonly used modulation system in digital telecommunication systems. The PCM signal is generated by sampling, quantizing, and coding an analog signal. The result is a stream of binary digits (bits), that is, an alternation of high and low voltage levels in the signal. This stream can then be applied, frequency modulation.

The process of sampling an analog voltage $V(t)$ consists of developing a pulse train in which the amplitude of the nth pulse equals the amplitude of $V(t)$ at $t = nT$[5]. In order for the pulse train to represent uniquely the information contained in $V(t)$, the sampling rate $f_c = 1/T$ must be at least twice as large as the highest frequency component in the spectrum of $V(t)$, the amplitudes of the pulses in the sampled signal are then quantized and converted into a set of bits, called a digital word.

The transmission of digital words in a practical PCM telecommunication system often utilizes time-division multiplexing (TDM). In a TDM system, the digital words taken from several channels are transmitted interlaced over the same line. In voice-frequency (telephone) systems, usually 24 or 32 voice channels are thus multiplexed onto a single pair of wires. The International Telegraph and Telephone Consultative Committee (CCITT) had recommended two main architectures ("hierarchies"), which now many nationwide PCM transmission network use. The first one, shown schematically in Fig. 1, has been adopted mostly in Europe, Africa, Australia, and South America. In this system, the input multiplexers (MUX) interleave 32 digital words. Of these, 30 words represent the signal amplitudes in 30 voice channels, while the remaining two time slots contain signaling and synchronization information. The second hierarchy, used mainly in the United States, Canada and Japan, is illustrated in Fig. 2. In this system, 24 voice channels are multiplexed at the input section.

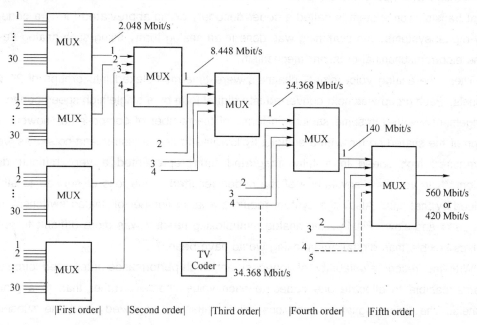

Fig. 1 The PCM Hierarchy Used in Europe, Africa, Australia and South America

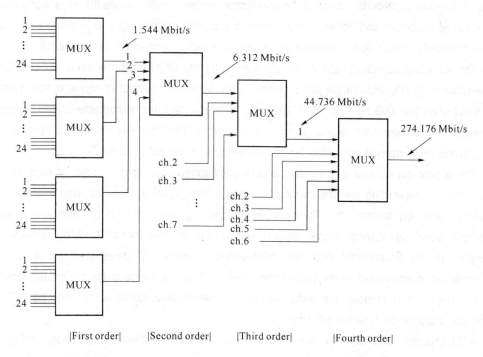

Fig. 2 The PCM Hierarchy Used in the United States, Canada and Japan

There are two main tasks performed in a digital telecommunication system: transmission and switching. Transmission involves sending the digitally coded voice signal from one location to another, while switching consists of establishing the desired connection between two voice channels which carry digital signals [6].

The unit which performs the pulse code modulation and demodulation of the signals in a digital transmission system is called a coder-decoder, or, in abbreviated form, a codec. In early digital systems, the switching was done in an analog form, using such analog devices as the electromechanical crossbar mechanism.

Then, the analog voice signal channels were time-multiplexed into groups of 24 or 30 channels. Each group was next converted into digital form by a single high speed codec. This arrangement resulted in some savings in terms of the number of components; however, the design of the shared codec with a sufficiently low line-to-line crosstalk and noise, as well as the required high speed in a fully integrated form represented a very difficult design problem [7]. In addition, any failure of the codec resulted in the loss of service to all lines serviced by that unit. Also, the system required a large number of analog switches, which were bulky and slow. Finally, the analog multiplexing needed was more difficult to perform and less flexible than digital multiplexing would have been [8].

With the recent availability of low-cost and high-performance integrated circuits, it became feasible to allocate one codec to each voice channel, rather than to a group of channels. The voice signal in each channel is thus first digitized, and the subsequent switching and multiplexing are performed by digital systems which can use low-cost digital logic and memory circuits. Such a "per-channel codec" system results in a considerable reduction of crosstalk and noise. Also, there is a significant saving in size and cost, due to the elimination of most of the bulky and expensive electromechanical components.

The standard sampling rate f_c recommended by the CCITT for the usual 300~3 400 Hz voice channel is 8 000Hz. In the per-channel codec system, the analog signal is thus sampled at intervals of 1/8 000 Hz = 1.25×10^{-4} s = 125 μs, and the amplitude of the sample is converted into an eight-bit digital word is then transmitted serially to the multiplexer. The 125-μs-long time interval available for the conversion is called a frame.

The digital multiplexer places all the bits corresponding to one sample of each of 24 or 30 channels (depending on the hierarchy used) into a single frame, and transmits the resulting serial bit stream [9]. To mark the beginning and the end of each frame at the receiver, some identifying signal should be added to the transmitted bit stream. For example, in the 24-channel eight-bit PCM system called D2 developed by AT&T, an additional bit is appended to the bits of each frame. Thus, a frame in the D2 system contains $24 \times 8 + 1 = 193$ bit. Hence, the data rate of the transmitted signal is 193 bits per 125 μs, which corresponds to 1.544×10^6 bit/s.

A 24-Channel Time-Division Multiplexed PCM telephone system is illustrated in Fig. 3.

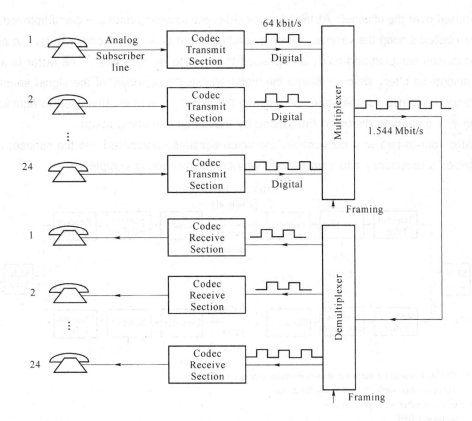

Fig. 3 A 24-Channel Time-Division Multiplexed PCM Telephone System

The components of a typical switching or transmission path are illustrated in Fig. 4. In the transmit direction, the subscribed line is connected to the subscriber-line interface circuit (SLIC). The SLIC performs the two-to-four wire conversion, the battery feed, the line supervision, and also provides ringing access and over voltage protection. The signal then passes through the transmit filter, which limits its spectrum to (approximately) 3 400 Hz. The transmit filter thus removes the part of the spectrum which extends over 4 kHz, and thus makes it possible to sample the signal at an 8 kHz rate without introducing aliasing. In addition, the low-frequency portion (below 300 Hz) of the spectrum is also suppressed by the transmit filter, to prevent power-line frequency (50 or 60 Hz) noise from being transmitted.

The filtered signal, now band limited to the 300~3 400 Hz range, is then sampled at an 8 kHz rate, and then converted (encoded) into eight-bit PCM data. This conversion is performed nonlinearly; that is, the resolution of the resulting digital signal is finer for small signals than for large ones.

The output of the nonlinear A/D converter is a specially coded eight-bit digital word. The first bit indicates the sign of the input x, with "1" representing positive and "0" negative polarity. The next seven bits provide the amplitude value of the signal.

Returning to the block diagram of Fig. 4 [10], the digital output of the encoder is then time-division multiplexed with the outputs from the other lines, and the resulting bit stream is transmitted over the channel. At the receiver side, the incoming data are demultiplexed, that is, distributed among the various channels, and decoded (i.e., D/A converted). The analog output is then sampled-and-held, and passed through the receive filter. The latter is a low-pass smoothing filter, which removes the high-frequency "side lobes" of the signal spectrum, and hence smoothes out the staircase noise in the signal. It is also often used to equalize for the $\sin x/x$ amplitude distortion introduced by the sample-and-hold stage.

After four-to-two wire convention, the voice signal is transmitted into the handset of the subscriber's telephone, and thus the one-way communication is completed.

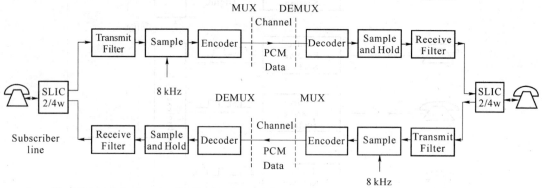

Note: The SLIC stands for the subscriber-line interface circuit.
This circuit performs the following functions:
① two-to-four wire conversion
② battery feed
③ line supervision
④ ring access
⑤ overvoltage protection

Fig. 4　Signal Path Through a Typical PCM System

NEW WORDS AND PHRASES

immune	adj.	免除的,不受影响的,可避免的
threshold	n.	门槛,门限
interlace	v.	使交织,使交错
hierarchy	n.	等级,体系,系列
abbreviate	v.	缩写
electromechanical	adj.	机电的
crosstalk	n.	串话
bulky	adj.	体积庞大的
feasible	adj.	可行的,行得通的
elimination	n.	消除,排除,淘汰
interval	n.	间隔时间
append	v.	附加,贴上,挂上
handset	n.	手机

supervision	n.	监督，监管
overvoltage	n.	超压，过电压
aliasing	n.	混淆
suppress	v.	抑制
nonlinearly	ad.	非线性地
resolution	n.	分析，分辨
sign	n.	符号
polarity	n.	极性
lobe	n.	叶片，瓣
staircase	n.	楼梯
in terms of		根据，按照，在……方面，从…方面（来说）

NOTES

[1] 本篇课文涉及数字通信领域，题目意思为"数字通信系统"。

[2] First, if digital rather than analog signals are transmitted, then the system remains nearly immune to noise as long as it is below a threshold level.

本句中，"rather than"是"而不是"之意；"immune to"意思是"可避免的，不受影响的"。

全句可译为：第一，如果传输的是数字信号而不是模拟信号，则只要噪声电平低于门限电平，系统就几乎不受影响。

[3] This is due to the fact that for long-distance transmission the digital signal can be regenerated at each repeater, creating a new, noise-free signal.

"creating a new, noise-free signal"是一个现在分词短语，作状语，可译为："从而产生一个新的、无噪声的信号"。

全句可译为：事实是因为，对于长距离传输，数字信号可以在再生器中重新生成，从而产生一个新的、无噪声的信号。

[4] There are various modulation schemes to accomplish this, including pulse-width modulation (PWM), pulse amplitude modulation (PAM), and pulse code modulation (PCM).

"including… code modulation"是现在分词短语，作定语，修饰"various modulation schemes"。

全句可译为：有多种调制手段以实现这种转换，包括脉宽调制、脉幅调制以及脉码调制。

[5] The process of sampling an analog voltage $V(t)$ consists of developing a pulse train in which the amplitude of the nth pulse equals the amplitude of $V(t)$ at $t = nT$.

句中的"sampling"和"developing"都是动名词，作其前面介词"of"的宾语。"in which … at $t = nT$"是带介词的限制性定语从句，修饰"a pulse train"。"which"表示"a pulse train"。

全句可译为：对模拟电压$V(t)$采样过程包括生成一个脉冲串，在这个脉冲串中，第n个脉冲的幅度等于$V(t)$在$t = nT$时的幅值。

[6] Transmission involves sending the digitally coded voice signal from one location to another, while switching consists of establishing the desired connection between two voice channels which carry digital signals.

本句是个并列复杂句,并列连词"while"前后的两个分句并列。第二个分句中,"which…signals"是限制性定语从句,修饰"voice channels"。第一个分句中,"sending"是动名词,作动词"involve"的宾语。"the digitally coded voice signal"可译为:"数字编码的语音信号"。

全句可译为:传输包括把数字编码的语音信号从一个地方发送到另一个地方,而交换包括建立两个话音信道的有效连接,这两个信道是(用来)承载数字信号的。

[7] This arrangement resulted in some savings in terms of the number of components; however, the design of the shared codec with a sufficiently low line-to-line crosstalk and noise, as well as the required high speed in a fully integrated form represented a very difficult design problem.

该句是并列句,即分号前和分号后的句子并列。第二个分句中,谓语为"represented",而"the design of the shared coded with a sufficiently low line-to-line crosstalk and noise, as welt as the required high speed in a fully integrated form"是主语部分,可译为:"具有足够低的线间串话和噪声,同时又具有所需很高速度的全集成(各路)共用编解码器的设计"。

全句可译为:这种排列导致了器件数量的一些减少,但是,具有足够低的线间串话和噪声,同时又具有所需很高速度的全集成(各路)共用编解码器的设计代表了一个很难的设计问题。

[8] Finally, the analog multiplexing needed was more difficult to perform and less flexible than digital multiplexing would have been.

本句主语为:"the analog multiplexing needed",意思是:"所需要的模拟多路复用"。这是一个含比较级的句子,"than"后是一个比较状语从句,比较的对象为"degital multiplexing would have been"。

全句可译为:最后,所需的模拟多路复用与数字多路复用相比,在实现上更为困难,灵活性亦更差。

[9] The digital multiplexer places all the bits corresponding to one sample of each of 24 or 30 channels (depending on the hierarchy used) into a single frame, and transmits the resulting serial bit stream.

句中的"corresponding"为现在分词,所引导的短语作定语,修饰"all the bits",译为:"对应于24路或30路各路的一个样值的全部比特"。

全句可译为:数字复用器把对应于24路或30路各路样值的全部比特放在一个帧中,然后传输结果串行比特流。

[10] Returning to the block diagram of Fig.4,…

"Returning"引导的现在分词短语作状语,可译为:"现在(我们)回到方框图中"。

EXERCISES

一、将下述词组译成中文

pulse code modulation   the highest frequency component
signaling and synchronization information per-channel codec system
two-to-four wire conversion   the lower-frequency portion of the spectrum
nonlinear A/D converter   amplitude distortion

to prevent power-line frequency noise from being transmitted
resolution of the resulting digital signal   the resulting serial bit stream
line-to-line crosstalk   in a fully integrated form

二、将下列短文译成中文

1. The unit which performs the pulse code modulation and demodulation of the signals in a digital transmission system is called a coder-decoder, or, in abbreviated form, a codec. In early digital systems, the switching was done in an analog form, using such analog devices as the electromechanical crossbar mechanism.

2. With the recent availability of low-cost and high-performance integrated circuits, it became feasible to allocate one codec to each voice channel, rather than to a group of channels. The voice signal in each channel is thus first digitized, and the subsequent switching and multiplexing are performed by digital systems which can use low-cost digital logic and memory circuits. Such a "per-channel codec" system results in a considerable reduction of crosstalk and noise. Also, there is a significant saving in size and cost, due to the elimination of most of the bulky and expensive electromechanical components.

3. At the receiver side, the incoming data are demultiplexed, that is, distributed among the various channels, and decoded (i. e., D/A converted). The analog output is then sampled-and-held, and passed through the receive filter. The latter is a low-pass smoothing filter, which removes the high-frequency "side lobes" of the signal spectrum, and hence smoothes out the staircase noise in the signal. It is also often used to equalize for the $\sin x/x$ amplitude distortion introduced by the sample-and-hold stage.

Unit 3

Pulse Code Modulation

TEXT

1. INTRODUCTION

One of the problems associated with the transmission of speech signals is that, as the distance over which the signal is transmitted is increased, so does the noise induced into the transmission circuit. Unfortunately, since the introduction of telephony just over a century ago, the number of sources of electro-magnetic noise have also increased considerably. Amplifying signals cannot be used as a technique to overcome noise because the noise gets amplified along with the signal.

Way back in 1937 Alec Reeves suggested that one way to overcome the problem of noise in long-distance telephony would be to convert the analogue speech signal into a signal represented by a sequence of digital pulses. Provided these pulses were regenerated before they become impaired beyond recognition, then it would be possible, in principle, to transmit the signal over infinitely long distances with no deterioration, except the approximation inherent in converting an analogue signal into a digital signal and back again[1]. This deterioration is known as quantization noise and will be discussed further in a subsequent section. Of course, regenerators are necessary, but these are no more difficult to build than amplifiers and it dose not appear necessary to provide these are no more difficult to build than amplifiers and it dose not appear necessary to provide these any more frequently than it is already necessary to provide amplifiers to overcome the transmission losses in the transmission path. The technique of converting the analogue signal into a digital pulse stream became known as Pulse-Code-Modulation (PCM). Let us now look at PCM in more detail.

2. SAMPLING

The basic principle of PCM is that the analogue signal representing the sound-wave is sampled at regular intervals and the value of the amplitude of the sample is digitally represented by a number. This involves a process of quantization whereby the continuously variable amplitude function is represented by a selection from a range of digitally quantized levels. This process is illustrated in Fig. 1.

The sampling theorem tells us that we need to sample the signal at a rate equivalent to at least twice the highest frequency present in the signal if we are to reconstitute the signal at the receiver without distortion [2]. Since telephone speech is generally band-limited to between 300 and 3 400 Hz, the sampling frequency chosen for PCM is 8 k samples/s.

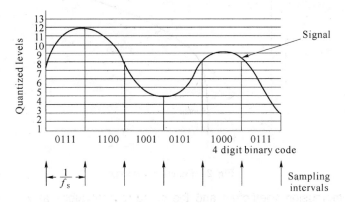

Fig. 1 Quantization of analogue signal

3. QUANTIZATION

The next question we have to answer is how many quantization levels do we need to provide in order to represent the signal amplitude with sufficient accuracy [3]? If the quantization is too coarse, then our signal will be unacceptably impaired by quantization noise. Quantization noise is a result of the difference between the actual signal and the reconstituted signal because of the approximation inherent in the quantization process. On the other hand, the number of binary digits required to represent the quantization levels is related to the number of levels in the quantization process. Thus too fine a quantization leads to an excessive requirement on the number of binary digits required to represent each amplitude sample. It has been found in practice that 256 amplitude levels is adequate for acceptable speech quality, which requires $\log_2 256 = 8$ binary digits per sample. The quantization levels, however, are not equally spaced throughout the full amplitude range of the signal, but are chosen to be of increasing coarseness as the signal amplitude increases. This ensures that the signal-to-quantization noise ratio remains substantially constant throughout the full dynamic range of speech signals. This is important as the range of speech signal amplitudes encountered is much greater than is immediately apparent because the human ear is highly adaptive to speech signal amplitude variations.

Because the effect of the non-linear quantization scale is to compress the large amplitude signals for transmission and to expand them again on receipt, the process has become known as " companding ".

4. COMPANDING

To obtain compression of the large amplitude signals, a logarithmic law would seem appropriate. Unfortunately, as we can see from Fig. 2, the function $y = \log x$ does not pass through the origin. It is therefore necessary to substitute a linear portion to the curve for lower values of x. Most practical companding systems are based on a law suggested by K. W. Cattermole, namely.

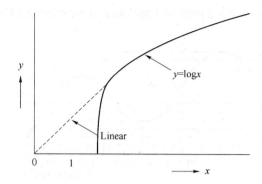

Fig. 2 Function $y = \log x$

A is the compression coefficient and the curve is continuous at $x = 1/A$. The law is illustrated in Fig. 3.

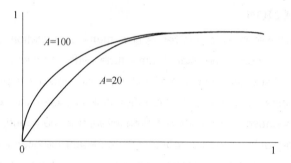

Fig. 3 Cattermoles's companding law

The practical implementation of this law would require nonlinear signal processing followed by linear quantization. The implementation of the non-linearity, together with the complementary non-linearity at the receiver, presents considerable problems, It is usual, therefore, to implement a piece-wise linear segmental approximation to the law. Two piece-wise linear laws are in general use. That used in Europe is known as the CCITT companding A-law. A-law companding consists of eight linear segments for each polarity, the slope halving for each segment, except for the lowest two segments. The law is illustrated in Fig. 4. Three bits are required to define the segment. Within each segment there are 16 linear steps, defined by a further 4 bits. Finally, the polarity of the signal is defined by a single bit, making a total of 8 bits in all. Because the full curve has 13 linear segments, A-law companding is sometimes referred to as 13 segment companding. The compression coefficient for A-law companding is approximately equal to 87.6. A slightly different companding law is used in the USA, known as μ-law companding. In μ-law companding the slope is halved over all eight segments as shown in Fig. 4, otherwise the procedure is very similar to A-law. Because the full curve comprises 15 linear segments. μ-law is sometimes referred to as 15 segment companding. It will be seen from Fig. 4 that there is hardly any difference between A-law and μ-law companding except at very low signal amplitudes.

The piece-wise linear companding rules can be readily implemented within the analogue-to-digital conversion process. As the signal sample passes up from one segment to another, all that is required is a doubling of the step size of the analogue-to-digital converter. This can be achieved by simply discarding the least significant bit of the converter output whenever a segment threshold is passed.

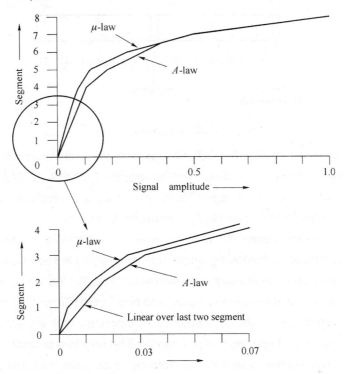

Fig. 4　A-law and μ-law companding

5. PCM FRAME STRUCTURES

With a sampling rate of 8 k samples and 8 bit required for each sample, the overall binary data rate required to transmit a PCM speech signal is 64 kbit/s. This digit rate forms the basis of all PCM transmission and is the accepted as international standard for PCM.

PCM has found its widest application in junction and trunk transmission in the telephone network. On junction and trunk links it is not usual to dedicate a transmission path to each single telephone conversation. Instead, several calls are "multiplexed" together to share a common transmission facility. The primary level of multiplexing used throughout Europe is to combine together 30 separate PCM telephone speech signals using Time-Division-Multiplexing (TDM). In TDM, 8 bit "octets", each representing a single sample, are taken from each signal in turn and transmitted sequentially along the transmission path, Besides the bits representing the speech signal, it is also necessary to send information that indicates the way in which the samples are assembled so that they can be disassembled and distributed to the correct recipient on completion of transmission. Also, information about the routing of the signals is required by the network. These are known respectively as synchronization and signaling data. This data is incorporated into the multiple signal by providing 32 time-slots instead of the 30 required for the speech signals. The 32 channel slots are normally numbered 0 to 1. The 0th slot is used for frame synchronization and the 16th slot is allocated for network signaling information. Thus slots 1 to 15 and 16 to 31 are available for speech signals. The basic frame structure is given in Fig. 5.

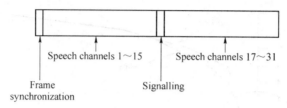

Fig. 5   PCM basic frame structure

Each frame consists of $32 \times 8 = 256$ bit and conveys one sample from each speech channel. The overall transmission rate required is therefore $256 \times 8 k = 2.048$ Mbit/s. This rate of 2.048 Mbit/s is often referred to as the "primary rate", since it represents the first level of multiplexing used in the Synchronous Digital Hierarchy(SDH).

In North America and Japan the primary level of multiplexing consists of 24 speech signals with a single bit of synchronizing information for every 24×8 kbit frame, giving a frame size of 193 bit[4]. The overall transmission rate required is thus $193 \times 8 k = 1.544$ Mbit/s. In this system the signaling information is incorporated into bits "stolen" from the information-bearing octets. An early system used in the UK also used 24 channels, with the 8 th bit of each octet being used for signaling and synchronization, leaving 7 bit only to represent each PCM sample of the signal. The quantization noise was therefore twice as great than that obtained using 8 bit quantization. The overall transmission rate for this system was $24 \times 8 \times 8 k = 1.536$ Mbit/s. However, all UK 24 channel systems have now been replaced with 30 channel systems to CCITT standards, although their impact is still felt, as will be seen later when we discuss the choice of line codes for transmission.

6. SIGNALING AND SYNCHRONIZATION

We now return to consider in a little more detail the signaling and synchronization signals incorporated into channels 0 and 16 of the 30 channel PCM frame. The frame alignment pattern contained in time slot 0 alternates between successive frames as shown in Fig. 6.

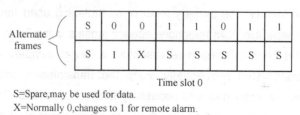

S=Spare,may be used for data.
X=Normally 0,changes to 1 for remote alarm.

Fig. 6   Frame alignment pattern

Some of the bits are not part of the specified pattern and these can be used to carry data. One bit in each alternate frame is available for remote alarm signaling purposes to signal loss of frame alignment to the distant station.

Two different methods are in common use for the channel signaling contained in time-slot 16, the earliest, and currently most widely used, method is that known as "channel associated signaling". Channel associated signaling is incorporated into a 16 frame multi-frame structure. The frame are numbered sequentially form 0 to 15. The first four bits of frame 0, time slot 16, contain the multi-frame alarming pattern of four consecutive zeros, as shown in Fig. 7 (a). Three of the other four bits are spare and are available for use for data. The eighth bit is used to signal remote loss of multi frame alignment.

In frames 1 to 15, the time-slot 16 octets are divided into two 4 bit sub-fields as shown in Fig. 7(b). The first four bits in frame N are used for channel N signaling and the second four bits for channel $N+16$ signaling. This gives four bits for signaling in each channel, the signaling information being updated, every 16 frame, that is, every 2 ms. The four bits per channel give the possibility of 15 signaling states. The all-zero combination is never used because of the possibility of confusion with the multiframe alignment pattern.

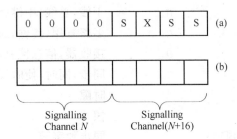

S=Spare, may be used for data.
X=Normally 0, changed to 1 for remote loss of multiframe aligment.

Fig. 7   Time-slot 16 digit assignment

With modern digital switching systems it is possible to make more efficient use of the signaling channel by using it simply as a message transmission facility, the formatting of the signaling information being the responsibility of the exchange equipment[5].

This means that signaling messages relating to a specific channel are only required when there is a change in status on that channel. The repetitive transmission of signaling messages, characteristic of channel associated signaling, is therefore avoided. This technique is known as common channel signaling. The CCITT common channel signaling standard for use with digital switching networks is known as signaling system No. 7(SS7). The No. 7 signaling system operates on a data packet concept. A more detailed study of signaling system No. 7 will have to be postponed until we have first considered the principles of operating digital switching networks.

NEW WORDS AND PHRASES

Pulse Code Modulation(PCM)   脉冲编码调制

regenerate	v.	还原,再生,更新,(使)恢复
impair	v. n	削弱,损害,减少
recognition	n.	认出,辨别,判明
beyond recognition		不能辨认,认不出来
deterioration	n.	变质,退化,变坏
quantization	n.	量化,分层
equivalent	adj.	相等的,等效的
signal-to-quantization noise ratio		信号量噪比
companding	n.	压扩,展缩,压伸
coefficient	n.	系数,折算率,程度
implementation	n.	装置,仪器,履行,实现
complementary	adj.	余的,补的,补充,互补,辅助
threshold	n.	槛,门限,定值
analogue-to-digital converter		模数转换器
junction	n.	接合,接续(线),中继线
trunk	n.	干线,总线,中继(线),连接线路
multiplex	n.	多路复用(传输,通信)
recipient	n.	接收器,信息接收器
synchronization	n.	同步,同时,使时间一致
time-slot		时隙
frame	n.	帧
Synchronous Digital Hierarchy(SDH)		同步数字网
incorporate	v.	(使)结合,包括,插(编)入
multi-frame		复帧
bipolar	adj.	两极的,双极(性)的,双向的

NOTES

[1] Provided these pulses were regenerated before they become impaired beyond recognition, then it would be possible, in principle, to transmit the signal over infinitely long distances with no deterioration, except the approximation inherent in converting an analogue signal into a digital signal and back again.

本句中,"provided…recognition"是以"provided"为引导词的条件状语从句,"provided"是"只要"的意思。主句是"it would be possible…deterioration",其中"in principle"为插入语;"except the…back again"是介词短语作状语。

全句可译为:只要在脉冲变得无法识别之前重新再生它,那么,除了把模拟信号转换为数字信号及把数字信号转换为模拟信号时内在的近似过程,原则上信号可以无衰减地传输无限长的距离。

[2] The sampling theorem tells us that we need to sample the signal at a rate equivalent

to at least twice the highest frequency present in the signal if we are to reconstitute the signal at the receiver without distortion.

本句是复杂句,句中"that we need…without distortion"是宾语从句;"if we…without distortion"是宾语从句中的条件状语从句。

全句可译为:抽样定律告诉我们:如果想要在接收端无失真地重建信号,抽样频率需要至少是信号中最高频率的两倍。

[3] The next question we have to answer is how many quantization levels do we need to provide in order to represent the signal amplitude with sufficient accuracy?

该句是个复杂句。"We have to answer"是"question"的定语从句(省略了关系代词"that")。"how many…with sufficient accuracy'"是表语从句,它与"is"一起构成复合谓语。为了加强语气,强调谓语动词"need"表示的动作,"do"提到"we need"之前。

全句可译为:我们要回答的下一个问题是:为了有足够的精确度来代表信号幅度,我们需要提供多少量化级?

[4] In North America and Japan the primary level of multiplexing consists of 24 speech signals with a single bit of synchronizing information for every 24×8 kbit frame, giving a frame size of 193 bit.

本句虽然较长,但是个简单句。为了强调地点状语"In north America and Japan",故将其放在句首。句中,"the primary…multiplexing"作主语;"consists"作谓语,"of 24 speech signals with…24×8 kbit frame"作状语;"giving…"是现在分词短语作伴随状语,其逻辑主语是句子的主语。

全句可译为:在北美和日本,复用的一次群包括24个语音信号和为每24×8 k比特帧同步的一个比特,(故)帧的大小为193比特。

[5] With modern digital switching systems it is possible to make more efficient use of the signaling channel by using it simply as a message transmission facility, the formatting of the signaling information being the responsibility of the exchange equipment.

该句中,"With…systems"是介词"with"引导的状语,"it"为形式主语,"to make more…facility"是真正的主语,"the signaling channel"作宾语,"efficient"是"use"的定语;"the formatting…equipment"是分词独立结构,作伴随状语。

全句可译为:利用现代数字交换系统,把信令信道仅仅作为信息传输工具(设备)使其利用率更高是可能的,信令信息的初始化是交换设备的功能。

EXERCISES

一、根据课文内容判断对错

1. The overall binary data rate required to transmit a PCM speech signal is 64 kbit/s.(　　)

2. The quantization levels are equally spaced throughout the full amplitude range of speech signals.(　　)

3. A PCM basis frame has 32 time-slots.(　　)

4. The spectrum of bipolar non-return-to-zero binary signals has no d.c. component.(　　)

5. The spectrum of HDB3 has no d.c. component. (　　)
6. In HDB3 the parity pulse violates the alternate mark inversion rule. (　　)
7. The "000" ternary code group is not used in 4B3T. (　　)

二、将以下短文译成中文

1. This deterioration is known as quantization noise and will be discussed further in a subsequent section. Of course, regenerators are necessary, but these are no more difficult to build than amplifiers and it dose not appear necessary to provide these are no more difficult to build than amplifiers and it dose not appear necessary to provide these any more frequently than it is already necessary to provide amplifiers to overcome the transmission losses in the transmission path. The technique of converting the analogue signal into a digital pulse stream became known as Pulse-Code-Modulation (PCM).

2. This means that signaling messages relating to a specific channel are only required when there is a change in status on that channel. The repetitive transmission of signaling messages, characteristic of channel associated signaling, is therefore avoided. This technique is known as common channel signaling. The CCITT common channel signaling standard for use with digital switching networks is known as signaling system No.7 (SS7). The No.7 signaling system operates on a data packet concept.

Unit 4

Common-Channel Signaling

TEXT

1. INTRODUCTION TO COMMON-CHANNEL SIGNALING

Common-channel signaling (CCS) uses message-based data communication. Signals are sent, as messages, between the control systems of SPC exchanges. Because the information in the data field of a message can be used not only to define the signal, but also to identify the call to which it refers, common-channel signaling can be removed from the speech path (hence its name). Thus, between two exchanges, the signaling for a number of speech circuits can take place over a single signaling circuit, as in Fig. 1. Further, because the handling of such signaling is at the speed of computer processing, the signaling circuit does not have to be a direct connection between the two exchanges. Indeed, once signaling is detached from speech transmission, there is the opportunity for an independent signaling network to exist. For example, Fig. 2 shows seven exchanges interconnected by separate speech and signaling networks. Dimensioning a signaling network is dependent not only on carrying capacity and economics, but also security, and so on.

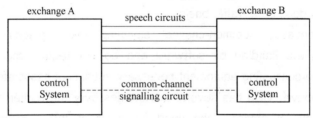

Fig. 1 Separate Speech and Signaling Circuits

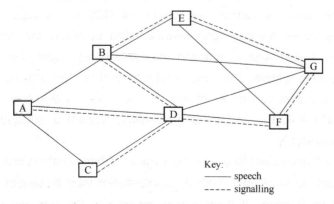

Fig. 2 Independent Speech Signaling Networks

Common-channel signaling overcomes all the limitations of channel-associated signaling. Considering these limitations, the advantages of common-channel signaling include:

(i) Being digital transmission directly between processors, it is extremely fast.

(ii) The signal repertoire, being dependent only on the size of the data field is potentially vast.

(iii) Given(ii),above, expansion will not be limited by technical constraints, but only by international agreement.

(iv) The large repertoire will provide signals for all services and not only for telephony.

(v) Network-management signals will be facilitated by the fact that they can be made available from the repertoire and by the speed and flexibility of the signaling network [1].

(vi) Because signals links are independent of speed paths signals may be sent at any time.

(vii) Because signals are not transmitted over the speech path, they are inaudible to subscribers.

(viii) Message transmission is dependent on accuracy in timing, but problems are immediately detected and automatically overcome, not only by the error checks built into individual messages, but also by a number of self-checking mechanisms in the network itself.

(ix) Because in common-channel signaling a single message of a few hundred bits contains all the information necessary to set up a call, a single signaling channel can accommodate the messages relating to a large number of speech channels. Signaling channels are, therefore, efficiently used; unlike in channel-associated signaling, there is no permanent allocation of the signaling-channel capacity to circuits. Signaling-channel dimensioning is thus done on a traffic basis.

In addition, because common-channel signaling takes places directly between processors, signals are handled by software and do not require the large amounts of expensive and space-consuming equipment necessary in channel-associated systems.

As described above, CCS has several advantages over the earlier channel-associated signaling. Importantly, it obviates the need for most of the percival circuit signaling equipment which is necessary when channel-associated signaling is used[2]. This in turn reduces its overall cost. A further key feature of CCS is its repertoire of signaling information. In the earlier analogue channel-associated systems, the number of different signals that could be sent was limited and the sending rate slow. For instance, in the multifrequency signaling system, there was a repertoire of only 16 different codes. A signal in this system is equivalent to 4 bit of information, and, as it would take about 100 ms to send it, the bit rate is 40 bit/s. The common-channel variant of subscriber-line signaling typically achieves 64 kbit/s.

This high speed(equivalent to a very high signaling bandwidth)is crucial to many new ISDN-based services, in which up to 1 000 bit of information must be sent between two nodes in order for a call to proceed. If these had to be sent at the signaling rates of channel-associated systems, the call set-up delay would be excessive and unacceptable to subscribers.

The development of CCS is the greatest quantum leap in the history of telephony signaling. Being interprocessor, it is independent of switch or transmission technology; so new signaling systems do not need to be introduced in parallel with every other development in telephony[3]. Standards can be laid down which are constant for all applications. Thus, for the first time, there can be a system which may be used in both national and international networks. Indeed, the CCITT signaling system No. 7, is already in use both nationally and internationally. It is also constantly being expanded to provide signaling for new services and network management. Common-channel signaling is also employed between subscribers and their local exchanges, using the ISDN architecture.

2. CCITT COMMON-CHANNEL SIGNALING SYSTEM No. 7

CCITT signaling system No. 7 is now the internationally accepted interrex change CCS system for use in both national and international networks. Fig. 3 shows a simplified block-schematic representation of a CCITT No. 7 signaling link between two exchanges. The signaling is transported in a dedicated time slot on one of the PCM systems carrying speech channels between the exchanges. In the case of two 2 Mbit/s systems, carrying up to 60 speech channels, one of the PCM systems carries the CCITT No. 7 link in its TS 16. The signaling is extracted from and inserted into the 2 Mbit/s(or 1.5 Mbit/s)system either via the exchange switch block, as shown in Fig. 3.

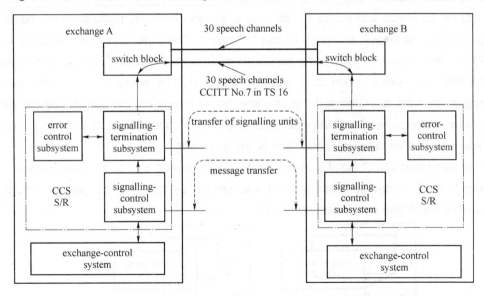

Fig. 3   Block-schematic Representation of CCITT No. 7 Signaling System

Signaling messages to be sent from one exchange to another are formulated by the exchange-control system and passed to the common-channel-signaling sender/receiver(CCS S/R)for CCITT No. 7(see Fig. 3). The CCS S/R consists of three subsystems: the signaling-control subsystem, the signaling-termination subsystem and the error-control subsystem all of which are microprocessor based. Information from the exchange-control system is received by the signaling-control subsystem, which structures the messages to be sent in the appropriate formats. Messages are then queued until they can be transmitted. When there are no messages to be sent, the signaling-control subsystem generates filler messages to keep the link active. On the Fig. 3, the dotted line labeled message transfer' indicates the source and destination of signaling messages.

Messages are then passed to the signaling-termination subsystem, where complete CCITT No. 7 signaling units are assembled, using sequence numbers and check bits generated by the error-control subsystem. In the Fig. 3, the dotted line labeled transfer of signaling units' shows the actual source and destination of the signaling units (as opposed to the messages containing the basic information to be transferred).

At the receiving exchange, the reverse sequence to that described above is carried out. Because of the importance of CCITT No. 7 to digital SPC exchange networks, its architecture and operation are explained in the following sections.

A technique used by designers of signaling systems is that of modeling the system as a stack of protocols. In this context, a "protocol" is a set of rules by which the communicating entities abide. A protocol stack employs the principle of data abstraction: each protocol layer in the stack is abstracted from those above and below it. A protocol stack thus allows the designer to divide the functions required for the signaling system into separate blocks, each of manageable proportions and with its information exchange with those above and below it defined, so that each block can be developed in isolation[4]. A protocol stack splits the design into several layers, forming a conceptual tower. The upper layer are then designed on the assumption that each of the lower layers performs certain defined functions without error. For instance, if a lower layer is responsible for correcting errors in the transmission of messages, then the layer above it can as some that all messages it sends or receives via the lower layer are error-free[5]. Thus, each layer depends on those below it, and, when layer N is referred to, the functions of layers 1 to N are assumed.

The traditional CCITT No. 7 protocol stack is represented by Fig. 4. It can be seen that the term "level" is used to describe what was termed a "layer" in the general description above. The traditional model has four levels.

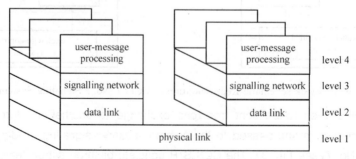

Fig. 4   The 4-level Architecture

(1) Lever 1: The Physical Carrier.

Level 1 is at the bottom of the protocol stack. In summary, it is the means of sending a stream of bits of information from one point to another, over a physical connection. At this level, there is no definition of, or requirement for, a structure to the information, other than that provided by the transmission equipment. Nor is there an error-detection mechanism. Such refinements are provided in higher levels.

(2) Level 2: The Data Link.

Level 2, supported by level 1, provides the basic signaling link. Specifically, the functions performed at level 2 are error control, link initialization, error-rate monitoring, flow control and delimitation of the signaling messages.

(3) Level 3: The signaling Network.

Within a national telecommunications network there may be several thousand public exchanges, and signaling messages must be routed flexibly and securely between them. The level 3 within the CCITT No. 7 system provides the functions necessary for the management of a signaling network.

(4) Level 4: The User Part

In the traditional architecture, level 4 of CCITT No. 7 was called the user part. This comprises those processes which are dedicated to handling the services being controlled by the signaling system. Three processes within the user part have been defined: the telephone-user part(TUP), the data-user part(DUP) and the integrated-services digital-network-user part(ISDN-UP), designed, respectively, to support telephony services, data services and ISDN-based services. The ability of the message-transfer part (MTP) to support a multiplicity of user parts is therefore crucial. With the flexibility and expandability which the user part provide, CCITT No. 7 will be able to handle new services as they are made available. This capability is essential if networks are to evolve into full ISDNS. Indeed, with new services controlled by the software of CCITT No.7, there will need only to be minimal change to the hardware of the exchanges, which will reduce the cost and complexity of the introduction of services. This was not possible with the earlier channel-associated signaling system, which were tailored to match the transmission and switching systems with which they worked, and whose message repertoires were extremely limited[6].

3. CCS Networks

Unlike channel-associated signaling, CCS offers administrations the possibility of developing a separate signaling network. This results from the detachment of signaling from its traffic channels, as shown Fig 2. A signaling network comprises signaling nodes, located in exchanges and normally forming a part of the exchange system, interconnected by signaling links which are provided by the transmission network.

The advantages to an administration of developing a separate CCS network are that it enables:

(i) The capabilities of CCS to be fully exploited.

(ii) The network of CCS links to be optimized for economy.

(iii) A high degree of resilience to be achieved, using both the security aspects of the CCS system and the alternative-routing possibilities of the line plant.

Signaling nodes(or, in CCIT No.7 terms "signaling points") may occur at the following locations:

(i) Switching units (local, trunk and international).

(ii) Operation, administration and maintenance centers.

(iii) Intelligent-network database sites.

(iv) Signal-transfer points.

In some cases a node is common to two networks; for example, an international gateway exchange is connected to both a national network and the international network. All signaling points are allocated a code by which they are addressed in CCS messages. In the case described above, the international exchange will have two signaling point codes, one national and the other international.

There are three ways in which the CCS links are associated with their dependent traffic channels. Briefly, these are as follows:

(i) Associated. In the associated mode, the messages relating to the traffic circuits connecting two exchanges are conveyed over signaling links directly connecting the two exchanges (see Fig.5a).

(ii) Non-associated. The non-associated mode is illustrated in Fig.5b. The signaling messages between A and B are routed through several signaling links, according to the network conditions at the time, while the traffic circuits are routed directly between A and B. At other times, the routing of the CCS messages may follow different paths. This method is not normally used because it is difficult to determine the exact routing of signaling messages at any given time.

(iii) Quasi-associated. This is a limited case of the non-associated mode, and the signaling messages between nodes A and B(see Fig.5c) follow a predetermined routing path through several signaling links in tandem, while the traffic circuits are routed directly between A and B. Usually, different transmission bearers are used for the CCS and their associated traffic links.

Associated working is normally used where the traffic route between two exchanges is large. For example, in the case of 200 circuits between two exchanges, seven 2 Mbit/s digital transmission systems would be required. One of which carried the single CCS link in its time slot 16(TS 16). However, where a network has many small-capacity traffic routes, the overheads of providing a CCS port for each one may be reduced by quasi-associated working. The most important use of quasi-associated working, however, is as a security back-up, as described below.

In the example above, failure of the PCM system carrying the CCS link would result in the loss not only of the 30 circuits of traffic but also of the signaling for the remaining 170 circuits, even through their transmission remained intact. In order to reduce to an acceptably low level the risk of this occurring, alternative means of carrying the CCS link are employed.

The most common is to re-route the CCS link over quasi-associated routings in the event of failure of the (associated) primary routing.

In addition to re-routing, which is programmed to operate automatically in the event of failure of the primary CCS link, network resilience is enhanced by permanently spreading the CCS messages over two (or more) parallel associated links. Thus, in the above example, the signaling for the 200 traffic circuits would be carried over two CCS links, in the TS 16s of different 2 Mbit/s digital transmission systems. Ideally, they would be carried on physically diverse paths to ensure maximum security.

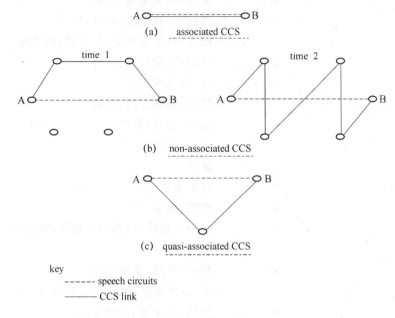

Fig. 5　Signaling Modes

An example of a resilient CCS network is shown in Fig. 6, in which nodes A to F are interconnected by a mesh network. Then, if CCS message from A to B are normally routed ACDB, and one of the links AC, CD or DB fails, the alternative paths AEFB, ACFB and ACDFB exist.

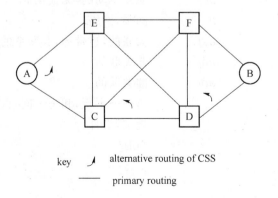

Fig. 6　Example of Signaling in a Mesh Network

NEW WORDS AND PHRASES

detach	vt.	分离,分开,移出
constraint	n.	制约,限制,约束
inaudible	adj.	听不见的,不可闻的
quantum	n.	量,数量,量子
obviate	vt.	消除,免除
crucial	adj.	关键的,关系重大的
schematic	adj.	图解的,概略的,示意的
formulate	vt	配置;按配方制造;公式化;格式化
termination	n.	终端(装置),终止,终点
abstraction	n.	分离,提取
refinement	n.	精制,明确表达,微调
delimitation	n.	定界,划界,界限
multiplicity	n.	多样,多样性
flexibility	n.	灵活性
expandability	n.	可扩充性
tailor	v.	修整,制造
match	v.	与……相适应,和……相符,匹配……
node	n.	节点,结点
exploit	vt.	利用,使用,发挥,开发
optimize	v.	最优,使最佳;确定……的最佳特性
resilience	n.	弹性,回弹能力,恢复力
database	n	数据库
failure	n.	故障,失败
bearer	n.	载体,运载工具,承载线路(信道)
overhead	n.	总开销
intact	adj.	原封不动的,无损伤的
mesh	n.	网眼,网络
associated	adj.	关联的,连带的,有联系的
non-associated	adj.	非关联的
quasi-associated	adj	准关联的
in parallel with		与……平行,和……同时,伴随着……
lay down		规定,设计
at the time		当时

NOTES

[1] Network-management signals will be facilitated by the fact that they can be made available from the repertoire and by the speed and flexibility of the signaling network.

句中"that"引导同位语从句,说明"the fact",翻译时,把同位语从句译为与主句并列的一个分句。

全句可译为:基于信令网的(高)速度和方便性,网管信号(传送)方便。

[2] Importantly, it obviates the need for most of the per circuit signaling equipment which is necessary when channel-associated signaling is used.

句中"for most of…equipment"短语作定语修饰"the need";"which"引导定语从句,修饰"the per circuit signaling equipment";"when"引导时间状语从句。翻译时,可把作状语的"importantly"和句子之间的关系译为表语从句形式,把"when"引导的状语从句译为句中的一个定语成分,使译文简洁明了。

全句可译为:重要的是,共路信令省略了大部分的噪声抑制电路信令设备,这些设备当使用随路信令时是必需的。

[3] Being interprocessor, it is independent of switch or transmission technology; so new signaling systems do not need to be introduced in parallel with every other development in telephony.

句中"Being interprocessor"为分词短语作原因状语;"so"引导并列分句;"in parallel with…in telephony"短语作状语,表示伴随情况。翻译时,为了上下文连贯,可把作状语的"Being interprocessor"增加主语成分译为原因状语从句。

全句可译为:因为共路信令是跨处理器的,它独立于交换或传输技术;所以新的信令系统不需要和电话系统的每个发展同步。

[4] A protocol stack thus allows the designer to divide the functions required for the signaling system into separate blocks, each of manageable proportions and with its information exchange with those above and below it defined, so that each block can be developed in isolation.

句中"required for the signaling system"是过去分词短语作定语,修饰"the functions";"A protocol…separate blocks"与"each of…it defined"为两个并列分句,其中"each of…its information"为第二个分句的主语;"so that"引导结果状语从句,全句是并列复杂句。

全句可译为:因此,协议栈允许设计者把信令系统所需的功能划分成单独的模块,每个可管理部分和它的上、下层之间进行信息交换,所以每个模块可以单独地进行开发。

[5] For instance, if a lower layer is responsible for correcting errors in the transmission of messages, then the layer above it can assume that all messages it sends or receives via the lower layer are error-free.

句中"if"引导条件状语从句,"that"引导宾语从句;"it sends or receives…layer"为省掉"that"的定语从句,"that"在从句中作宾语,代表"all messages"。

全句可译为:例如,如果低层负责信息传输中的错误纠正,则它的上层就会假设它通过低层传输或接收的信息是没有错误的。

[6] This was not possible with the earlier channel-associated signaling system, which were tailored to match the transmission and switching systems with which they worked, and whose message repertoires were extremely limited.

本句中多次使用了定语从句:"which"引导的定语从句修饰"the earlier channel-associated signaling system"; "with which" 引导的定语从句修饰"the transmission and switching systems"; 而"whose"引导的定语从句修饰"the earlier…signaling system"。翻译时可把定语从句拆译成并列分句。tailored to…译为根据……调整。

全句可译为:这在早期的随路信令系统中是不可能的。早期的随路信令被调整到与它协同工作的传输和交换系统相匹配,并且它的信息指令的使用受到了极大的限制。

EXERCISES

一、根据课文选择最佳答案

1. In a signaling network, signaling nodes are interconnected by _____.
   A. signaling points   B. signaling routes
   C. signaling transfer points D. signaling links

2. Signaling nodes may occur at _____.
   A. switching unit
   B. intelligent-network database sites signaling transfer points
   C. operation, administration and maintenance centers
   D. all of above

3. In Fig. 6, if one of the links AE, EF or FB fails, CCS messages from A to B are alternatively routed via _____.
   A. ACDB   B. AEDB
   C. AEFDB   D. ACDB, AEDB and AEFDB

二、根据课文判断对错

1. All signaling points are allocated two signaling point codes, one national and the other international. (   )

2. The CCS links are associated with their dependent traffic channels only in the associated mode. (   )

3. Non-associated working is easy to determine the exact routing of signaling messages at any given time. (   )

4. Quasi-associated working is normally used when the traffic route between two exchanges is large. (   )

三、回答下列问题

1. What are the advantages to administration of developing a separate CCS network?

2. What is the most important use of quasi-associated working? Why?

Unit 5

The Sampling Theorem

TEXT

Under certain conditions, a continuous signal can be completely represented by and recoverable from a sequence of its values, or samples, at points equally spaced in time[1]. This somewhat surprising property follows from a basic result that is referred to as the sampling theorem. This theorem is extremely important and useful. It is exploited, for example, in moving pictures, which consist of a sequence of individual frames, each of which represents an instantaneous view (i.e., a sample in time) of a continuously changing scene[2]. When these samples are viewed in sequence at a sufficiently fast rate, we perceive an accurate representation of the original continuously moving scene.

Much of the importance of the sampling theorem also lies in its role as a bridge between continuous-time signals and discrete-time signals. The fact that under certain conditions a continuous-time signal can be completely recovered from a sequence of its samples provides a mechanism for representing a continuous-time signal by a discrete-time signal[3]. In many contexts, processing discrete-time signals is more flexible and is often preferable to processing continuous-time signals[4]. This is due in large part to the dramatic development of digital technology over the past few decades, resulting in the availability of inexpensive, lightweight, programmable, and easily reproducible discrete-time signal, process the discrete-time system. We exploit sampling to convert a continuous-time signal to a discrete-time signal, process the discrete-time signal using a discrete-time system, and then convert back to continuous-time signal.

Sampling theorem can be started as follows:

Let $x(t)$ be a band-limited signal with $X(j\omega) = 0$ for $|\omega| > \omega_m$. Then $x(t)$ is uniquely determined by its samples $x(nT)$, $n = 0, \pm 1, \pm 2, \cdots$, if

$$\omega_s > 2\omega_m$$

where

$$\omega_s = 2\pi/T$$

Given these samples, we can reconstruct $x(t)$ by generating a periodic impulse train in which successive impulses have amplitudes that are successive sample values. This impulse train is then processed through an ideal lowpass filter with gain T and cutoff frequency greater than ω_m and less than $\omega_s - \omega_m$. The resulting output signal will exactly equal $x(t)$[5].

The frequency $2\omega_m$, which, under the sampling theorem, must be exceeded by the sampling frequency, is commonly referred to as the Nyquist rate.

In previous discussion, it was assumed that the sampling frequency was sufficiently high that the conditions of sampling theorem were met[6]. As illustrated in Fig. 1, with $\omega_s > 2\omega_m$, the spectrum of the sampled signal consists of scaled replications of the spectrum of $x(t)$, and this forms the basis for the sampling theorem. When $\omega_s < 2\omega_m$, $X(j\omega)$, the spectrum of $x(t)$, is no longer replicated in $X_P(j\omega)$ and thus is no longer recoverable by lowpass filtering. The reconstructed signal will no longer be equal to $x(t)$. This effect is referred to as aliasing.

Sampling has a number of important applications. One particularly significant set of applications relates to using sampling to process continuous-time signals with discrete-time systems, by means of minicomputers, microprocessors, or any of a variety of devices specifically oriented towards discrete-time signal processing.

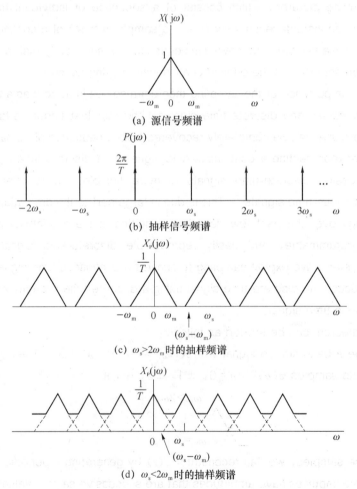

Fig. 1 Effect in the frequency of domain of sampling in the time domain

NEW WORDS AND PHRASES

theorem	n.	定理,定律,法则
exploit	vt.	开拓,开发,利用
sequence	n.	次序,顺序,序列
instantaneous	adj.	瞬间的,即刻的,即时的
reproducible	adj.	能繁殖的,可再生的,可复制的
cut off	n.	截止,中止,切掉
replication	n.	复制,重现
perceive	v.	感知,感到,认识到
aliasing	n.	混淆现象,混叠
Nyquist rate	n.	奈奎斯特抽样率

NOTES

[1] Under certain conditions, a continuous signal can be completely represented by and recoverable from a sequence of its values, or samples, at points equally spaced in time.

本句可译为：在一定的条件下，一个连续时间信号完全可以由该信号在时间等间隔点上的瞬时值或样本值来表示，并且能用这些样本值恢复出原信号来。

本句中过去分词 equally spaced in time 作定语，修饰 points，译为：在时间上等分的点。can be completely represented by and recoverable from 这一结构中，and 与 recoverable 之间省略了 be 动词，翻译时可分开翻译。

[2] It is exploited, for example, in moving pictures, which consist of a sequence of individual frames, each of which represents an instantaneous view (i.e., a sample in time) of a continuously changing scene.

本句可译为：例如，抽样定理在电影里得到了利用。电影由一组按时序排列的单个画面所组成，其中每一个画面都代表着连续变化景象中的一个瞬时画面（即时间样本）。

句中有两个定语从句，第一个 which 引导的定语从句修饰 moving pictures，第二个 which 引导的定语从句修饰 individual frames，这一定语从句嵌套在第一个定语从句之中。本句中的主语是 it，指前面提到的 sampling theorem，谓语是 is exploited，其余的作状语。

[3] The fact that under certain conditions a continuous-time signal can be completely recovered from a sequence of its samples provides a mechanism for representing a continuous-time signal by a discrete-time signal.

本句可译为：在一定的条件下，可以用信号的时序样本值完全恢复出原连续时间信号，这就提供了用一个离散时间信号来表示一个连续时间信号的机理。

本句中主语是 the fact，谓语是 provides，that 引导的同位语从句解释 fact 的内容。

[4] In many contexts, processing discrete-time signals is more flexible and is often preferable to processing continuous-time signals.

在许多方面，处理离散时间信号要更加灵活些，因此往往比处理连续时间更为可取。

句中 is preferable to 是固定搭配，意思是"比……更为可取"。

[5] Given these samples, we can reconstruct $x(t)$ by generating a periodic impulse train in which successive impulses have amplitudes that are successive sample values. This impulse train is then processed through an ideal lowpass filter with gain T and cutoff frequency greater than ω_m and less than $\omega_s - \omega_m$. The resulting output signal will exactly equal $x(t)$.

本句可译为：已知这些样本值，我们可以用以下方法重新构造 $x(t)$：产生一个周期的冲激串，其冲激的强度就是依次而来的样本值，然后将冲激串通过一个增益为 T，截止频率大于 ω_m，而小于 $\omega_s - \omega_m$ 的理想低通滤波器，该滤波器的输出就等于 $x(t)$。

[6] In previous discussion, it was assumed that the sampling frequency was sufficiently high that the conditions of sampling theorem were met.

本句可译为：在前面的讨论中，假设抽样频率足够高，因而满足抽样定理的条件。

句中 that the sampling frequency was sufficiently high 是 that 引导的主语从句，it 是形式主语，that the conditions of sampling theorem were met 中 that 相当于 so that，引导目的状语从句。

EXERCISES

一、请根据课文内容回答以下问题

1. How is the sampling theorem exploited in moving picture?
2. Why does the sampling theorem lie in its role as a bridge between continuous-time, signals and discrete-time signals?
3. Please state the sampling theorem and tell what the Nyquist rate is.
4. What is the spectrum of the sampled signal when $\omega_s > 2\omega_m$ and when $\omega_s < 2\omega_m$ where ω_s is sampling frequency and ω_m is bandwidth of original signal?

二、将以下短文译成中文

The circuit consists of a transistor switch, a capacitor with a large capacitance, and two voltage followers. The voltage followers are used to shield the capacitor to eliminate the loading problem. The switch is controlled by control logic. When the switch is open, the capacitor voltage remains roughly constant. Thus the output of the sampled-and-hold circuit is stepwise. Using this circuit, the problem due to the conversion time can be eliminated. Therefore, a sample-and-hold circuit is often used, either internally or externally, with an A/D converter.

Unit 6

Evolution of Lightwave Systems

TEXT

The research phase of fiber-optic communication systems started around 1975. The enormous progress over the 25-year period extending from 1975 to 2000 can be grouped into several distinct generations[1]. Fig. 1 shows the increase in the BL product over this time period as quantified through various laboratory experiments. The straight line corresponds to a doubling of the BL product every year. In every generation, BL increases initially but then begins to saturate as the technology matures. Each new generation brings a fundamental change that helps to improve the system performance further.

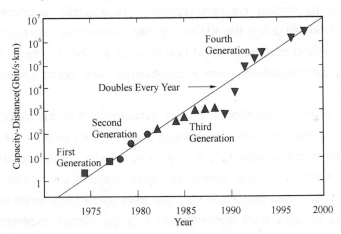

Fig. 1 Increase in the BL product over the period 1975 to 2000 through several generations of lightwave systems. Different symbols are used for successive generations.

The first generation of lightwave systems operated near 0.8 μm and used GaAs semiconductor lasers. After several field trials during the period 1977-1979, such systems became available commercially in 1980. They operated at a bit rate of 45 Mbit/s and allowed repeater spacing of up to 10 km. The larger repeater spacing compared with 1-km spacing of coaxial systems was an important motivation for system designers because it decreased the installation and maintenance costs associated with each repeater.

It was clear during the 1970s that[2] the repeater spacing could be increased considerably by operating the lightwave system in the wavelength region near 1.3 μm, where fiber loss is below 1 dB/km. Furthermore, optical fibers exhibit minimum dispersion in this wavelength region. This realization led to a worldwide effort for the development of InGaAsP semiconductor lasers and detectors operating near 1.3 μm. The second generation of fiber-optic communication systems became available in the early 1980s, but the bit rate of early systems was limited to below 100 Mbit/s because of dispersion in multimode fibers. This limitation was overcome by the use of single-mode fiber. A laboratory experiment in 1981 demonstrated transmission at 2 Gbit/s over 44 km of single-mode fiber. The introduction of commercial systems soon followed. By 1987, second-generation lightwave systems, operating at bit rates of up to 1.7 Gbit/s with a repeater spacing of about 50 km, were commercially available.

The repeater spacing of the second-generation lightwave systems was limited by the fiber losses at the operating wavelength of 1.3 μm (typically 0.5 dB/km). Losses of silica fibers become minimum near 1.55 μm. Indeed, a 0.2-dB/km loss was realized in 1979 in this spectral region. However, the introduction of third-generation lightwave systems operating at 1.55 μm was considerably delayed by large fiber dispersion near 1.55 μm. Conventional InGaAsP semiconductor lasers could not be used because of pulse spreading occurring as a result of simultaneous oscillation of several longitudinal modes. The dispersion problem can be overcome either by using dispersion-shifted fibers designed to have minimum dispersion near 1.55 μm or by limiting the laser spectrum to a single longitudinal mode. Both approaches were followed during the 1980s. By 1985, laboratory experiments indicated the possibility of transmitting information at bit rate of up to 10 Gbit/s. The best performance is achieved using dispersion-shifted fibers in combination with lasers oscillating in a single longitudinal mode.

A drawback of third-generation 1.55 μm systems is that the signal is regenerated periodically by using electronic repeaters spaced apart typically by 60~70 km. The repeater spacing can be increased by making use of a homodyne or heterodyne detection scheme because its use improves receiver sensitivity. Such systems are referred to as coherent lightwave systems. Coherent systems were under development worldwide during the 1980s, and their potential benefits were demonstrated in many system experiments. However, commercial introduction of such systems was postponed with the advent of fiber amplifiers in 1989.

The fourth generation of lightwave systems makes use of optical amplification for increasing the repeater spacing and of wavelength-division multiplexing (WDM) for increasing the bit rate[3]. In most WDM systems, fiber losses are compensated periodically using erbium-doped fiber amplifiers spaced 60~80 km apart. Such amplifiers were developed after 1985 and became available commercially by 1990. A 1991 experiment showed the possibility of data transmission over 21 000 km at 2.5 Gbit/s and over 14 300 km at 5 Gbit/s, using a recirculating-loop configuration. This performance indicated that an amplifier-based, all optical, submarine transmission system was feasible for intercontinental communication. By 1996, not only transmission over 11 300 km at a bit rate of 5 Gbit/s had been demonstrated by using actual submarine cables, but commercial transatlantic and transpacific cable systems also became available[4]. Since then, a large number of submarine lightwave systems have been deployed worldwide.

The 27 000 km fiber-optic link around the globe (known as FLAG) became operational in 1998, linking many Asian and European countries. Another major lightwave system, known as Africa One was operating by 2000; it circles the African continent and covers a total transmission distance of about 35 000 km. Several WDM systems were deployed across the Atlantic and Pacific oceans during 1998-2001 in response to the Internet-induced increase in the data traffic; they have increased the total capacity by orders of magnitudes. A truly global network covering 250 000 km with a capacity of 2.56 Tbit/s (64 WDM channels at 10 Gbit/s over 4 fiber pairs) is scheduled to be operational in 2002. Clearly, the fourth-generation systems have revolutionized the whole field of fiber-optic communication.

The fifth generation of fiber-optic communication systems is concerned with extending the wavelength range over which a WDM system can operate simultaneously. The conventional wavelength window, known as the C band, covers the wavelength range $1.53 \sim 1.57$ μm. It is being extended on both the long- and short-wavelength sides, resulting in the L and S bands, respectively. The Raman amplification technique can be used for signals in all three wavelength bands. Moreover, a new kind of fiber, known as the dry fiber has been developed with the property that fiber losses are small over the entire wavelength region from 1.30 to 1.65 μm. Availability of such fibers and new amplification schemes may lead to lightwave systems with thousands of WDM channels.

The fifth-generation systems also attempt to increase the bit rate of each channel within the WDM signal. Starting in 2000, many experiments used channels operating at 40 Gbit/s; migration toward 160 Gbit/s is also likely in the future. Such systems require an extremely management of fiber dispersion. An interesting approach is based on the concept of optical soliton-pulse that preserve their shape during propagation in a lossless fiber by counteracting the effect of dispersion through the fiber nonlinearity. Although the basic idea was proposed as early as 1973, it was only in 1988 that a laboratory experiment demonstrated the feasibility of data transmission over 4 000 km by compensating the fiber loss through Raman amplification[5]. Erbium-doped fiber amplifiers were used for soliton amplification starting in 1989. Since then, many system experiments have demonstrated the eventual potential of soliton communication systems. By 1994, solitons were transmitted over 35 000 km at 10 Gbit/s and over 24 000 km at 15 Gbit/s. Starting in 1996, the WDM technique was also used for solitons in combination with dispersion management. In a 2 000 experiment, up to 27 WDM channels, each operating at 20 Gbit/s, were transmitted over 9 000 km using a hybrid amplification scheme.

Even though the fiber-optic communication technology is barely 25 years old, it has progressed rapidly and has reached a certain stage of maturity. This is also apparent from the publication of a large number of books on optical communications and WDM networks since 1995.

NEW WORDS AND PHRASES

evolution	n.	进展，发展，演变，进化
commercially	adv.	商业上，通商上
dispersion	n.	色散
drawback	n.	缺点，缺陷，瑕疵，障碍
sensitivity	n.	灵敏度，灵敏性
magnitude	n.	大小，数量，巨大，广大，量级
counteract	v.	抵消，中和，阻碍
nonlinearity	n.	非线性
soliton	n.	孤立子，孤波
maturity	n.	成熟，完备

NOTES

[1] The enormous progress over the 25-year period extending from 1975 to 2000 can be grouped into several distinct generations.

本句为被动语态，其主语是 the enormous progress，短语 extend from…to…表示"从……延续（一直）到"，全句可译为：从1975年一直到2000年这25年期间的巨大发展可以划分为不同的几代。

[2] It was clear during the 1970s that the repeater spacing could be increased considerably by operating the lightwave system in the wavelength region near 1.3 μm, where fiber loss is below 1 dB/km.

全句可译为：在20世纪70年代，通过使光波系统工作在损耗低于 1 dB/km 的 1.3 μm 附近的波长范围内可以显著增加中继距离，这一点是很明确的。

it 为形式主语，真正的主语是后面 that 引导的从句。

[3] The fourth generation of lightwave systems makes use of optical amplification for increasing the repeater spacing and of wavelength-division multiplexing (WDM) for increasing the bit rate.

全句可译为：第四代光波系统利用光放大器来增加中继距离；利用波分复用来增加比特率。

makes use of：利用，使用。

[4] By 1996, not only transmission over 11 300 km at a bit rate of 5 Gbit/s had been demonstrated by using actual submarine cables, but commercial transatlantic and transpacific cable systems also became available.

全句可译为：到1996年，不仅可以用实际的海底光缆以 5 Gbit/s 的速率传播 11 300 km，而且穿越大西洋和太平洋的光缆系统也开始商用。

该句为"not only…but also"句型。

[5] Although the basic idea was proposed as early as 1973, it was only in 1988 that a laboratory experiment demonstrated the feasibility of data transmission over 4 000 km by

compensating the fiber loss through Raman amplification.

全句可译为：虽然早在 1973 年就提出了这种基本思想，但直到 1988 年在实验室中进行的一次试验才证明，通过拉曼放大来补偿光纤损耗，使数据传输 4 000 km 成为可能。

as early as：早在。it was only in 1988 that…为强调句型。

EXERCISES

一、将下述词组译成英文

光波系统　　　　中继距离　　　　半导体激光器　　　　光纤放大器
波分复用　　　　光纤损耗　　　　光纤色散　　　　　　掺铒光纤放大器

二、将下述词组译成中文

coaxial systems　　　　multimode fiber　　　　　　single-mode fiber
fiber dispersion　　　　coherent lightwave systems　　fiber amplifiers
wavelength-division multiplexing　　　　　　　　　erbium-doped fiber amplifier
optical soliton-pulse　　fiber losses

三、将下述短文译成中文

1. The first generation of lightwave systems operated near 0.8 μm and used GaAs semiconductor lasers. After several field trials during the period 1977-1979, such systems became available commercially in 1980. They operated at a bit rate of 45 Mbit/s and allowed repeater spacing of up to 10 km. The larger repeater spacing compared with 1km spacing of coaxial systems was an important motivation for system designers because it decreased the installation and maintenance costs associated with each repeater.

2. It was clear during the 1970s that the repeater spacing could be increased considerably by operating the lightwave system in the wavelength region near 1.3 μm, where fiber loss is below 1 dB/km. Furthermore, optical fibers exhibit minimum dispersion in this wavelength region. This realization led to a worldwide effort for the development of InGaAsP semiconductor lasers and detectors operating near 1.3 μm.

3. Even though the fiber-optic communication technology is barely 25 years old, it has progressed rapidly and has reached a certain stage of maturity. This is also apparent from the publication of a large number of books on optical communications and WDM networks since 1995.

Unit 7

Fiber Optic

TEXT

Optical fiber transmission has come of age as a major innovation in telecommunications. Such systems offer extremely high bandwidth, freedom from external interference, immunity from interception by external means, and cheap raw material (silicon, the most abundant material on the Earth).

1. Fundamentals of Fiber Optic System

Optical fibers guide light rays within the fiber material. They can do this because light rays bend or change direction when they pass from one medium to another. They bend because the speed of propagation of light in each medium is different. This phenomenon is called refraction. One common example of refraction occurs when you stand at the edge of a pool and look at an object at the bottom of the pool. Unless you are directly over the object, it appears to be farther away than it really is. This effect occurs because the speed of the light ray from the object increases as the light ray passes from the water to the air. This causes them to bend, changing the angle at which you perceive the object. You can obtain an appreciation for the manner by which light flows by focusing upon Snell's Law.

2. Snell's Law

How optical fibers work can be explained by Snell's Law, which states that the ratio of the sine of the angle of incidence to the sine of the angle of refraction is equal to the ratio of the propagation velocities of the wave in the two respective media[1]. This is equal to a constant that is the ratio of the refractive index of the second medium to that of the first. Written as an equation, Snell's Law looks like this:

$$\frac{\sin A_1}{\sin A_2} = \frac{v_1}{v_2} = K = \frac{n_2}{n_1} \tag{1}$$

In this equation, A_1 and A_2 are the angles of incidence and refraction, respectively v_1 and v_2 are the velocities of propagation of the wave in the two media, n_1 and n_2 are the indices of refraction of the two media.

The parameters are demonstrated graphically in Fig. 1. In each case, A_1 is the angle of incidence, and A_2 is the angle of refraction. The index of refraction of material 1, n_1, is greater than the index of refraction of material 2, n_2. This means that the velocity of propagation of light is greater in material 2 than in material 1.

Fig. 1(a) demonstrates how a light ray passing from material 1 to material 2 is refracted in material 2 when A_1 is less than the critical angle. Fig. 1(b) demonstrates the condition that exists when A_1 is at the critical angle and angle A_2 is at 90[dg][2]. The light ray is directed along the boundary between the two materials.

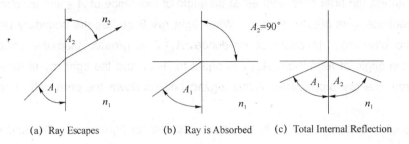

(a) Ray Escapes　　(b) Ray is Absorbed　　(c) Total Internal Reflection

Fig. 1　The index of refraction ($n_1 > n_2$)

As shown in Fig. 1 (c), any light rays that are incident at angles greater than A_1 of Fig. 1 (b) will be reflected back into material 1 with angle A_2 equal to A_1. The condition in Fig. 1 (c) is the one of particular interest for optical fibers.

3. Fiber Composition

An optical fiber is a dielectric (nonconductor of electricity) waveguide made of glass or plastic. It consists of three distinct regions: a core, a cladding, and a sheath or jacket. The sheath or jacket protects the fiber but does not govern the transmission capability of the fiber.

The index of refraction of the assembly varies across the radius of the cable, and the core has a constant or smoothly varying index of refraction called n_c. The cladding region has another constant index of refraction called n. The core possesses a high refractive index, whereas the cladding is constructed to have a lower refractive index. The result of the difference in the refractive indices keeps light flowing through the core after it gets into the core, even if the fiber is bent or tied into a knot. For a fiber designed to carry light in several modes of propagation at the same time (called a multimode fiber), the diameter of the core is several times the wavelength of the light to be carried. Wavelength is a measure of the distance between two cycles of the same wave measured in nanometers (nm), or billionths of a meter, and the cladding thickness will be greater than the radius of the core[3]. Following are some typical values for a multimode fiber:

➢ An operating light wavelength of 0.8 μm
➢ A core index of refraction n_c of 1.5
➢ A cladding index of refraction n of 1.485 (= $0.99n_c$)
➢ A core diameter of 50, 62.5 or 100 μm
➢ A cladding thickness of 37.5 μm

The clad fiber would have a diameter of 125μm, and light would propagate as shown in Fig. 2.

A light source emits light at many angles relative to the center of the fiber. In Fig. 2, light ray A enters the fiber perpendicular to the face of the core and parallel to the axis. Its angle of incidence A_1 is 0; therefore, it is not refracted, and it travels parallel to the axis. Light ray B enters the fiber core from air at an angle of incidence of A_{1B} and is refracted at an angle A_{2B} because n_2 is greater than n_1. When light ray B strikes the boundary between the core and the cladding, its angle of incidence, $A_{1'B}$, is greater than the critical angle. Therefore, the angle of refraction, $A_{2'B}$, is equal to $A_{1'B}$, and the light ray is reflected back into the core. The ray propagates in this zigzag fashion down the core until it reaches the other end.

If the angle of incidence, A_{1C}, is too large, as it is for light ray C, the light ray strikes the boundary between the core and the cladding with an angle of incidence, $A_{1'C}$, less than the critical angle. The ray enters into the cladding and propagates into, or is absorbed into, the cladding and jacket (which is opaque to light).

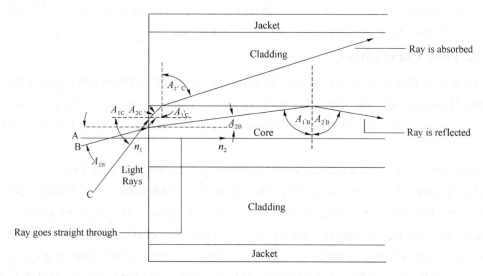

Fig. 2　Light ray paths in multimode fiber ($n_1 > n_2$)

4. Modal Delay

For optical fibers in which the diameter of the core is many times the wavelength of the light transmitted, the light beam travels along the fiber by bouncing back and forth at the interface between the core and the cladding. Rays entering the fiber at differing angles are refracted varying angles numbers of times as they move from one end to the other and consequently do not arrive at the distant end with the same phase relationship as when they started[4]. The differing angles of entry are called modes of propagation (or just modes), and a fiber carrying several modes is called a multimode fiber. Multimode propagation causes the rays leaving the fiber to interfere both constructively and destructively as they leave the end of the fiber. This effect is called modal delay spreading.

Because most optical communications systems transmit information in digital form consisting of pulses of light, the effect of modal delay spreading limits the capability of the fiber to transport recognizable pulses[5]. This is because modal delay spreading broadens the pulses in the time domain, as illustrated in Fig. 3.

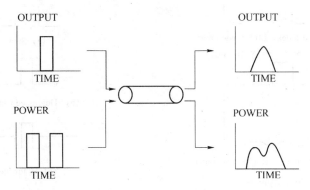

Fig. 3 Pulse Spreading

The effect of pulse spreading is to make it difficult or impossible for an optical receiver to differentiate one pulse from another after a given transmission distance. Thus, after a predefined transmission distance, a multimode fiber either causes a very high bit error rate or precludes the capability of the pulse to be recognized and terminates the capability of the cable to be used for communications.

If the diameter of the fiber core is only a few times the wavelength of the transmitted light (say, a factor of 3), only one ray or mode will be propagated, and no destructive interference between rays will occur[6]. These fibers, called single-mode fibers, are the media that are used in most transmission systems. Fig. 4(a) and Fig. 5(b) show the distribution of the index of refraction across, and typical diameters of, multimode and single-mode fibers[7]. One of the principal differences between single-mode and multimode fibers is that most of the power in the multimode fiber travels in the core, whereas, in single-mode fibers, a large fraction of the power is propagated in the cladding near the core. At the point where the light wavelength becomes long enough to cause single-mode propagation, about 20 percent of the power is carried in the cladding, but if the light wavelength is doubled, more than 50 percent of the power travels in the cladding.

5. Refractive Index

Fiber can also be classified by its type of refractive index. Fig. 5 illustrates a few of the classifications, which are outlined here:

- Stepped-index fiber—The fiber cores has a uniform refractive index throughout with a sudden change of the refractive index at the core-cladding boundary.
- Graded-index fiber—The fiber core has a refractive index that gradually decreases as

the distance from the center of the fiber increases.

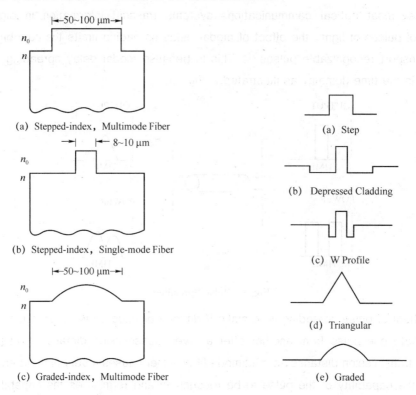

Fig. 4 Refractive index profiles

Fig. 5 Different refractive index profile

> Single-mode fiber—Also known as monomode, this has a uniform refractive index. This type of fiber permits only a single light ray to pass through the cable.

> Graded-index multimode fiber—The index of refraction varies smoothly across the diameter of the core but remains constant in the cladding. This treatment reduces the intermodal dispersion by the fiber because rays traveling along a graded-index fiber have nearly equal delays.

Other refractive index profiles have been devised to solve various problems, such as reduction of chromatic dispersion. Some of these profiles are shown in Fig. 5; the step and graded profiles are repeated for comparison.

Fig. 6 compares the flow of light through stepped-index, graded-index, and single-mode fiber. A stepped-index fiber typically has a core diameter between 100 μm and 500 μm. A graded-index fiber commonly has a core diameter of 50 μm or 62.5 μm, while single-mode fibers have core diameters between 8 μm and 10 μm. Both stepped-index and graded-index fiber supports multimode transmission.

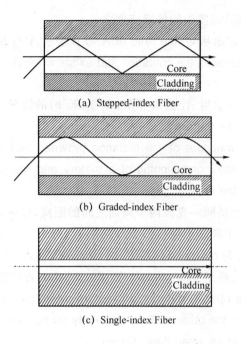

Fig. 6 Light flow through different refractive index fibers

NEW WORDS AND PHRASES

propagate	v.	传播
refraction	n.	折射,折射度
interception	n.	截取,窃听,监听
critical	adj.	临界的
waveguide	n.	波导,波导管
perpendicular	adj.	垂直的
zigzag	adj.	之字形的,Z 字形的
opaque	adj.	不传导的,不透明的
mono-		(前缀)单,单一,一
dispersion	n.	色散
profile	n.	曲线,分布图
error rate		误码率
destructive interference		破坏性干扰,干涉相消

NOTES

[1] How optical fibers work can be explained by Snell's Law, which states that the ratio of the sine of the angle of incidence to the sine of the angle of refraction is equal to the ratio of the propagation velocities of the wave in the two respect media.

本句可译为:光纤的工作原理可用斯涅尔折射定律来解释:入射角与折射角的正弦值之

比等于光波在这两种(传输)媒质中的传播速度之比。

Which 引导非限定性定语从句;the ratio of A to B 表示 A 与 B 之比。

[2] Fig. 1(b) demonstrates the condition that exists when A_1 is at the critical angle and angle A_2 is at 90[dg].

本句可译为:图 1(b)表示当 A_1 为临界角,A_2 为 90°时的情况。

[dg]表示角度单位,dg = degree 度。

[3] Wavelength is a measure of the distance between two cycles of the same wave measured in nanometer (nm), or billionths of a meter, and the cladding thickness will be greater than the radius of the core.

本句可译为:波长指的是同一光波两个周期之间的距离,以纳米即一米的十亿分之一来表示。光纤包层厚度要大于纤芯半径。

nanometer 纳米,简写为 nm;nano-(前缀)纳(诺)、毫微(10^{-9}),这种单位前缀在科技文中很常见,例如本课中还出现了 micrometers(微米)、gigabit(吉比特)等。

[4] Rays entering the fiber at differing angles are refracted varying numbers of times as they move from one end to the other and consequently do not arrive at the distant end with the same phase relationship as when they started.

本句可译为:光线从光纤的一端传至另一端时,以不同的角度入射的光线发生折射的次数不同。因而,到达远端时,其相位关系也与开始时不同。

[5] Because most optical communications systems transmit information in digital form consisting of pulse of light, the effect of modal delay spreading limits the capability of the fiber to transport recognizable pulses.

本句可译为:由于大部分光纤通信系统都是以光脉冲这种数字方式传输信息的,所以模式延迟限制了光纤传输可识别脉冲的容量。

[6] If the diameter of the fiber core is only a few times the wavelength of the transmitted light (say, a factor of 3), only one ray or mode will be propagated, and no destructive interference between rays will occur.

本句可译为:如果光纤纤芯的直径仅仅是传输光波波长的几倍(比如说 3 倍),那么只有一种光或传输模式可以传输,并且在光线之间不会产生干涉相消。

Factor 表示"因数、倍"。

[7] Fig. 4(a) and Fig. 4(b) show the distribution of the index of refraction across, and typical diameters of, multimode and single-mode fibers.

本句可译为:图 4(a)和图 4(b)给出了折射率沿多模光纤和单模光纤的分布,以及它们典型的直径值。

EXERCISE

一、将下列单词(词组)译成中文

propagation mode	refractive index profile	optical receiver
dielectric	destructive interference	stepped-index fiber

二、在下列空白处填上缺少的单词(词组)

1. Optical fiber transmission has come _____ age as a major innovation in telecommunications.

2. Light ray A enters the fiber perpendicular _____ the face of the core and parallel to the axis.

3. This is because modal delay spreading broadens the pulses _____ the time domain.

4. The effect of pulse spreading is to make it difficult or impossible for an optical receiver to differentiate one pulse _____ another after a given transmission distance.

5. Because most optical communications systems transmit information _____ digital form consisting of pulses of light, the effect of modal delay spreading limits the capability of the fiber recognizable pulse.

Unit 8

Synchronous Digital Hierarchy[1]

TEXT

SDH is an International Standard for high-speed synchronous optical telecommunication networks—a Synchronous Digital Hierarchy.

Work started on SDH standards in CCITT's Study Group XVIII in June 1986. The objective was to produce a worldwide standard for synchronous transmission systems which can provide network operators with a flexible and economic network.

In November 1988 the first SDH standards were approved—G. 707, G. 708, G. 709. These standards define transmission rates, signal format, multiplexing structures and tributary mappings for the Network Node Interface (NNI)—the international standard interface for Synchronous Digital Hierarchy.

In addition to defining standards covering the NNI, CCITT also embarked on series of standards governing the operation of synchronous multiplexers (G. 781, G. 782, G. 783) and SDH Network Management[2] (G. 784). It is the standardization of these aspects of SDH equipment that will deliver the flexibility required by network operators to cost-effectively manage the growth in bandwidth and provisioning of new customer services expected in the next decade[3].

The SDH standards are based on the principles of direct synchronous multiplexing which is the key to cost-effective and flexible telecommunication networking. In essence, it means that individual tributary signals may be multiplexed directly into a higher rate SDH signal without intermediate stages of multiplexing. SDH Network Elements can then be interconnected directly with obvious cost and equipment savings over the existing network.

Advanced network management and maintenance capacities are required to effectively manage the flexibility provided by SDH. Approximately 5% of the SDH signal structure is allocated to supporting advanced network management procedures and practices.

The SDH signal is capable of transporting[4] all the common tributary signals found in today's telecommunication networks. This means that SDH can be deployed as an overlay to the existing signal types of customer service signals that network operators will wish to support in the future.

SDH can be used in all traditional telecommunications application areas. SDH therefore makes it possible for a unified telecommunication network infrastructure to evolve. The fact that SDH provides a single common standard for this telecommunications network means that equipment supplied by different manufacturers may be interconnected directly.

Now, let's take a look at the network "building blocks" and how they are configured. These network elements are now all defined in CCITT standards and provide multiplexing or switching functions.

Line Terminal Multiplexer (LTM): LTM can accept a number of tributary signals and multiplex them to the appropriate optical SDH rate carrier, i.e. STM-4 or STM-16. The input tributaries can either be the existing PDH signals such as 2, 34, and 140 Mbit/s or lower rate SDH signals. LTM forms the main gateway from the PDH to the SDH.

Add-drop Multiplexer (ADM)[5]: a particular type of terminal multiplexer designed to operate in a through mode fashion. Within the ADM it is possible to add channels to, or drop a variety of tributary signals, i.e. 2, 34 or 140 Mbit/s.

The ADM function is one of the major advantages resulting from the SDH since the similar function within a PDH network, required banks of hardwired back-back terminals.

Synchronous DXC: these devices will form the cornerstone of the new synchronous digital hierarchy. They can function as semi-permanent switches for transmission channels and can switch at any level from 64 kbit/s up to STM-1. Generally such devices have interfaces at STM-1 or STM-4. The DXC can be rapidly reconfigured, under software control, to provide digital leased lines and other services of varying bandwidth.

For clarity, a single frame in the STM-1 can be represented by a 2-dimensional map (see Fig. 1). The 2-dimensional map comprises 9 rows and 270 columns of boxes. Each box represents a single 8-bits byte within the synchronous signal. Six framing bytes appear in the top left corner of the 2-dimensional map. These framing bytes act as a marker, allowing[6] any byte in the frame to be easily located.

The signal bits are transmitted in a sequence starting with those in the first row. The order of transmission is from left to right. After transmission of the last byte in the frame (the byte located in row 9, column 270), the whole sequence repeats starting with the 6 framing bytes of the following frame.

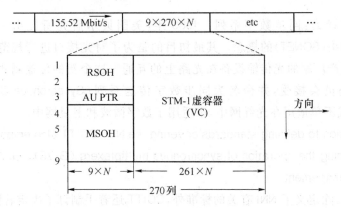

Fig. 1 Synchronous Transport Frame for STM-1

A synchronous transport frame comprises two distinct and readily accessible parts within the frame structure—a virtual container part and a section overhead part. Virtual Container (VC) is arranged mainly for user's information to be transmitted through the network, but the Section Overhead (SOH) provides the facilities required to support and maintain the transportation of a VC between nodes in a synchronous network, such as alarming monitoring, bit-error monitoring and data communication channels.

NEW WORDS AND PHRASES

hierarchy	n.	体系,分层结构
synchronous	adj.	同步的
tributary	adj.	支流的,从属的,辅助的
map	v.	绘制,设计,映射,变换
embark	v.	从事,开始搞
provision	v.	准备,预备
essence	n.	本质,精华,核心
accommodate	v.	供应,提供,容纳
configure	v.	使成形,使具体,构成
gateway	n.	门口,入口,通道
variety	n.	变化,多样化,各种各样
cornerstone	n.	基石,柱石,基础
permanent	adj.	永久的,持久的
dimensional	adj.	维的,度的
marker	n.	记号,符号,标志
overhead	n.	开销,经常性开支
assemble	v.	集合,装配,聚集

NOTES

[1] 题目可译为:同步数字系列。1986年,美国贝尔研究所提出一种新的传输制式——光同步网络(SONET)的概念。其最初目的是为了对光接口进行规范化,以实现美国电信网上不同生产厂家的光传输设备在光路上的互通。这个新的传输制式1988年为国际电报电话咨询委员会接受,并命名为同步数字传送系列(Synchronous Digital Hierarchy, SDH)。这种制式不单适用在光纤网中,也适用于数字微波和卫星网中。

[2] In addition to defining standards covering the NII, CCITT also embarked on series of standards governing the operation of synchronous multiplexers (G.781, G.782, G.783) and SDH Network Management.

全句可译成:除定义了NNI有关的标准外,CCITT还着手制订了决定着同步复用设备的运行以及SDH网络管理的一系列标准。

本句中,defining为动名词,作介词宾语;covering为现在分词,作standard的定语;

governing 引起的现在分词短语亦作定语,修饰 a series of standard。

[3] It is the standardization of these aspects of SDH equipment that will deliver the flexibility required by network operators to cost-effectively manage the growth in bandwidth and provisioning of new customer services expected in the next decade.

全句可译为:正是由于 SDH 设备在这些方面的标准化,才提供了网络运营者所期待的灵活性,以便能低价高效地应付带宽方面的增长并为今后十年中将出现的新用户业务做好准备。

这是一个强调句。强调句的基本形式为:It is(was)+ 强调部分 + that(which,who,when,where)+ 谓语及其他成分。强调句一般可译成:"正是……"。另外,本句的 to cost-effectively manage the growth in bandwidth and provisioning of new customer services expected in the next decade 是一个动词(manage)不定式短语,在句中作目的状语。

[4] be capable of doing…能够做……

[5] Add-drop Multiplexer(ADM)

本句译成:分插复用单元——一种特殊类型的终端复用单元,它是以"透传"模式运行的。

add-drop multiplexer 中的 add-drop 意为"上下话路",可译为"分插复用单元"。Designed 为过去分词,作定语,修饰 a particular type of terminal multiplexer。

[6] These framing bytes act as a marker, allowing any byte in the frame to be easily located.

全句可译成:这些成帧字节起着标志的作用,它使帧中的任何字节极易被确定位置。

本句中的 allowing 为现在分词,作定语,用以修饰 marker。

EXERCISES

一、将下述词组译成英文

同步数字系列	支路信号	数字交叉连接	网络维护
支路映射	同步传输帧	线路终端复用器	灵敏度
虚容器	成帧字节	段开销	端到端传输
误码监视	信号处理节点	净负荷	指针

二、将下述词组译成中文

1. synchronous transmission system
2. the equipment supplied by different manufacturers
3. terminal multiplexer
4. synchronous DXC
5. individual tributary signals
6. section overhead

三、将下述短文译成中文

1. In November 1988 the first SDH standards were approved—G.707, G.708, G.709. These standards define transmission rates, signal format, multiplexing structures and

tributary mappings for the Network Node Interface (NNI)—the international standard interface for Synchronous Digital Hierarchy. It is the standardization of these aspects of SDH equipment that will deliver the flexibility required by network operators to cost-effectively manage the growth in bandwidth and provisioning of new customer services expected in the next decade.

2. The SDH standards are based on the principles of direct synchronous multiplexing which is the key to cost-effective and flexible telecommunication networking. In essence, it means that individual tributary signals may be multiplexed directly into a higher rate SDH signal without intermediate stages of multiplexing. SDH Network Elements can then be interconnected directly with obvious cost and equipment savings over the existing network.

3. The SDH signal is capable of transporting all the common tributary signals found in today's telecommunication networks. This means that SDH can be deployed as an overlay to the existing signal types of customer service signals that network operators will wish to support in the future.

Unit 9

WDM[1]

TEXT

Even visionaries such as Albert Einstein and Isaac Newton, who contributed significantly to our understanding of the properties of light and its fundamental importance, would not likely imagine the communications networks of today. Highways of light span the globe, transmitting massive amounts of information in the twinkling of an eye[2]. The equivalents of millions of telephone calls are transmitted on a single fiber, thinner than a human hair. Astounding as these advances may seem, we are only at the beginning of what is possible[3].

The current explosion of traffic in the worldwide networks is ample evidence of the speed with which we are adopting new communications technologies. The growth of wireless systems and the Internet are well-documented phenomena. No matter what application it is that is generating traffic, most of this traffic will be carried by the unifying optical layer[4]. For this reason, the growth of various applications such as telephony (whether cellular or fixed), Internet, video transmission, computer communication and database access leads directly to an increase in the demand placed on the optical network. It is very likely that the optical network will be used to convey large amounts of video information in the future.

The most striking recent advances in optical networking have taken place in the field of Wavelength Division Multiplexing (WDM). These advances have benefited both terrestrial and submarine systems, increased available capacities by several orders of magnitude and correspondingly[5], reduced costs.

Until quite recently, it was possible to send only one wavelength, or color, of light along each fiber[6]. A lot of effort has therefore been concentrated in maximizing the amount of information that can be transmitted using a single wavelength. Commercial systems will soon be able to carry 40 Gbit/s on a single wavelength, while in the labs 320 Gbit/s systems have already been demonstrated.

WDM, on the other hand, makes it possible to transmit a large number of wavelengths using the same fiber[7], effectively sending a "rainbow" of colors, where there was only one color before[8]. Already today, commercially available systems can transmit 400 Gbit/s of information on a single fiber. That is equivalent to transmitting approximately 200 feature-length films per second. Recently, a team of researchers from Bell Labs demonstrated long-distance, error-free transmission of 3.28 Tbit/s over a single optical fiber.

The major advance that has led to the WDM revolution has been the invention of the Optical Amplifier (OA). Before the invention of the OA, after having traveled down a fiber for some distance, each individual wavelength had to be converted into the electronic form, then back into optical form and then transmitted into the next span of fiber. This was relatively expensive, since the optical components involved are highly specialized devices[9]. The OA, however, can boost the signal power of all wavelengths in the fiber, thus eliminating the need for separate regenerators, and allowing many wavelengths to share the same fiber. Advances in optical amplifier design have been considerable. First, the operating window has expended from 12 nm, in the first generation, to about 80 nm today. This allows the OA to amplify more signals simultaneously. Second, the development of gain equalization techniques has enabled a much flatter response and allows a number of these amplifiers to be connected in series. There have also been advances in the fibers themselves. In the early days of optical systems, optical fibers were not built for multi-wavelength transmission. Today's fibers, on the other hand, are designed to have wide transmission windows and are optimized for high-capacity, multiple-wave-length transmission.

The growing demand on optical network is a complex issue. On the one hand, the growth in capacity demand is extraordinary, and this in itself[10] would be a big enough challenge to meet. However, this is accompanied by an increasing variety of services and applications, as well as much more exacting requirements for quality differentiation. For example, there is quite a difference in the quality requirement for a signal being used to transmit an emergency telephone call or live video converge of a medical operation, as compared with an E-mail that is not urgent and can arrive after several hours.

However, the same optical infrastructure is expected to support this wide variety of services. Internet Protocol (IP) traffic, in particular, is growing exponentially. In some parts of the world, it is expected that IP will constitute the majority of traffic in the near future. Therefore, existing networks will have to be progressively optimized to handle various types of traffic. WDM has a major advantage in this regard, which is that the different types of traffic can be assigned to different wavelengths, as required.

Fortunately, we will soon be in a position to route individual wavelengths flexibly through an optical network. Features such as add/drop and cross-connection in the optical domain are being made possible by advance in photonics[11]. I would like to draw attention to a few recent advances in this area. Firstly, the so-called digital wrapper is in the process of being standardized in the international bodies. A second significant development is the all-optical cross-connect. Bell Labs has recently unveiled its all-optical cross connect called the Lambda Router. Based on Micro Electro Mechanical Switching (MEMS) technology, it consists of microscopic mirrors that bit, and thus re-direct optical signals. It is such a technology that will enable us to build networks that are purely optical[12]. As more routing functions are implemented in the optical plane, more sophisticated intelligence is needed to control and manage the network. Control systems are being developed for these optical routers with which it will be able to demand[13], and which also have self-healing properties and fast restoration times in the order of fifty to a hundred milliseconds, much the same as today's SDH and SONET networks.

A further aspect to consider[14] is access to the optical network. Most users would like to have direct access to the optical network and the enormous capacity it provides. This will take place in stages. Multi-wave-length optical systems are rapidly spreading out from the core towards the end user. In regional and metropolitan areas, the requirements are somewhat different from the long-distance area. The dream of Fiber To The Home (FTTH) or desktop is yet to materialize, mainly because of the cost-sensitive nature of this part of the network. In the near future, residential access may remain copper-based, using technologies such as ADSL to boost the capacity of traditional copper lines. However, for business offices, optical technology will be used to bring bandwidth to the end-used. Currently, a lot of Fiber To The Building (FTTB) networks are being developed involving ATM and SDH access equipment at customer premises. The next step is to use WDM technology for these applications. WDM will first be used in industrial and campus Local Area Network (LAN) environments.

We are at the beginning of a revolution in communication networks, where increasing capacity, variety of applications, and quality of service are placing enormous demands on the optical network. The revolution of optical network is just beginning, and is advancing vary swiftly towards a future online world in which bandwidth is essentially unlimited, reliable and low-cost.

NEW WORDS AND PHRASES

visionary	n.	幻想家,梦想家
striking	adj.	引人注意的,显著的
demonstrate	v.	示范,展示,演示
boost	v.	上推,增加,提高
eliminate	v.	除去,淘汰
differentiation	a.	分化,变异,演变
infrastructure	n.	基础,基础结构
exponential	adj.	指数的,幂的
standardize	v.	使与标准比较,使合标准,使标准化
twofold	adj.	两倍的,两重的
identify	v.	使等同于,识别,鉴定
unveil	v.	使公之于众,揭露,展出
microscopic	adj.	显微镜的,微小的,细微的
implement	v.	贯彻,完成,履行
sophisticate	v.	使复杂,使精致

restoration	*n.*	恢复,复位,复员
enormous	*adj.*	巨大的,庞大的
metropolitan	*adj.*	大城市的,大都市的
residential	*adj.*	居住的,长住的,居留的

NOTES

[1] 题目可译成:波分复用。波分复用是目前光纤通信扩容的主要手段之一。是采用合波器在发送端将多个不同波长的光载波合并起来并送入一根光纤进行传输,在接收端,再由分波器将这些不同波长承载不同信号的光载波分开的复用方式。

[2] Highways of light span the globe, transmitting massive amounts of information in the twinkling of an eye.

本句可译为:光的高速公路穿越整个地球,眨眼之间便可传输海量的信息。

transmitting massive…分词短语在此表示结果状语,表示一种伴随的情况。

[3] Astounding as these advances may seem, we are only at the beginning of what is possible.

本句可译为:尽管这些发展使人惊讶,我们还仅仅位于(光纤拥有的无限)可能的起点。

Astounding as these…, as 在此引导让步状语从句,可译为"尽管、虽然"。

[4] No matter what application it is that is generating traffic, most of this traffic will be carried by the unifying optical layer.

No matter what…引导让步状语从句,译为"无论什么"。

[5] These advances have benefited both terrestrial and submarine systems, increased available capacities by several orders of magnitude and correspondingly, reduced costs.

本句可译为:这些优点同时惠及了陆地和海底系统,使其可能的通信容量增加了好几个数量级,相应的也降低了成本。

correspondingly 插入语,译为"因而,相应的"。

[6] Until quite recently, it was possible to send only one wavelength, or color, of light along each fiber.

it 作形式主语,可以代替不定式短语,真正的主语是后面的不定式短语。这时 it 只是形式上的主语,本身没有词汇意义,不必译出。句型为:It is(was) + 形容词+不定式。

[7] WDM, on the other hand, makes it possible to transmit a large number of wavelengths using the same fiber.

本句可译为:另一方面,波分复用技术使得利用一根光纤传输大量不同波长成为可能。

makes it possible to transmit…, it 在此是形式宾语,没有词汇意义,代替后面的不定式短语 to transmit。当动词不定式短语或从句在句中作宾语,而这种宾语又带有补语时,通常要用 it 作为引导词放在宾语补足语之前,而把真正的宾语,即不定式短语或从句放在补足语之后。

[8] where there was only one color before…

where there was only…, where 在此引导地点状语从句,译为"而在以前只有一种颜色"。

[9] This was relatively expensive, since the optical components involved are highly specialized devices.

since 引导原因状语从句,译为"因为……"。since 只表示事物内在联系上的一种合乎逻辑的自然结果。从语气上来说,because 语气最强,since 次之,for 最弱。

[10] On the one hand, the growth in capacity demand is extraordinary, and this in itself would be a big enough challenge to meet.

这里 in itself 译为"本身"。

[11] Features such as add/drop and cross-connection in the optical domain are being made possible by advance in photonics.

are being made 为被动语态,其构成为"助动词 be + 过去分词",时态通过 be 的各种形式来体现,在英语中共有 10 种形式,在此为被动语态进行时。

[12] It is such a technology that will enable us to build networks that are purely optical.

本句可译为:正是这样一种技术,使我们可以构建全光网络。

It is…that 强调句,句型为"It is(was)+ 被强调的部分 + that(which, who)",一般可用"正是……"来翻译。

[13] Control systems are being developed for these optical routers with which it will be able to demand…

with which…句型为"介词 + which + 句子其他成分"。一般有几种形式,在此构成状语。that 引出定语从句,并在从句中作主语。

[14] A further aspect to consider…不定式作后置定语,修饰 aspect。

EXERCISES

一、选择合适的答案填空

1. Highways of light span the globe, _____ massive amounts of information in the twinkling of an eye.

  A. to transmit   B. transmitting   C. transmitted   D. be transmitted

2. The equivalent of millions of telephone calls are _____ on a single fiber, thinner than human hair.

  A. transmitted   B. transmitting   C. to transmitted   D. to transmit

3. WDM, on the other hand, makes it possible _____ a large number of wavelengths using the same fiber, effectively sending a, "rainbow" of color, where there are only one color before.

  A. to transmit   B. to transmitting   C. transmitted   D. to transmitted

4. Before the invention of the OA, after having traveled down a fiber for electronic form, then back into optical form and then retransmitted into the next span of fiber.

  A. to convert   B. converted   C. converting   D. to converting

5. In the near future, residential access may remain copper-based, _____ technologies such as ADSL to boost the capacity of traditional copper lines.

  A. to use   B. use   C. using   D. used

二、根据课文内容选择正确答案填空

1. As more routing function are implemented in the optical place, we need _____.
   A. more sophisticated intelligence to control and manage the network
   B. self-healing properties and fast restoration times
   C. direct access to the optical network
   D. live video coverage of a medical operation

2. Therefore, to handle various types of traffic, _____.
   A. this in itself would be big enough challenge to meet
   B. this allow the OA to amplify more signals simultaneously
   C. today's network will have to be progressively optimized
   D. the different types of traffic can be assigned to different wavelength, as required

3. Second, the development of gain equalization techniques has enabled a much flatter response and allow _____.
   A. much more exacting requirements for quality differentiation
   B. a number of these amplifiers to be connected in series
   C. the majority of traffic in the near future
   D. our understanding of the properties of light

4. For this reason, the growth of various applications, such as telephony, Internet, video transmission, computer communication and database access _____ on the network.
   A. would not likely to imagine the communication network of today
   B. be only at the beginning of what is possible
   C. have already been demonstrated
   D. leads directly to an increase in the demand placed

5. The major advance that has led to the WDM revolution _____.
   A. can boost the power of all wavelengths
   B. will be used to convey large amount of video information in the future
   C. has been the invention of OA
   D. is access to the optical work

6. As more routing functions are implemented in optical plane, more sophisticated intelligence _____.
   A. are being developed for these optical router
   B. can be easily configured in response to demand
   C. are being made possible by advance in photonics
   D. is needed to control and massage the network

三、将下述短文译成中文

1. The most striking recent advances in optical networking have taken place in the field of Wavelength Division Multiplexing (WDM). These advances have benefited both terrestrial and submarine systems, increased available capacities by several orders of magnitude and

correspondingly, reduced costs.

2. The OA, however, can boost the signal power of all wavelengths in the fiber, thus eliminating the need for separate regenerators, and allowing many wavelengths to share the same fiber.

3. A further aspect to consider is access to the optical network. Most users would like to have direct access to the optical network and the enormous capacity it provides. This will take place in stages. Multi-wave-length optical systems are rapidly spreading out from the core towards the end user.

4. Although DWDM technology is still evolving and technologists and standards bodies are addressing many issues, systems are being offered with few of wavelengths in the fiber. However, it is reasonable to assume that in the near future we will see DWDM systems with several hundreds of wavelengths in a single fiber. Theoretically, more than 1 000 channels may be multiplexed in a fiber. DWDM technology with more than 200 wavelengths has already been demonstrated.

Unit 10

Introduction to Computer Networks

TEXT

During the 1950s, most computers were similar in one respect. They had a main memory, a central processing unit (CPU), and peripherals. The memory and CPU were central to the system. Since then a new generation of computing has emerged in which computation and data storage need not be centralized. A user may retrieve a program from one place, run it on any of a variety of processors, and send the result to a third location.

A system connecting different devices such as PCs, printers, and disk drives is a network. Typically, each device in a network serves a specific purpose for one or more individuals. For example, a PC may sit on your desk providing access to information or software you need. A PC may also be devoted to managing a disk drive containing shared files. We call it a file server. Often a network covers a small geographic area and connects devices in a single building or group of buildings. Such a network is a local area network (LAN). A network that covers a larger area such as a municipality, state, country, or the world is called a wide area network (WAN).

Generally speaking, most networks may involve many people using many PCs, each of which can access any of many printers or servers. With all these people accessing information, their requests inevitably will conflict[1]. Consequently, the devices must be connected in a way that permits an orderly transfer of information for all concerned. A good analogy is a street layout in a large city. With only one person driving it matters little where the streets are, which ones are one-way, where the traffic signals are, or how they are synchronized. But with thousands of the cars on the streets during the morning rush hour, a bad layout will create congestion that caused major delays. The same is true of computer networks. They must be connected in a way that allows data to travel among many users with little or no delay. We call the connection strategy the network topology. The best topology depends on the types of devices and user needs. What works well for one group may perform dismally for another.

Some common network topologies are described as following.

Fig. 1 shows a common bus topology (or simply bus topology) connecting devices such as workstations, mainframes, and file servers. They communicate through a single bus (a collection of parallel lines). A common approach gives each device an interface that listens to the bus and examines its data traffic. If an interface determines that data are destined for the device it serves, it reads the data from the bus and transfers it to the device. Similarly, if a device wants to transmit data, the interface circuit sense when the bus is empty and then transmit data. This is not unlike waiting on a freeway entrance ramp during rush hour. You sense an opening and either quickly dart to it or muscle your way through, depending on whether you're driving a subcompact or a large truck.

Sometimes, two devices try to transmit simultaneously. Each one detects an absence of traffic and begins transmitting before becoming aware of the other device's transmission. The result is a collision of signals. As the devices transmit they continue to listen to the bus and detect the noise resulting from the collisions. When a device detects a collision it stops transmitting, waits a random period of time, and tries again. This process, called Carrier Sense, Multiple Access with Collision Detection (CSMA/CD) will be discussed later.

One popular common bus network is an Ethernet. Its common bus typically is Ethernet cable, which consists of copper, optical fiber, or combinations of both. Its design allows terminals, PCs, disk storage systems, and office machines to communicate. A major advantage of an Ethernet is the ability to add new devices to the network easily.

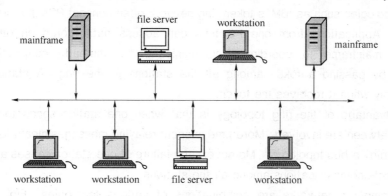

Fig. 1 A common bus topology

Another common connecting arrangement is the star topology, shown in Fig. 2. It uses a central computer that communicates with other devices in the network. Control is centralized; if device wants to communicate, it does so only through the central computer. The computer, in turn, routes the data to its destination. Centralization provides a focal point for responsibility, an advantage of the star topology. The bus topology, however, has some advantages over a star topology. The lack of central control makes adding new devices easy because no device needs to be aware of others. In addition, the failure or removal of a device in a bus network does not cause the network to fail. In a star topology, the failure of the central computer brings down the entire network.

Star topologies often involve a single mainframe computer that services many terminals and secondary devices. With appropriate terminal emulation software, PCs can communicate with the mainframe. Data transfers between terminals or between terminals and storage devices occur only through the main computer.

In a ring topology shown in Fig. 3, devices are connected circularly. Each one can communicate directly with either or both of its neighbors but nobody else[2]. If it wants to communicate with a device farther away, it sends a message that passes through each device in between.

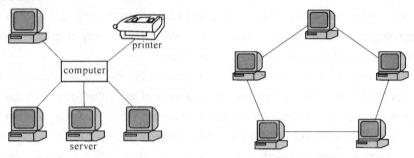

Fig. 2　The star topology　　　Fig. 3　A ring topology

A ring network may be either unidirectional or bidirectional. Unidirectional means that all transmissions travel in the same direction. Thus, each device can communicate with only one neighbor. Bidirectional means that data transmissions travel in either direction, that is, a device can communicate with both neighbors.

Ring topologies such as IBM's token ring network often connect PCs in a single office or department. Applications from one PC thus can access data stored on others without requiring a mainframe to coordinate communication[3]. Instead, communications are coordinated by passing a token among all the stations in the ring. A station can send something only when it receives the token.

A disadvantage of the ring topology is that when one station sends to another, all stations in between are involved. More time is spent relaying messages meant for others than in, for example, a bus topology[4]. Moreover, the failure of one station causes a break in the ring that affects communications among all the stations.

Many computer networks are combinations of various topologies. Fig. 4 shows a possible combination.

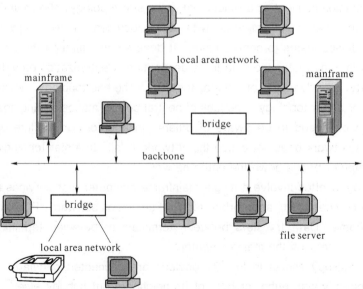

Fig. 4　Combinations of various topologies

NEW WORDS AND PHRASES

peripheral	n.	外围设备
congestion	n.	充满,拥塞
topology	n.	拓扑
dismally	adv.	忧郁地,无力地
mainframe	n.	大型机
dart	v.	猛冲
muscle	v.	强行侵入
Ethernet	n.	以太网
circularly	adv.	圆形地,循环地
bidirectional	adj.	双向的
token	n.	令牌

NOTES

[1] With all these people accessing information, their requests inevitably will conflict.

本句可译为:在这么多人存取信息的情况下,不可避免地会产生冲突。

本句中的 With 表示"在……的情况下",而 accessing information 是现在分词短语,修饰前面的 these people。

[2] Each one can communicate directly with either or both of its neighbors but nobody else.

本句可译为:每一个设备只能与它相邻的一边或两边之间进行通信,而不能与除此之外的其他设备直接通信。

[3] Applications from one PC thus can access data stored on others without requiring a mainframe to coordinate communication.

本句可译为:一个 PC 上的应用程序可以访问其他机器上的数据,而用不着大型机对通信进行协调。

stored on others 是过去分词短语,作定语修饰它前面的名词"数据",而 without requiring a mainframe to coordinate communication 表示条件。

[4] More time is spent relaying messages meant for others than in, for example, a bus topology.

本句可译为:这样,比起总线拓扑来,要花更多的时间来为其他的站点转发数据。

本句中,relaying messages 是一个现在分词短语作状语,表示原因;而 meant for others 是一个过去分词短语,修饰 messages。

EXERCISES

一、将下列词组译成中文

Central processing unit　　Local area network
Network topology　　Token ring network

二、根据课文为下列句子选择合适单词

1. During the 1950s, most computers were _____ in one respect. They had a main memory, a central processing unit (CPU), and peripherals.

  A. same   B. different   C. similar   D. the same as

2. A PC may also be devoted to managing a disk drive containing shared _____. We call it a file server.

  A. files   B. devices   C. printer   D. peripherals

3. With all these people accessing information, their requests _____ will conflict.

  A. usually   B. often   C. sometimes   D. inevitably

4. Sometimes, two devices try to transmit simultaneously. Each one detects an absence of traffic and begins _____ before becoming aware of the other device's transmission.

  A. transmit   B. to send   C. transfer   D. transmitting

5. Star topology often _____ a single mainframe computer that services many terminals and secondary devices.

  A. evolve   B. covers   C. involve   D. revolve

三、将下述短文译成中文

With only one person driving it matters little where the streets are, which ones are one-way, where the traffic signals are, or how they are synchronized. But with thousands of the cars on the streets during the morning rush hour, a bad layout will create congestion that caused major delays. The same is true of computer networks. They must be connected in a way that allows data to travel among many users with little or no delay. We call the connection strategy the network topology. The best topology depends on the types of devices and user needs. What works well for one group may perform dismally for another.

Unit 11

Share the Internet Wealth

TEXT

Matt Haughey has a day job as a web designer, but in his spare time he nurtures a borderline obsessive relationship with his TiVo video recorder. So, mostly as a lark, he created a personal Web log (www.pvrblog.com), where he archives TiVo[1] news and offers tips about what he has discovered on the Internet. The day after launching the blog in July 2003, Haughey signed up for an automated service called Google AdSense[2] to run small text advertisements on the site. Each time one of his readers clicks on an ad, Google pays Haughey a small fee. "My goal was to cover the monthly cost of hosting the site—about $20," he says.

Haughey's expectations were way off. Soon after the ads began running on the site, he checked his online reports and found that he had made $150 in one day. "I thought to myself, 'If anyone ever finds out that you can just sit around in your underwear writing stupid blog and make $150 a day, the world will be ruined,'" he jokes. "I mean, money ruins everything, right?"

Not necessarily. We used to measure the impact of the Internet by the vast fortunes made: Amazon's Jeff Bezos, eBay's Pierre Omidyar. But those billions were an old story updated for a new medium. Every major media revolution—newspapers, radio, film, television—has created moguls. Now Matt Haughey's $150 points to another possibility: financial reward for the little guys, the amateurs, and the hobbyists. If you're looking for a trend that truly suggests the power of this new medium, ignore the twenty something entrepreneur who just bought his first private jet. Pay attention, instead, to the guy who's getting his rent money from *the Lord of the Rings* fan site he maintains.

Why should we care about such small change? Because most of us, whether we recognize it or not, have a passion about something. Maybe you're an armchair astronomer or a guy who restores 1964-1965 Corvettes. Maybe you follow cricket religiously or know more about the Battler of Antietam than academic historians. Or maybe you can wire a home theater system in your sleep. That wisdom may be genuinely useful or interesting to other people, yet chances are you've never shared it with more than family and friend.

Now that expertise has a place to go. Bit by bit over the past 10 years, the Web has erected a global platform for personal wisdom. Services like AdSense—along with other advertising outfits, including one called Blogads, which focuses exclusively on blogs—are simply the final plank. You can now compose, design, publish, promote, and make money from your writing without ever leaving your desk. Some high-profile bloggers—particularly in the world of political commentary—have attracted hundreds of thousands of people to their personal sites, making enough money form AdSense or Blogads to quit their day jobs[3]. The liberal commentary site Daily Kos has a monthly audience that exceeds that of venerable magazines like *The New Republic and the Nation*. But most of the 4.5 million blogs created in the past few years have audiences confined to dozens or hundreds of visitors. That may not sound like a lot, but don't underestimate the wonder of suddenly having a platform to discuss your Civil War arcana with 500 fellow buffs after years of boring your friends and family to tears. As tech commentator Dave Weinberger astutely puts it, "on the Web, everyone will be famous to 15 people." The rise of service like AdSense suggests a corollary: Everyone will make 15 extra bucks a day talking to those 15 people.

How do these new advertising systems work? The key to the AdSense program is Google's ability to analyze the content of a Web page and determine with reasonable accuracy the topics that are crucial to that content[4]. Having this ability, of course, is why Google is so good already at instantaneously delivering pages that match your search requests. AdSense tweaks the original model: Instead of finding Web pages that correspond to a search query, the technology finds Web pages that correspond to advertisements.

Let's say you're an advertiser trying to sell a new diet book. You create a brief description of the product with a compelling sales line and a URL[5] pointing to your Web site, and you purchase an ad campaign from Google. Instead of randomly running the book promo on every Web page in its inventory, Google tries to place the ad exclusively on pages that have some semantic connection to food-related issues—health sites, for example, or personal blogs recounting someone's battle to lose weight. The idea is logical enough. Someone surfing the Internet for information about complex carbohydrates is likely to be interested in a book about diets.

Google tracks more than 4 billion pages on the Web. Say, for the sake of argument, that a million of those mention the word *diet*, and a thousand of them are devoted almost exclusively to diet issues. Google searches through those thousand pages and identifies the ones that are signed up for the AdSense program. Within a matter of minutes, those specific pages will be running the ads for your new book.

From the perspective of someone who signs up to run AdSense on a Web site, the whole system is simple. Once you join the program, you insert a few line of HTML[6] code in your Web page, and almost instantly advertisements appear on your site. If enough people click on the ads, a check will arrive in the mail a month or two later. Google doesn't talk publicly about its rates, but individual clicks range from paying out a few cents to a few dollars, depending on what's advertised. Because the company uses a bidding process to determine click value, topics that have a lot of advertisers are more expensive than less popular topics. Someone selling home video equipment will pay more per click than someone selling used copies of Hegel's *Phenomenology of Spirit*.

Google's ads are smart enough to shift in response to your own changing interests. If Haughey suddenly started posting tributes to the music of Burt Bacharach, the ads would almost immediately start linking to online music sites selling Bacharach records, this may be the most uncanny thing about AdSense: watching the ads shift, chameleon-like, in response to text posted on the site. Shortly after the service was launched, I experimented with it for a few months on my own blog. When I commented on the presidential primaries, the site filled with political ads. When I wrote about editing home movies on my PC, it teemed with ads for digital video recorders. Then one day I posted a short entry about Rush Limbaugh's battle with the painkiller OxyContin. The next morning I found my blog covered with ads for detox centers.

One of the strange side effects of programs like AdSense is the intrusion of commercial messages into what can be remarkably intimate spaces. Bloggers often post first-person accounts of their life: stories about their kids, their romances, their struggles to find new jobs, or the loss of loved ones. You're just as likely to find someone writing about a difficult breakup as you are likely to find someone writing a love song to their TiVo[7]. Encountering advertising in that personal space can be unsettling—particularly advertising that contorts itself to match the day's subject matter. It's not unlike opening a snail-mail[8] letter from an old friend and having a few supermarket coupons drop out of the envelope.

Of course no one is forcing bloggers to run ads on their sites; many choose to keep free of commercial messages. And in the long run, creating financial rewards for solo publishers is a healthy development for the Web ecosystem. The Blogads service has generated some significant revenue for political bloggers whose sites were swarming with traffic in the election season, but Henry Copeland, the founder of the service, is just as bullish on a few dozen baseball bloggers who pocket up to $200 a month: "My hunch is, in the next year the sports blogs will be where the politics blogs are today."

Matt Haughey doesn't quite pull in $150 a day anymore—first-day spikes are not unusual for online ads because the novelty tends to wear off for return visitors to a site—but he's still making far more money than he initially hoped to make. It's not enough to quit his day job yet, but that's partly the point. Most blogs aren't full-time occupations. They're hobbies, diversions, places for people to share their wisdom with strangers. Before the Web, finding a venue to write about personal passions was almost impossible. Now you can publish your thoughts to a global audience—and get rewarded for it in the process. Haughey calls the new generation of amateur Web publishers the "thousandaires". "There are going to be a lot of people making a thousand bucks from writing about stuff that interests them," he says. "That's awesome".

NEW WORDS AND PHRASES

chunk	n.	相当大的部分或数量
mogul	n.	显要人物,有权势的人
erect	v.	树立,建立
astutely	adv.	敏捷地,伶俐地
corollary	n.	必然的结果,推论
instantaneously	adv.	瞬间地,即刻,突如其来地
promo	n.	商品推销
exclusively	adv.	排外地,专有地
semantic	adj.	语义的
recount	v.	细述,讲述
carbohydrate	n.	碳水化合物
tribute (to)	n.	赞词,颂词,礼物
intrusion	n.	闯入,侵扰
contort	v.	扭曲,歪曲
ecosystem	n.	生态系统
revenue	n.	收入,国家的收入,税收
hunch	n.	直觉,预感
spike	n.	聚增,上涨
diversion	n.	转移,转换

NOTES

[1] TiVo：1997年在美国问世,被称为硬盘数字录像机。它的外形就像是电视机的机顶盒一样,自身带有硬盘,能够连接上闭路电视线路,通过信号的转换把电视节目录制在硬盘里,想看的时候随时能看。

[2] Google AdSense：是网络会员联盟的一种形式,如果一个网站加入Google AdSense,即成为Google的内容发布商,可以在自己的网站上显示Google关键广告词,Google会根据会员网站上显示的广告被点击的次数支付佣金,当某个月底佣金累计达到100美元时即可向用户支付广告佣金。

[3] Some high-profile bloggers—particularly in the world of political commentary—have attracted hundreds of thousands of people to their personal sites, making enough money form AdSense or Blogads to quit their day jobs.

该句的主干为 Some high-profile bloggers have attracted hundreds of thousands of people to their personal sites；particularly in the world of political commentary 为插入语,修饰 bloggers；making enough money form AdSense or Blogads to quit their day jobs 为结果状语。本句可译为：一些盈利颇高的博主们,特别是那些专注于政坛评论的博客,吸引了成千上万人浏览他们的个人网站,这样他们从AdSense或Blogads上挣够了钱从而辞去了白天的工作。

［4］The key to the AdSense program is Google's ability to analyze the content of a Web page and determine with reasonable accuracy the topics that are crucial to that content.

该句中 key to 和 crucial to 中的 to 为介词，ability to 中的 to 为不定式。determine 与 analyze 并列作定语，省去了前面的 to。

本句可译为：AdSense 的关键技术在于 Google 能够对网页内容进行分析，并相当准确地分辨出与其内容相符的关键话题。

［5］URL（Uniform Resource Locator）：统一资源定位器。是 WWW 的地址，是 Internet 上用来指定一个位置（site）或网站（Web Page）的标准方式。

［6］HTML（hypertext markup language）：超文本标记语言。是用于创建 Web 文档的编程语言。

［7］You're just as likely to find someone writing about a difficult breakup as you are likely to find someone writing a love song to their TiVo.

该句中 be likely to = be probable to，writing about a difficult breakup 和 writing a love song to their TiVo 为分词短语作定语，分别修饰 someone。

本句可译为：有可能你能搜寻到某个人述说自己苦涩的分手过程，同样也有可能找到有人为自己 TiVo 谱写的情歌。

［8］snail-mail：由邮递员分发传递的传统信件。其速度较慢（像蜗牛似的）。

EXERCISES

将下述短文译成中文

How do these new advertising systems work? The key to the AdSense program is Google's ability to analyze the content of a Web page and determine with reasonable accuracy the topics that are crucial to that content. Having this ability, of course, is why Google is so good already at instantaneously delivering pages that match your search requests.

Unit 12

Introduction to 3G[1]

TEXT

The mobile communications industry has evolved in three stages:

Analog→Digital→Multimedia

Three generations of mobile phones have emerged so far, each successive generation more reliable and flexible than the last.

Analog: You could only easily use analogue cellular to make voice calls, and typically only in any one country. Digital mobile phone systems added fax, data and messaging capabilities as well as voice telephone service in many countries. Multimedia services add high speed data transfer to mobile devices, allowing new video, audio and other applications through mobile phones—allowing music and television and the Internet to be accessed through a mobile terminal[2].

With each new generation of technology, the services which can be deployed on them becomes more and more wide ranging and truly limited only by imagination. We are reaching that stage with 3G.

During the first and second generations different regions of the world pursued different mobile phone standards, but are converging to a common standard for mobile multimedia called Third Generation (3G) that is based on CDMA technology[3]. 3G will bring these incompatible standards together.

The Third Generation of mobile communications systems will soon be implemented. Following on the heels of analog and digital technology, the Third Generation will be digital mobile multimedia offering broadband mobile communications with voice, video, graphics, audio and other information. This transition is shown below:

- First Analog 1980s Voice centric, multiple standards (NMT, TACS etc.).
- Second Digital 1990s Voice centric, multiple standards (GSM, CDMA, TDMA).
- 2.5G Higher Rate Data Late 1990s Introduction of new higher speed data services to bridge the gap between the Second and Third Generation, including services such as General Packet Radio Service (GPRS) and Enhanced Data Rates for Global Evolution (EDGE).
- Third Digital Multimedia 2010s Voice and data centric, single standard with multiple modes.

1. **3G Features**

3G has the following features.

(1) Packet Everywhere

With Third Generation (3G), the information is split into separate but related packets before being transmitted and reassembled at the receiving end. Packet switching is similar to a jigsaw puzzle—the image that the puzzle represents is divided into pieces at the manufacturing factory and put into a plastic bag. During transportation of the now boxed jigsaw from the factory to the end user, the pieces get jumbled up. When the recipient empties the bag with all the pieced, they are reassembled to form the original image. All the pieces are all related and fit together, but the way they are transported and assembled varies.

Packet switched data formats are much more common than their circuit switched counterparts. Other examples of packet-based data standard include TCP/IP, X.25, Frame Relay and Asynchronous Transfer Mode (ATM). In the mobile world, CDPD (Cellular Digital Packet Data), PDCP (Personal Digital Cellular Packet), General Packet Radio Service (GPRS) and wireless X.25 technologies have been in operation for several years. X.25 is the international public access packet radio data network standard.

(2) Internet Everywhere

The World Wide Web is becoming the primary communications interface—people access the Internet for entertainment and information collection, the intranet for accessing company information and connecting with colleagues and the extranet for accessing customers and supplier[4]. These are all derivatives of the World Wide Web aimed at connecting different communities of interest. There is a trend away from storing information locally in specific software packages on PCs to remotely on the Internet. Web browsing is a very important application for packet data.

(3) High Speed

Speeds of up to 2 Megabits per second (Mbit/s) are achievable with Third Generation (3G). The data transmission rates will depend upon the environment the call is being made in—it is only indoors and in stationary environments that these types of data rates will be available. For high mobility, data rates of 144 kbit/s are expected to be available—this is only about three times the speed of today fixed telecoms modems.

(4) New Application, Better Applications

Third Generation (3G) facilitates several new applications that have not previously been readily available over mobile networks due to the limitations in data transmission speeds. These applications range from Web Browsing to file transfer to Home Automation—the ability to remotely access and control in-house applications and machines. Because of the bandwidth increase, these applications will be even more easily available with 3G than they were previously with interim technologies such as GPRS.

2. **Timescales for 3G**

So when will mobile multimedia actually arrive? Here's your inside track on when and where we will see 3G.

Whenever a new service is introduced, there are a number of stages before it becomes established. 3G service developments will include standardization, infrastructure development, network trials, contracts placed, network roll out, availability of terminals, application development, and so on.

These stages for 3G are shown below:

Data Milestone

- Throughout 1999: 3G radio interface standardization took place, and initial 3G live technical demonstrations of infrastructure and concept terminals shown.
- 2000: Continuing standardization with network architectures, terminal requirements and details standards.
- May, 2000: the formal approval of the IMT-2000 Recommendations will be made at the ITU Radio communication Assembly in early May.
- 2000: 3G licenses for phase 1 spectrum are awarded by governments around Europe and Asia.
- 2000: WRC 2000 Spectrum Review of 3G Phase 2 spectrums.
- 2001: 3G trial and integration commence 2001 3G launched in Japan (by NTT DoCoMo and others).
- Summer of 2001: First commercial deployment of 3G services becomes available in Europe.
- Start of 2002: Basic 3G capable terminals begin to be available in commercial quantities.
- Throughout 2002: Network operators launch 3G services commercially and roll out 3G—Vertical market and executive 3G early adopters begin using 3G regularly for no voice mobile communication.
- 2002/3: New 3G specific applications, greater network capacity solutions, more capable terminals become available, fuelling 3G usage.
- 2004: 3G will have arrived commercially and reached critical mass in both corporate and consumer sectors.
- 2005: 3G Phase 2 spectrum expected to be available, subject to WRC 2000 decisions.

NEW WORDS AND PHRASES

evolutionary	adj.	进化的
intertwine	v.	(使)纠缠,(使)缠绕
underlying	adj.	根本的,优先的
ubiquitous	adj.	普遍存在的
paradigm	n.	范例
resolvable	adj.	可分解的
rudimentary	adj.	基本的;初步的,未来发展的

overlay	n.	覆盖,覆盖图
cellular	adj.	细胞的,细胞状的;蜂窝状的;单元的
counterpart	n.	极相似的人或物,相对物
timescale	n.	时间表(尺度),时标,时间量程

NOTES

[1] 题目可译为:3G 简介。3G (3rd Generation):是国际电信同盟(ITU)定义的第三代移动通信技术(第一代为模拟蜂窝移动通信,第二代为数字式移动通信),能够支持更宽带宽的通信,在室内、室外和行车环境中能够分别支持不同的传输速率。

[2] Multimedia services add high speed data transfer to mobile devices, **allowing** new video, audio and other applications through mobile phones—**allowing** music and television and the Internet to be accessed through a mobile terminal.

本句可译为:多媒体服务为移动设备增加了高速数据传输的能力,从而通过移动电话可以进行新的视频、音频和其他应用,即可以通过移动终端收听音乐、电视或接入因特网。

现在分词"allowing"引导的是结果状语从句,其特点是分词的逻辑主语不是句子的主语,而是其前面的整个句子。译为汉语时,可以增译"从而"、"使得"、"以"等。

[3] During the first and second generations different regions of the world pursued different mobile phone standards, but are converging to a common standard for mobile multimedia called Third Generation (3G) that is based on CDMA technology.

本句可译为:对于(移动通信的)第一代和第二代而言,世界上不同地域采用不同的移动电话标准,但是对基于 CDMA 技术,被称为 3G 的移动多媒体达成一个共同的标准。

[4] The World Wide Web is becoming the primary communications interface—people access the Internet for entertainment and information collection, the intranet for accessing company information and connecting with colleagues and the extranet for accessing customers and supplier.

本句可译为:万维网正日益成为主要的通信接口,人们在因特网上娱乐、获取信息;在内联网上共享公司资讯、联系同事;在外联网上联系客户与供应商。

EXERCISE

一、写出下列缩写词汇的原文并翻译成汉语
CDMA   ATM   GPRS   PDCP

二、将下述短文译成中文
Packet switching is similar to a jigsaw puzzle—the image that the puzzle represents is divided into pieces at the manufacturing factory and put into a plastic bag. During transportation of the now boxed jigsaw from the factory to the end user, the pieces get jumbled up. When the recipient empties the bag with all the pieced, they are reassembled to form the original image. All the pieces are all related and fit together, but the way they are transported and assembled varies.

Unit 13

Comparison between GSM and CDMA[1]

TEXT

Using CDMA/FDD technology, subscribers of CDMA cellular mobile communication system can transmit their information simultaneously through the same channel. On the other hand, the GSM system adopts TDMA/FDD method to transmit and distinguish information from different GSM mobile stations. In addition, in favor of QCELP arithmetic, RAKE receiver, power control and soft switching etc., CDMA shows more advantages in its system performance than the GSM, such as greater anti-interference capability, bigger system capacity, higher successful connection ratio, fewer off-line chances, low probability of intercept(LPI),and so on.

1. Power Control and RAKE Receiver

When different subscribers send their information to the same BS (base station), different signal power caused by different transmitting distances will consequentially cause interference with each other, especially for those MSs(mobile station) being far away from BS will be seriously disturbed because of their almost submerged signals by signals of the close-to-BS MSs[2].

In order to solve this problem and keep high system performance, power control technique is introduced in CDMA communication system, which can effectively overcome this cross-disturbance. As one of the core techniques in CDMA cellular mobile communication system, power control can make the signal power from all subscribers to the BS equivalent through adjusting the transmitting power from each subscriber.

Power control can be not only divided to open-loop control and closed-loop control, but also to forward (down) power control and backward (up) power control. For open-loop control method, subscriber adjusts emitting power according to the measured frame error probability, while for the closed-loop power control, base station measures the signal-to-noise ratio of received signals and then adjust the transmitting power of corresponding MS.

The backward power control in CDMA system can be divided into two kinds of control technique, the open-loop backward power control only used by mobile stations, and the closed-loop backward power control that can be adopted by both base station and mobile stations. On the other hand, the forward power control is just used to reduce the disturbance from small adjacent districts.

RAKE Reception Technique

Fading and distortion are inevitable for signals transmitted in mobile communication channel because of the unideal characteristics of channel, and then make bad influence on system performance. The basic theory of RAKE reception technique is: by means of collecting all transmitted signals from multi-path and uniting them, the received signal power can obtain an effective enhancement, which can improve the output SNR and system performance[3].

Three, four RAKE receivers are respectively set in each MS, BS in CDMA system in order to receive the arriving branch signals of the same original from different transmitting routes, and then combine them to get an incresent output SNR after their respectively independent demodulation. Thus, in favor of RAKE reception technique, the disadvantageous factor that signal transmitted in multi-path becomes an advantageous factor in CDMA cellular mobile communication system.

2. Better Performance of CDMA

(1) Greater Anti-interference Capability

Because of spread spectrum modulation, bandwidth of user's signal (B_N) is extremely broadened by the assigned unique pseudo-random (PN) sequence, thus the modulated broad band (B_B) signal owns spectral properties close to Gaussian white noise. Receiving this kind of spread spectrum signal, all the CDMA receivers try to demodulate it using PN sequence created locally, but only one receiver with the same local PN sequence as that in the received signal can convert the broad band noise-like signal into narrowband useful signal, while other receivers without the unique local PN sequence couldn't. Thus, output from demodulator of each receiver is still the insignificant broadband noise except the relative demodulator with the unique local PN sequence.

In addition, as far as the narrow band meaningless signal additive to the received signal by the relative receiver with the same unique pseudo-random sequence, it is modulated into broad band signal with extremely lessened power spectral density. Thus, the relative receiver can filter the broad band signal from other users and majority of the meaningless signal out of the filter bandwidth just through a narrowband filter. Therefore, reservation in relative receiver only consists of the narrowband useful signal and little meaningless signal within the filter bandwidth. As a consequent result, the output Signal-to-Noise ratio is improved largely, that will necessarily leads to greater system anti-interference capability.

It can be proved that the more high value of B_N/B_B, the more great system anti-interference capability.

(2) Bigger System Capacity and Higher Successful Access Ratio

Unlike the TDMA multi-access mode in GSM mobile communication system, signal of each CDMA subscriber is distinguished by the assigned unique PN sequence based on the CDMA technology. Thus, each signal of CDMA subscriber can be transmitted synchronously occupying the entire sub-channel bandwidth divided from the FDD method. So under the equal frequency resource condition, in other word, for the same channel bandwidth, capacity of CDMA system is 4~5 times larger than that of GSM system.

In the nature of things, a communication system with big capacity must have high successful access ratio.

In addition, using CELP (Code Excited Linear Predictive) arithmetic for voice code, audio signal in CDMA system can be transmitted with variable speed, with the maximum CELP coded audio signal transmitting velocity is 9.6 kbit/s while the subscriber is talking, and the minimum velocity of 1.2 kbit/s for the conversation pause. This technique called Voice Activation can reduce the background disturbance among subscribers communicating on one channel at the same time, and enhances the system capacity. For GSM system, this Voice Activation technique cannot be used because of the signal transmitting delay at conversation pause.

(3) Better Voice Quality

Using advanced CELP (Code Excited Linear Predictive) arithmetic for its digital audio signal code, and 3 RAKE receivers in a handset to receive signals from different directions simultaneously, it is made extremely abundant and dimensional for audio signal spectrum from CDMA handset. Furthermore, vocoder based on the CELP arithmetic in CDMA system can adjust its transmitting velocity and choose corresponding sending power level automatically to reduce the disturbance of noise. Thus, even under the circumstance with loud noise, we can make conversation of good quality without any cacophony.

(4) Lower Probability of Intercept (LPI)

It is necessary for eavesdropping somebody's conversation that the transmitted conversation information must be captured and then decoded. For CDMA system, signal with user's information must be spread spectrum modulated before sent to the common channel with extremely spread spectrum and very low power spectral density. Thus, it is too difficult to detect this kind of CDMA signal for the listener-in because its power spectral density is even lower than ambient noise, and it's almost impossible for him to distinguish the signal from background noise.

Moreover, even if the signal is captured, what the listener-in can get is only broad band noise of insignificance from his demodulator because of his inaccurate local pseudo-random sequence. The probability of right PN sequence pattern necessary for spread spectrum demodulation is one of more than one thousand billion! What a low probability for listener-in to eavesdrop other's conversation through CDMA cellular mobile communication system!

(5) Fewer Off-line Chances

Because of the soft-switching technique, which means "connect-before-break", it's overcome for CDMA that the frequent occurrence of off-line.

In mobile communication system, BS is the guarantee for conversation. When subscribers during conversation moving close to the edge of the BS's demesne, the BS should maintain the communication through its active switching, otherwise the process will be interrupted. During switching period, BS's dominion should shift from "demesne of the local BS (such as A)" to "demesne of A and its neighboring BS (B)" to "demesne of B", and signal from the moving mobile station will automatically switch to a relatively idle neighboring BS. Thus, only when it is approved that the moving MS has moved to the "demesne of B", can the connection between the moving MS and its original BS (A) be switched off. So it is not easy for a CDMA conversation to be interrupted by off-line.

Unlike the above soft-switching technique in CDMA, hard-switching method adopted in GSM system executes switching process as "break-before-connect", which happen to be the reversed processing sequence with that of CDMA. That is to say, when a GSM subscriber during conversation moving close to edge of the BS's demesne, the local BS (A) cut off connection with the MS at first, then the MS set new connection with the neighboring BS (B) once again. Thus, communication during this switching will have to be interrupted, that consequently leads to a high off-line ratio.

(6) Simple Frequency Layout

CDMA subscribers are distinguished by the assigned unique pseudo-random sequence, so neighboring channels can be used for signals transmitting with the same carrier frequency. Thus, it's quite flexible to program the system frequency layout, and so for the system expansion.

NEW WORDS AND PHRASES

fading	n.	衰减
lessen	v.	减少，减轻
vocoder	n.	声音合成机
cacophony	n.	刺耳的音调，不和谐音，杂音
listener-in	n.	窃听者，收听者
ambient	adj.；n.	周围的；周围环境
insignificance	n.	无意义
demesne	n.	土地之所有，领地，私有地

NOTES

[1] 本文题目可译为：GSM 与 CDMA 之比较。GSM (Global System for Mobile Communications,)中文为全球移动通讯系统,俗称"全球通",是一种起源于欧洲的移动通信技术标准,是第二代移动通信技术,其开发目的是让全球各地可以共同使用一个移动电话网络标准,让用户使用一部手机就能行遍全球。CDMA(Code Division Multiple Access)中文是码分多址,其技术原理是基于扩频技术,即将需传送的具有一定信号带宽的信息数据,用一个带宽远大于信号带宽的高速伪随机码进行调制,使原数据信号的带宽被扩展,再经载波调制并发送出去。接收端使用完全相同的伪随机码,与接收的宽带信号作相关处理,把宽带信号换成原信息数据的窄带信号即解扩,以实现信息通信。

[2] When different subscribers send their information to the same BS (base station),

different signal power caused by different transmitting distances will consequentially cause interference with each other, especially for those MSs(mobile station) being far away from BS will be seriously disturbed because of their almost submerged signals by signals of the close-to-BS MSs.

本句可译为:不同用户向同一基站发送信息时,由于到达基站的传输距离不同,其信号功率大小有所差异,这必然会引起信号之间的相互干扰。对于那些远离基站的移动台来说,其信号几乎淹没在基站附近的移动台的信号之中,这种干扰尤为严重。

[3] The basic theory of RAKE reception technique is: by means of collecting all transmitted signals from multi-path and uniting them, the received signal power can obtain an effective enhancement, which can improve the output SNR and system performance.

本句可译为:RAKE 接收技术的基本原理是通过收集并合并多径信道上的信号,有效增强接收到的信号功率,从而提高输出信噪比,改善系统的性能。

RAKE 接收技术是第三代 CDMA 移动通信系统中的一项重要技术。在 CDMA 移动通信系统中,由于信号带宽较宽,存在着复杂的多径无线电信号,通信受到多径衰落的影响。RAKE 接收技术实际上是一种多径分集接收技术,可以在时间上分辨出细微的多径信号,对这些分辨出来的多径信号分别进行加权调整,使之复合成加强的信号。这种作用有点像把一堆零乱的草用"耙子"把它们集拢到一起那样,英文"RAKE"是"耙子"的意思,因此被称为 RAKE 技术。

EXERCISE

一、将下述词组译成英文

离线率　软交换　功率谱密度　开环功率控制　抗干扰能力　拦截率

二、将下述短文译成中文

Receiving this kind of spread spectrum signal, all the CDMA receivers try to demodulate it using PN sequence created locally, but only one receiver with the same local PN sequence as that in the received signal can convert the broad band noise-like signal into narrowband useful signal, while other receivers without the unique local PN sequence couldn't. Thus, output from demodulator of each receiver is still the insignificant broadband noise except the relative demodulator with the unique local PN sequence.

Unit 14

Packet Switching

TEXT

Packet switching was invented in the late 1960s for data communications. Data communications applications were mainly interactions between dumb terminals and a shared mainframe computer. These Interactions were command traffic generated by humans and the corresponding responses from the mainframe. Such data transmissions occurred randomly and infrequently, and in bursts of arbitrary duration. Hence, data communications had (and still have) a very bursty pattern. If circuit switching was used to support data communications, the dedicated resources for a connection would be idle most of the time—very inefficient use of band-width[1]. Therefore, packet switching was invented to achieve more efficiency to support the bursty traffic pattern of data communications.

The packet switched network can have the same architecture as the switched point-to-point network architecture, in which case the switch is called a packet switch (see Fig. 1). The basic idea of packet switching is to not dedicate network resources statically as in circuit switching. Instead, packet switching allocates network resources to communicating parties on demand—only when they have information to send. This is sometimes referred to as bandwidth on demand. This allows more efficient sharing of network resources especially when the activity ratio of each source is low.

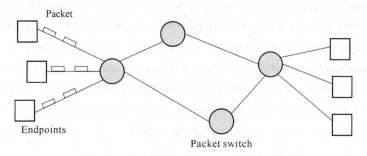

Fig. 1 A packet switch network

To provide such a fine level of network resource sharing, packet switching quantizes the network resource into small units of transmission bandwidth. The unit of bandwidth request is the amount of data to be transferred at a given instant. This is achieved by encoding user information in separate blocks. Data are sent in the form of packets; each consists of a header followed by a block of data as the payload (see Fig. 2). Each packet represents the basic transmission unit and the quanta of communications bandwidth in the packet switched network.

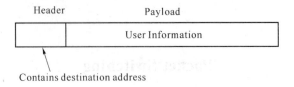

Fig. 2 A packet

The packet header contains the address of the destination endpoint (plus other control information), The destination address is used by the packet switches for forwarding the packet along the path to its destination. Determining the right output of the packet switch for each packet is called packet routing. Each packet switch has a routing table that translates destination addresses into the outgoing ports of the switch. The routing table is set up via a routing protocol operated among packet switches. Packets can be sent to the network without first setting up a connection. Instead, the route of each packet is determined by the packet switches along the path using its destination address. The packet switched network essentially gives the resource to each communicating party on a per packet basis; no bandwidth is used by two communicating parties that are idle. In contrast, circuit switched networks dedicate network resources on a per connection (or circuit) basis and last for the entire connection, even if the communicating parties are idle.

The routing tables in packet switches can change dynamically by the routing protocol, as a result of topological or loading changes in the network, for example. Hence, different packets between two communicating parties may travel different paths. There is no guarantee that they will arrive in the same order they were sent.

The packet switch has four core functions: routing, switching, buffering and multiplexing. Again, routing determines the desired output port for the incoming packet. Then, the switching function delivers the packet from its input port to the desired output port. Since packet transmissions from different sources are not coordinated, multiple packets arriving simultaneously at the packet switch on different input ports can all be destined to the same output port (see Fig. 3) [2]. Since only one of the packets can be transmitted on each output port, the other packets must be buffered for subsequent transmission. Hence, packet switches must provide buffering as its normal operation.

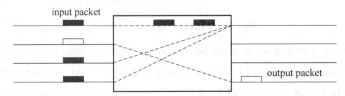

Fig. 3 A packet switch

Although instantaneous overload is normal for packet switching, such an overload can be severe enough as to exceed the buffer capacity of the packet switch. In this case, packets will be dropped. Occasional packet drops due to buffer overflow (though these should be avoided) are normal for packet switched networks, because applications running over packet switched network are expected to handle lost packets. This can be achieved using various error control mechanisms, such as error detection with retransmission, if data integrity is important. However, if such packet losses become excessive for a long period of time, it means that there is network congestion and applications can have significant performance degradation in throughput and delay. Hence, congestion control algorithms must be provided for packet switched networks, to avoid congestion occurring in the first place, and to control congestion when it does occur.

The multiplexing methodology for packet switching is based on statistical multiplexing, a dynamic form of time division multiplexing (TDM). The packet switch is responsible for multiplexing packets from different sources arriving on different input ports destined to the same output port using time division.

The TDM mechanism used in packet switching is different from that in circuit switching. In packet switching, it requires an explicit label (destination address) on the header of each packet to associate it with its destination node, while the position of the packet in time does not correspond to any channel information [3]. In fact, there is no concept of a frame to define position. No time slots are reserved and any time slots are ready for use by any packets arriving at that time. (Again, if more than one packet arrives or is buffered, only one is transmitted in the current time slot, while the rest is buffered for transmission in following time slots.) Hence, the transmission resources on each output link are only allocated to active communicating parties; no bandwidth is wasted for idle parties. In contrast, each time slot in TDM-based circuit switching belongs to a particular logical channel. Once a connection is accepted, a logical channel is assigned to it for the entire duration. If the connection is idle, it results in idle slots that cannot be used by other active parties. Therefore, packet switching is much more efficient in supporting bursty traffic than circuit switching.

Note that even for voice communications, circuit switching may not be that efficient. The reason is that a typical voice conversation is active for only 40% of the duration; the rest of the time the parties are silent and hence there is no need for sending any information. Therefore, voice over packet switched networks or packet voice communication has been explored extensively in the past two decades. In fact, voice over the Internet is intrinsically more efficient than over the PSTN.

In addition to using switched point-to-point architecture, packet switching can be implemented over a broadcast shared medium. A broadcast shared medium packet switched network does not need a packet switch, as switching is achieved in a distributed fashion among the endpoints. Packet switching over a broadcast network is discussed later in the chapter.

Connectionless and connection-oriented packet switching

In the basic form of packet switching discussed above, no explicit connection setup is required before packet transmission. As a matter fact, there is no notion of a connection from the network point of view. Furthermore, there is no guarantee in bandwidth, delay or loss rate for any packet transfer, which means that there is no quality of service (QoS) guarantees. (In any case, there is no notion of a connection to associate a bandwidth to it.) This form of packet switching is known as connectionless packet switching.

However, there is another form of packet switching that requires an explicit connection setup and tear-down. This is called connection-oriented packet switching. In this case, the packet header contains a connection identifier for indicating the connection to which the packet belongs. The connection-oriented packet switch has a connection table that translates connection identifiers into output port numbers. The purpose of connection setup is to reserve network resources. The basic network resource is the support of a connection itself, because each packet switch can support a limited number of connections. The reason is that each connection requires memory space in the connection table to hold connection-related information. Hence, the number of connections that can be supported on a packet switch is memory-limited. In addition, the connection setup can reserve other network resources, such as bandwidth and buffer for guaranteeing performance of applications.

Connection-oriented packet switching still maintains the statistical multiplexing property of connectionless packet switching and corresponding efficiency in supporting bursty traffic. Hence, connections in packet switched network are known as virtual connections or VCs, to distinguish them from nailed up connections with dedicated resources in circuit switched networks[4]. The VC paradigm allows the creation of a virtual private network across a public data network for corporations. VCs can be set up between different corporate locations to emulate a private network connectivity X.25 and its follow on, frame relay are examples of a connection-oriented packet switched network and are used exactly for the purpose of virtual private networking.

Today, data communications applications are very different, as the centralized computing paradigm based on mainframes transformed into a distributed computing paradigm based on PCs and workstations. However, data traffic remains bursty because today's data applications (such as file transfer, printing and electronic mail) exhibit similar bursty behavior. Therefore, packet switching is still very important for data communications for both local area networks (LANs) and wide area networks (WANs).

Permanent Connections

Although both circuit switching and connection-oriented packet switching require connection setup before information transfer, the protocol for establishing such connection setup (known as a signaling protocol) might not be available at the endpoints of the network.

Without signaling support to set up connections dynamically, the network has to provide connections on subscription basis (permanent connections), for which the connection is established by network management protocol at the beginning of the network service. Permanent (or non-switched) connections are common for circuit switched connections (leased line service) and packet switched connections (permanent virtual connections or PVCs in X.25, frame relay or ATM), either because they simplify network design, or there is no standard signaling protocol implementations. In fact, a fully connected point-to-point network can be logically constructed by these permanent connections over circuit switched and packet switched networks as if they were point-to-point links. Nevertheless, such fully connected permanent connections suffer from disadvantages similar to those of the fully connected point-to-point networks, such as scalability problems.

NEW WORDS AND PHRASES

mainframe	n.	[计]主机
arbitrary	adj.	任意的
quantize	vt.	[数]用基本数的倍数表示
quanta	n.	量
forward	vt.	转发,转寄
topological	adj.	拓扑的
core	n.	(果实的)核
instantaneous	adj.	瞬间的
methodology	n.	方法学
emulate	vt.	仿真
reserve	vt.	储备
TDM(Time Division Multiplexing)		时分复用
PSTN(Public Switched Telephone Network)		公众交换电话网
QoS(Quality of Service)		服务质量
VC(Virtual Circuit)		虚电路

NOTES

[1] If circuit switching was used to support data communications, the dedicated resources for a connection would be idle most of the time—very inefficient use of band- width.

本句是一个祈使句,If…,主语 would be…

全句可译为:如果在数据通信中使用电路交换,那么在大部分时间里(电路交换)连接的专用资源将是空闲的——非常不经济的带宽使用。

[2] Since packet transmissions from different sources are not coordinated, multiple packets arriving simultaneously at the packet switch on different input ports can all be destined to the same output port.

这是一个由 since 引导的复合句。destined to 去往……的。

全句可译为：尽管不同来源的分组传输不同步，但是同时到达交换机不同端口的很多分组可能是去往同一个输出端口的。

[3] In packet switching, it requires an explicit label (destination address) on the header of each packet to associate it with its destination node, while the position of the packet in time does not correspond to any channel information.

全句可译为：在分组交换中需要每个分组的头部有一个显式(明确的)地址(目的地址)把分组和其目的节点联系起来，而分组在时间上的位置与任何信道信息并不对应。

[4] Hence, connections in packet switched network are known as virtual connections or VCs, to distinguish them from nailed up connections with dedicated resources in circuit switched networks.

此句是一个简单句。to distinguish…不定式短语用来表示 hence 后结果的原因。

全句可译为：为了和电路交换网中有专用资源的固定连接区别，因此，将分组交换网中的连接命名为虚连接或 VC。

EXERCISES

一、将下述词组译成英文

虚电路　　　　　　　时隙
时分复用　　　　　　局域网
服务质量　　　　　　广域网
公众交换电话网　　　分组交换

二、将下述短文译成中文

1. To provide such a fine level of network resource sharing, packet switching quantizes the network resource into small units of transmission bandwidth. The unit of bandwidth request is the amount of data to be transferred at a given instant. This is achieved by encoding user information in separate blocks. Data are sent in the form of packets; each consists of a header followed by a block of data as the payload. Each packet represents the basic transmission unit and the quanta of communications bandwidth in the packet switched network.

2. The connection-oriented packet switch has a connection table that translates connection identifiers into output port numbers. The purpose of connection setup is to reserve network resources. The basic network resource is the support of a connection itself, because each packet switch can support a limited number of connections. The reason is that each connection requires memory space in the connection table to hold connection-related information.

3. In addition to using switched point-to-point architecture, packet switching can be implemented over a broadcast shared medium. A broadcast shared medium packet switched network does not need a packet switch, as switching is achieved in a distributed fashion among the endpoints. Packet switching over a broadcast network is discussed later in the chapter.

Unit 15

Residential Broadband

TEXT

1. The Problem With The Subscriber Loop

The communications channels installed between residences and the telephone office were designed for analog voice traffic that requires a modest amount of bandwidth; typically, 0.3 to 3.5 kHz [1]. As data applications became more prominent, modems were designed with sophisticated coding and modulation techniques that permitted transfer rates up to approximately 33 kbit/s to furl on the loop [2]. Increasingly, the subscriber at the residence has migrated to the V.34 modem, which operates at 28.8 kbit/s.

This transmission speed is adequate for some applications but insufficient for many others. As an example, to transmit a single page of text with a 28.8 kbit/s speed takes only one second of transmission time. However, a single video image requires 120 seconds at the V.34 rates and to downline load one second of uncompressed video for subsequent playback requires 840 seconds of time with this technology. Clearly, the user can benefit from technologies that provide higher bandwidths than the current modems.

The situation has not improved much with the ISDN technology, but some relief is provided. For example, most metropolitan areas in North America and Europe have local loop ISDN services that provide bandwidths of 64 kbit/s or 128 kbit/s. Nonetheless, this technology is too limiting for the support of multimedia traffic and provides only marginal improvement over V.34.

2. The Proposed Solutions: Two Interlocking Approaches, Coding/Modulation and Wiring

Simply stated, the local loop requires more bandwidth. Currently, the proposed solutions to this problem are focusing on (a) making better use of the existing copper wire with enhanced coding/modulation techniques, and/or (b) replacing or augmenting the copper wire with higher bandwidth media (i.e., rewiring parts of the distribution plant with optical fiber and/or coaxial cable).

A number of new coding and/or modulation specifications have been published to standardize the operations across the communications link for high bandwidth performance. In addition, several subscriber loop wiring options are under development or implementation, some of which use the coding and modulations schemes. The organization of these schemes is depicted in Fig. 1. The coding/modulation schemes are shown on the left side of the figure, and the wiring options (subscriber loop options) are shown on the right. Also, for the coding/modulation schemes, the main body of this chapter covers HDSL and ADSL/VDSL.

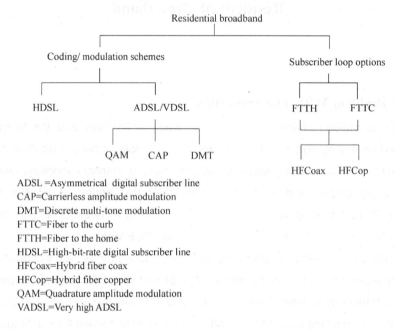

ADSL =Asymmetrical digital subscriber line
CAP=Carrierless amplitude modulation
DMT=Discrete multi-tone modulation
FTTC=Fiber to the curb
FTTH=Fiber to the home
HDSL=High-bit-rate digital subscriber line
HFCoax=Hybrid fiber coax
HFCop=Hybrid fiber copper
QAM=Quadrature amplitude modulation
VADSL=Very high ADSL

Fig. 1 New technologies for the subscriber loop

3. Coding and Modulation

The most prominent coding and modulation techniques that are examined in this section follow. Subscriber loop options are discussed in the next section of this chapter.

① High-bit-rate Digital Subscriber Line(HDSL)

② Asymmetrical Digital Subscriber Line(ADSL) and Very High ADSL(VADSL)

4. HDSL

The past several years have witnessed several notable "new technologies" in the local loop. One of these technologies is called the High-bit-rate Digital Subscriber Line (HDSL), depicted in Fig. 2. It is based in the ISDN 2B + D line coding (2B1Q). It operates up to 12 kft on 24 gauge copper wire, or up to 9 kft on 26 gauge. The lines are two full-duplex pairs that support bit rates of 784 kbit/s.

HDSL is viewed by its supporters as a simple, inexpensive technology that provides quick and easy provisioning. The copper wires chosen can be any pair; they do not have to be especially treated (conditioned). Bellcore is enthusiastic about HDSL because of its ease of installation and maintenance.

Notwithstanding, it is restricted to kbit/s transfer rates, so other solutions are underway; the most notable is ADSL.

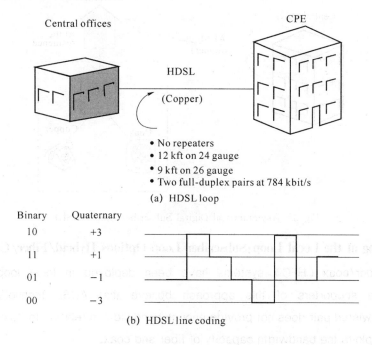

Fig. 2 High-bit-rate Digital Subscriber Line (HDSL)

5. ADSL

Another relatively new technology is known as Asymmetrical Digital Subscriber Line (ADSL), depicted in Fig. 3. It uses improved coding and modulation techniques on the local loop between the local telephone office and the subscriber to support multimedia applications.

The ADSL technology was originally set up as a downstream and upstream technology where the downstream signal was a 1.5 Mbit/s channel and the upstream channel operated at 16 kbit/s. Conventional telephone services were supported on the same wire pair. In 1994, a 6 Mbit/s system was introduced that provides for four TV channels over 12 kft of copper wire.

As just mentioned, the installation of ADSL on the local loop does not disturb the existing cable in the distribution plant, nor does it necessitate taking the customer's phone service out for a long time. These interfaces allow the existing copper wire to be split into multiple channels: (a) forward-central office to customer (down-stream), and (b) return-customer to central office (upstream).

The return channel operates at much lower frequency than the forward channel(s) (an asymmetrical configuration). Consequently, crosstalk is not so great a problem in comparison to conventional symmetrical configurations. And, this approach takes advantage of the asymmetrical nature of many applications in existence today.

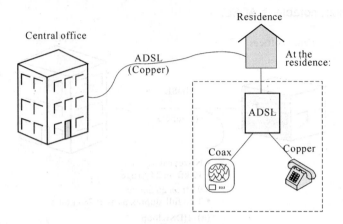

Fig. 3　Asymmetrical Digital Subscriber Line(ADSL)

6. Wiring at the Local Loop:Subscriber Loop Options Hybrid/Fiber/Coax (HFC)

Hybrid/fiber/coax (HFC) systems have been deployed in local loops in several countries. The supporters of this approach believe that ADSL technology over the conventional twisted pair does not provide enough bandwidth in relation to its costs. The HFC technology exploits the bandwidth capacity of fiber and coax.

As shown in Fig. 4, The HFC network has an optical fiber facility running from the central office(the head end) to a node in the residential neighborhood. The node has forward and return paths. At the node, users are connected by coaxial cable. The idea is to take the optical fiber deep into the neighborhood, and connect to the fiber from the home with a relatively short coaxial bus[3]. This approach is designed to balance the costs of using fiber and coax and provide adequate bandwidth for full-service multimedia traffic.

The goals of HFC are to provide a transport technology to support these types of services: (a) telephony, (b) ISDN, (c) broadcast video (analog), (d) broadcast video (digital), (e) interactive video(data), (f) and high-speed full duplex data (digital).

7. Fiber to the Curb (FTTC) and Fiber to the Home (FTTH)

Two other technologies to upgrade the local loop are fiber to the curb (FTTC) and fiber to the home (FTTH). FTTC entails the running of fiber closer to the subscriber than is done with HFC. The run is to a pedestal that serves between eight and sixteen homes. In initial plans, FTTC provides 96 voice channels, or data/video equivalents. Power is provided to the system by a separate coax cable. Presently, FTTC is more expensive than HFC.

FTTH entails running the fiber all the way into the home for business. While this technology provides for the most bandwidth. It is quite expensive at this stage of the local loop evolution. Each subscriber must be fitted with its own laser, and the analog signals emanating from the TV must be converted to optical digital signals. In comparison to FTTC and HFC, there is little interest in FTTH.

The HFC proponents do not think FTTC solutions will prove as cost effective as HFC. Other studies claim that the FTTC technology is capable of supporting multimedia broadband when CAP is employed, and that it is a viable alternative to HFC.

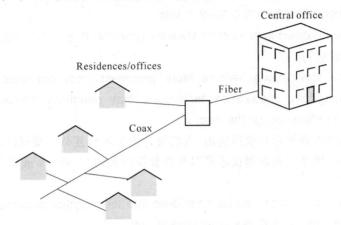

Fig. 4 Hybrid fiber/coax (HFC)

NEW WORDS AND PHRASES

interactive	adj.	交互式的
interface	n.	分界面，接触面
downstream	adv. adj.	下游地；下游的
gauge	n.	标准尺，规格，量规，量表
	v.	测量
prominent	adj.	卓越的，显著的，突出的
dwell	vi.	居住，踌躇
marginal	adj.	记在页边的，边缘的，边际的
metropolitan	adj.	首都的，主要都市的，大城市
migrate	vi. vt.	移动，移往，移植，（鸟类的）迁徙
sophisticate	vt.	篡改，曲解，使变得世故，掺和，弄复杂
	n.	久经世故的人，老油条，精于……之道的人
hybrid	n.	杂种，混血儿，混合物
	adj.	混合的，杂种的
duplex	adj.	[计] 双方的
coaxial	adj.	同轴的，共轴的
embryonic	adj.	[生] 胚胎的，开始的
at the node		在节点上
hybrid/fiber copper		混合电缆/光纤

NOTES

[1] The communications channels installed between residences and the telephone office

were designed for analog voice traffic that requires a modest amount of bandwidth; typically, 0.3 to 3.5 kHz.

本句可译为：居民和电话局之间的通信信道是为模拟话音业务设计的，话音业务需要一个适当的带宽，典型的带宽范围为 0.3～3.5 kHz。

"that requires a modest amount of bandwidth; typically, 0.3 to 3.5 kHz." 是修饰 analog voice traffic 的定语从句。

[2] As data applications became more prominent, modems were designed with sophisticated coding and modulation techniques that permitted transfer rates up to approximately 33 kbit/s to furl on the loop.

本句可译为：随着数据业务变得突出，人们设计出了具有复杂的编码技术和调制技术的调制解调器，这些编码技术和调制技术可以允许数据以大约 33 kbit/s 或更高的速率在用户线上传送。

[3] The idea is to take the optical fiber deep into the neighborhood, and connect to the fiber from the home with a relatively short coaxial bus.

本句可译为：这种方法的思想是把光纤引入邻里（范围），并使用一根相对较短的同轴总线把家庭和光纤连接在一起。

EXERCISES

一、将下述短语译成中文

ADSL(Asymmetrical digital subscriber line)

CAP (Carrierless amplitude modulation)

DMT (Discrete multi-tone modulation)

FTTC (Fiber to the curb)

FTTH (Fiber to the home)

HDSL(High-bit-rate digital subscriber line)

HFCoax (Hybrid fiber coax)

HFCop(Hybrid fiber copper)

QAM (Quadrature amplitude modulation)

VADSL (Very high ADSL)

二、将下述短文译成中文

As just mentioned, the installation of ADSL on the local loop does not disturb the existing cable in the distribution plant, nor does it necessitate taking the customer's phone service out for a long time. These interfaces allow the existing copper wire to be split into multiple channels: (a) forward-central office to customer (down-stream), and (b) return-customer to central office(upstream).

The return channel operates at much lower frequency than the forward channel(s) (an asymmetrical configuration). Consequently, crosstalk is not so great a problem in comparison to conventional symmetrical configurations. And, this approach takes advantage of the asymmetrical nature of many applications in existence today.

Unit 16

Frame Relay and ATM

TEXT

As the speed and number of local area networks (LANs) continue their relentless growth, increasing demand is placed on wide area packet-switching networks to support the tremendous throughput generated by these LANs [1]. In the early days of wide area networking, X.25 was designed to support direct connection of terminals and computers over long distances. At speeds of up to 64 kbit/s, X.25 copes well with these demands. As LANs have come to play an increasing role in the local environment, X.25, with its substantial overhead, is an inadequate tool for wide area networking. Fortunately, several new generations of high-speed switched services for wide area networking have moved rapidly from research lab and the draft standard stage to the commercially available, standardized-product stage[2]. There are a number of such high-speed WAN services available.

Indeed, the network manager may now be faced with too many choices for slowing capacity problems. In this text, we begin with an overview of various wide area networking alternatives, and show where the strengths and weaknesses lie. We then focus on perhaps the two most important WAN technologies: frame relay and ATM.

1. WIDE AREA NETWORKING ALTERNATIVES

In considering wide area networking strategies for business and other organizations, two distinct but related trends should be analyzed. The first is the distributed processing architecture used to support applications and to meet an organization's needs, and the second is the wide area networking technologies and service available to meet those needs.

WAN Offerings

To meet the demands of the new corporate computing paradigm, service and equipment providers have developed a variety of high-speed services. These include faster multiplexed line schemes, such as T-3 and SONET/SDH, as well as faster switched networks schemes, including frame relay and ATM.

Fig. 1 lays out the primary alternatives available from public U.S. carriers; a similar mix is available in other countries. A nonswitched, or dedicated, line is a transmission link leased for a fixed price. Such lines can be leased from a carrier and used to link offices of an organization. Common offerings include the following:

① **Analog**: the least expensive option is to lease a twisted-pair analog link. The necessary dedicated private line modems, data rates of 4.8 to 56 kbit/s are common.

② **Digital data services**: High-quality digital lines that require digital signaling units rather than modems are more expensive but can be leased at higher data rates.

Nonswitched(leased)	Rate
Analog	4.8~56 kbit/s
Digital Data Service	2.4~56 kbit/s
T-1	1.54 Mbit/s
Frame Relay	1.54~44.736 Mbit/s
T-3	44.736 Mbit/s
SONET	51.84 Mbit/s~2.488 Gbit/s
Switched(networked)	Rate
Dial-up/modem	1.2~56 kbit/s
X.25 packet switching	2.4~56 kbit/s
ISDN	64 kbit/s~1.54 Mbit/s
ADSL	16 kbit/s~9 Mbit/s
Frame relay	1.54~44.736 Mbit/s
SMDS	1.54~44.736 Mbit/s
ATM	25~155 Mbit/s

Fig. 1 primary alternatives available from public U.S. carriers

- **T-1, T-3**: For many years, the most common leased line for high-traffic voice and data needs was the T-1 line, which is still quite popular. For greater needs, the T-3 is widely available.
- **Frame relay**: Although frame relay is a switched network technology, the frame relay protocol can be used over a dedicated line to provide a convenient and flexible multiplexing technique [3]. Frame relay devices are required at the customer's premises for this approach.
- **Sonet**: The highest-speed leased lines that are available use SONET/SDH.

Public switched services include the following:

- **Dial-up/modem**: Modems connected to the public telephone network provide a relatively inexpensive way to obtain low-speed data services. The modems themselves are inexpensive, and the telephone rates are reasonable for modest connect times. This is the near-universal access technique for residential users. In organizations, many LANs and PBXs are equipped with modem banks to provide low-cost, supplemental data transmission service.

- **X.25 packet switching:** This elderly standby is still used to provide a switched data transfer service. With the increasing use of graphic and multimedia applications, X.25 at its traditional data rates is becoming increasingly inadequate. Typically, network charges are on based on the volume of data transferred.
- **ISDN:** The Integrated Services Digital Network provides both circuit switching and X.25 packet switching over 64 kbit/s B channels. Higher data rates are also achievable. Typically, network charges are based on the duration of the call regardless of the amount of data transferred.
- **Frame relay:** Provides switched capability at speeds equivalent to the leased T-1 rate and, in some offering, higher rates up to T-1, its low overhead makes it suitable for interconnecting LANs and high-speed stand-alone systems.

Choosing among the various leased and switched alternatives is no easy task, and the proliferation of alternatives has increased the difficulty comparable practices are used in other countries. As can be seen, the pricing structures of various services are not directly comparable. This is one complication. Other issues that complicate the selection process include the difficulty of forecasting future traffic volumes by organizations with wide area networking requirements, and difficulty in forecasting traffic distributions given the flexibility of applications and the mobility of users [4].

2. FRAME RELAY

Frame relay is designed to provide a more efficient transmission scheme than traditional packet switching. The standards for frame relay matured earlier than those for ATM, and commercial products also arrived earlier. Accordingly, there is a large installed base of frame relay products.

Background

The traditional approach to packet switching makes use of a protocol between the user and the network known as X.25. X.25 not only determines the user-network interface but also influence the internal design of the network. Several key features of the X.25 approach are as follows:

- Call control packets, used for setting up and terminating virtual circuits, are carried on the same channel and same virtual circuit as data packet. In effect, inband signaling is used.
- Multiplexing of virtual circuits takes place at layer 3.
- Both layer 2 and layer 3 include flow control and error control mechanisms.

The X.25 approach results in considerable overhead. At each hop through the network, the data link control protocol involves the exchange of a data frame and an acknowledgment frame. Furthermore, at each intermediate node, state tables must be maintained for each virtual circuit to deal with the call management and flow control/error control aspects of the X.25 protocol. All of this overhead may be justified when there is a significant probability of error on any of the links in the network. This approach is not the most appropriate for modern digital communication facilities. Today's networks employ reliable digital transmission technology over high-quality, reliable transmission links, many of which are optical fiber. In addition, the use of optical fiber and digital transmission, high data rates can be achieved. In this environment, the overhead of X.25 is not only unnecessary but degrades the effective utilization of the available high data rates.

Frame relay is designed to eliminate much of the overhead that X.25 imposes on end user systems and on the packet-switching network. The key differences between frame relaying and a conventional X.25 packet-switching service are as follows:

- Call control signaling is carried on a separate logical connection from user data. Thus, intermediate nodes need not maintain state tables or process messages relating to call control on an individual per-connection basis.
- Multiplexing and switching of logical connections takes places at layer 2 instead of layer 3, eliminating one entire layer of processing.
- There is no hop-by-hop flow control and error control. End-to-end flow control and error control are the responsibility of a higher layer, if they are employed at all.

Thus, with frame relay, a single user data frame is sent from source to destination, and an acknowledgment, generated at a higher layer, may be back in a frame. There are no hop-by-hop exchanges of data frames and acknowledgments.

Let us consider the advantages and disadvantages of this approach. The principal potential disadvantage of frame relaying, compared to X.25, is that we have lost the ability to do link-by-link flow and error control. (Although frame relay does not provide end-to-end flow and error control, this is easily provided at a higher layer.) In X.25, multiple virtual circuits are carried on a single physical link, and the link-layer protocol provides reliable transmission from the source to the packet-switching network and from the packet-switching network to the destination [5]. In addition, at each hop through the network, the link control protocol can be used for reliability. With the use of frame relaying, this hop-by-hop link control is lost. However, with the increasing reliability of transmission and switching facilities, this is not a major disadvantage.

The advantage of frame relaying is that we have streamlined the communications process. The protocol functionality required at the user-network interface is reduced, as is the internal network processing. As a result, lower delay and higher throughput can be expected. Studies indicate an improvement in throughput using frame relay, compared to X.25, of an order of magnitude or more. The ITU-T Recommendation I.233 indicates that frame relay is to be used at access speeds up to 2 Mbit/s. However, frame relay service at even higher data rates is now available.

NEW WORDS AND PHRASES

relentless   adj.   不间断的

throughput	n.	生产量,生产能力,吞吐量
substantial	adj.	大量的,相当大的
overhead	n.	开销,额外开销;系统开销
infrastructure	n.	下部构造,基础下部组织
intranet	n.	企业内部互联网
paradigm	n.	范例
supplemental	adj.	补足的,追加的
standby	n.	可以信任的人,使船待命的信息;备用
proliferation	n.	增殖,分芽繁殖
degrade	v.	(使)降级,(使)堕落,(使)退化
intermediate	adj.	中间的
ATM(Asynchronous Transfer Mode)		异步传输模式
ISDN(Integrated Services Digital Network)		综合业务数字网
Frame Relay		帧中继

NOTES

[1] As the speed and number of local area networks (LANs) continue their relentless growth, increasing demand is placed on wide area packet-switching networks to support the tremendous throughput generated by these LANs.

"to support the tremendous throughput generated by these LANs"是不定式短语作目的状语。"generated by these LANs"是分词短语作 throughput 的后置定语。

全句可译为:随着局域网(LAN)的速率和数量的不断增长,为了满足它巨大吞吐量(对网络)的需要,对广域分组交换网的要求也在提高。

[2] Fortunately, several new generations of high-speed switched services for wide area networking have moved rapidly from research lab and the draft standard stage to the commercially available, standardized-product stage.

全句可译为:幸运的是,一些新生代的广域网高速交换业务(技术)已经迅速从实验室草图标准阶段进入到可商业化的、标准化产品阶段。

[3] Although frame relay is a switched network technology, the frame relay protocol can be used over a dedicated line to provide a convenient and flexible multiplexing technique.

全句可译为:尽管帧中继是一种交换网技术,(但是)帧中继(也)可作为一种在专用线路上便捷、灵活的复用技术。

[4] Other issues that complicate the selection process include the difficulty of forecasting future traffic volumes by organizations with wide area networking requirements, and difficulty in forecasting traffic distributions given the flexibility of applications and the mobility of users.

全句可译为:使选择过程复杂化的其他因素包括:根据广域网(发展)要求预测各组织机构未来通信容量的困难以及预测满足业务灵活性和用户移动性的通信分布的困难。

[5] In X.25, multiple virtual circuits are carried on a single physical link, and the link-

layer protocol provides reliable transmission from the source to the packet-switching network and from the packet-switching network to the destination.

全句可译为：在 X.25(网络)中，单个物理链路承载多个虚拟电路；链路层协议提供从源(主机)到分组交换网络以及从分组交换网络到目的(主机)的数据的可靠传输。

EXERCISES

一、将下述词组译成英文

异步传输模式　综合业务数字网　帧中继　物理链路　虚电路　可靠传输

二、将下述短文译成中文

1. The X.25 approach results in considerable overhead. At each hop through the network, the data link control protocol involves the exchange of a data frame and an acknowledgment frame. Furthermore, at each intermediate node, state tables must be maintained for each virtual circuit to deal with the call management and flow control/error control aspects of the X.25 protocol. All of this overhead may be justified when there is a significant probability of error on any of the links in the network. This approach is not the most appropriate for modern digital communication facilities. Today's networks employ reliable digital transmission technology over high-quality, reliable transmission links, many of which are optical fiber. In addition, the use of optical fiber and digital transmission, high data rates can be achieved. In this environment, the overhead of X.25 is not only unnecessary but degrades the effective utilization of the available high data rates.

2. In the early days of wide area networking, X.25 was designed to support direct connection of terminals and computers over long distances. At speeds of up to 64 kbit/s, X.25 copes well with these demands. As LANs have come to play an increasing role in the local environment, X.25, with its substantial overhead, is an inadequate tool for wide area networking.

3. Frame relay is designed to provide a more efficient transmission scheme than traditional packet switching. The standards for frame relay matured earlier than those for ATM, and commercial products also arrived earlier. Accordingly, there is a large installed base of frame relay products.

Unit 17

Introduction to SPC Digital Telephone Exchanges

TEXT

Modern SPC exchanges, which use digital-switching technology, are making a major impact on the telecommunications networks of the world. Whether introduced as parts of integrated digital transmission and switching networks, or as straight replacements for analogue switching units, such exchanges offer many advantages. The telecommunications administrations benefit from operational savings and features available from such systems, while the subscribers enjoy an improved quality of service and a range of new services and facilities.

1. The development of SPC digital exchange

The current fully electronic SPC digital exchanges represent the successful coupling of electronic and computer technology with telephony. The first signs of success of such a marriage came in the early 1960s. There then followed two decades of development, in which successive generations of exchange systems contained increased quantities of electronics. This development was motivated by the desire to improve upon the cost, quality, maintainability and flexibility of electromechanical telephone exchange by exploiting the proven advantages of the rapidly evolving electronic and computer technologies [1].

The first application of electronic devices to telephone exchanges was in the control area: stored-program control. The first public SPC exchange, the No. 1ESS, developed by AT&T Bell Laboratories, was introduced at Succasunna, New Jersey, USA, in May 1965. This historic event initiated worldwide interest in SPC, which resulted in the introduction during the 1970s of a range of new exchange systems incorporating various degrees of computer-control technology [2]. However, these early systems all used electromechanical switching devices (e.g. crossbar and reed relay) because of the problems in developing suitable semiconductor switching arrays for public telephony applications. (Such hybrid-exchange systems were thus "semi-electronic", although, for reasons of prestige they were often introduced.)

There were two obstacles hindering the use of semiconductor switches for telephony. The first was the difficulty of producing large semiconductor switch matrices with adequately low crosstalk characteristics. The switches forming such matrices require very high off-resistances if interference between circuits is to be eliminated. Working in the analogue mode, semiconductor switches were unable to compete with the transmission linearity and the near-infinite off-resistances of existing electromechanical switches. The second obstacle was the inability of the available semiconductor devices to handle the high voltages and ringing currents required by the conventional telephone [3].

It is interesting to note that some small PABXs were successfully developed with analogue electronic switches (using PAM/TDM techniques). Their small size, typically terminating a maximum of 200 extensions, enabled crosstalk to be kept adequately low, while the high-voltage obstacle was minimized by the use of special telephones. Clearly, such conditions did not exist in public telephone switched networks (PSTNs). The application of semiconductor devices to switching in public telephony had to await the use of digital technology. The shift towards digital technology, and the overcoming of the two obstacles, was influenced by the introduction of digital transmission into the PSTNs and developments in semiconductor integrated-circuit (IC) devices[4].

Many countries began to introduce digital transmission, in the form of pulse-code modulation (PCM), into their networks during the late 1960s. The PCM systems were used originally in the junction networks to expand the capacity of existing audio-pair cables by virtue of their 24- or 30-channel multiplexing known as 'pair gain.' The application of digital transmission to long-distance routes did not start until the late 1970s, when higher-capacity systems, multiplexed from 24- or 30-channel groups, were used on coaxial cable. Now, microwave-radio and optical-fiber digital transmission systems are also being deployed.

The first application of digital technology to exchange systems was in the role of tandem switching between digital (PCM) junction routes. This overcame the problem of crosstalk because digital signals were sufficiently insusceptible to it. Thus, large semiconductor switching matrices could be used. Clearly, tandem and toll exchanges were not affected by the second obstacle because, with no subscriber lines involved, there were no high voltages or ringing currents to deal with. Hence, it was possible for an experimental digital junction-tandem exchange to be installed in London by the British Post Office in 1968. This carried live traffic successfully for a number of years. CIT-Alcatel led the world with the first public digital tandem system (E10) in 1970 in Lannion, France. In the USA, Bell introduced full public all-electronic digital toll and tandem exchanges, using the 4ESS system, from January 1976 onwards.

A key advantage of digital switching is the elimination of the multiplexing equipment normally associated with the PCM digital-transmission systems terminating at the exchange [5]. Thus, one of the major incentives for the introduction of digital switching into PSTNs was the potential for the elimination of analogue-to-digital conversion equipment from the trunk (toll) and junction networks. The planning aspects of coordinating the introduction of digital switching and transmission into a PSTN, to form an 'integrated digital network (IDN).

However, successful application of digital semiconductor technology to local exchanges depended on a solution to the second obstacle, namely the handling of the high voltages and currents associated with subscriber lines. The solution adopted universally was to handle all the high-voltage and DC-path requirements of subscriber lines in interface units at the periphery of the exchange. This enabled the electronic switches to be developed unhindered by the demanding requirements of the subscriber lines.

Thus, successful application of semiconductor technology to subscriber-line switching required economical designs of subscriber-line interfaces. The main cost component was the analogue-to-digital conversion equipment. Until the early 1980s, the cost of subscriber line interfaces made digital switches unattractive compared to the standard analogue switches then available (e. g. crossbar and reed relay). Therefore, the first generation of digital local exchanges (e. g. E10, System X, and AXE10) each comprised two forms of switching systems. One was an analogue reed, relay unit which terminated the subscriber lines and concentrated their traffic on to internal highly loaded trunks that could economically be connected to analogue-to-digital convertors [6]. The second form of switch was a digital system which interconnected the internal digital trunks with external trunk and junction digital routes. This hybrid analogue-digital architecture had the advantage of avoiding the provision of expensive PCM-encoding equipment for each subscriber's line and it exploited the inherent DC metallic path through reed relays to perform the subscriber-line support functions. The exception to this approach was Northern Telecom, who, in 1980, produced the world's first all-digital local exchange system (the DMS 100), which exploited the analogue-to-digital convertors developed for their digital PABX system (SLI).

The advent, in the early 1980s, of generally available integrated-circuit devices, that provided cheap analogue-to-digital conversion, enabled the cost of subscriber-line interfaces to decrease sufficiently for all-digital switching systems to be competitive with the analogue-digital hybrids [7]. Thus, the current generation of SPC exchanges (local, toll, trunk and international) comprise stored-program control and electronic digital switching. With the exception of some of the components within the subscriber-line interfaces, these exchanges use only digital technology.

However, the rapid rate of progress in semiconductor technology is continuing to broaden the options for SPC digital-exchange designers. For example, the AT&T 5ESS system uses specially developed analogue semiconductor devices for some of the subscriber.

SPC digital exchanges offer many advantages to the administration and its subscribers (see the following Sections). However, it is fair to say that some of these result from the virtues of SPC, so analogue SPC exchanges would also offer them. In addition, the full range of advantages does not accrue until the SPC digital exchanges are incorporated into a digital transmission environment.

2. Advantages of stored-program control

① **Flexibility**. In an SPC exchange, the hardware is controlled by programs and data held in electrically alterable storage. This control process offers a high degree of flexibility in the way that the exchange hardware is made to operate. Flexibility has long-and short-term aspects.

The long term will be considered first. At the switching-system-development stage, a range of programs may be produced to enable a basic exchange system to provide a variety of capabilities and facilities to suit the requirements of an administration. This software tailoring covers generic characteristics of local exchanges in the network, e. g. numbering, charging and routing rules, types of call offered, administrative and subscriber facilities.

An important aspect of the long-term flexibility provided by SPC systems is the ability for established exchanges to be upgraded without disruption to the service. This enables new capabilities and facilities not known or specified earlier to be incorporated during the life of an exchange system. Some of these enhancements may be achieved merely by the incorporation of new software, e. g. the introduction of a closed user-group facility for a certain class of subscriber. Other enhancements such as the introduction of digital data switching, also require the addition of new hardware. SPC offers short-term flexibility due to its ability to alter the status of exchange equipment simply by changes to data. Thus, the operation of an exchange can be made to react rapidly to network conditions. For example, routing algorithms may be changed so that calls are re-routed to avoid congestion in the network. The short-term flexibility of SPC enables a wide range of administration and subscriber facilities to be provided economically and with ease of operation.

② **Subscriber facilities.** SPC exchanges enable a wide range of subscriber facilities to be provided more cheaply and easily than in non-SPC exchanges. The facilities are allocated by the administration, as appropriate. Thereafter, many may be invoked by subscribers on a call-by-call basis.

③ **Administration facilities.** An SPC exchange offers an administration wide range of operational facilities which would otherwise be expensive or labour-intensive to provide. Most of the day-to-day operations on the exchange involve the use of these facilities, accessed via computer terminals associated with the exchange, either locally or at remotely located operational-control centres.

NEW WORDS AND PHRASES

impact(on)	n.	碰撞，冲击，冲突，影响，效果
	vt.	挤入，撞击，压紧，对……发生影响
couple(with)…	n.	（一）对，（一）双，夫妇
	vt.	联合，连接，结合
incorporate	adj.	合并的，结社的，一体化的
	vt.	合并，使组成公司，具体
prestige	n.	声望，威望，威信
matrices(matrix 的复数)	n.	矩阵

off-resistance	n.	断开电阻
linearity	n.	线性,直线性
insusceptible (to)	adj.	不受影响的
onwards	adv.	空前地,在先地
incentive	n.	动机
periphery	n.	外围
advent	n.	出现,到来
SPC(stored-program control)		存储程序控制

NOTES

[1] This development was motivated by the desire to improve upon the cost、quality、maintainability and flexibility of electromechanical telephone exchanges by exploiting the proven advantages of rapidly evolving electronic and computer technologies.

"by exploiting the proven advantages of rapidly evolving electronic and computer technologies"是分词短语作方式状语。

全句可译为:快速发展的电子和计算机技术的优势激发了(人们)降低成本、提高服务质量、提高机电式电话交换机的可维护性和灵活性的欲望。

或:这种发展是受到降低成本、提高服务质量、提高机电式电话交换机的可维护性和灵活性的欲望的激发(产生的),(这种发展)是通过利用快速发展的电子和计算机技术的优势(而获得的),这种技术优势是已经证明了的。

[2] This historic event initiated worldwide interest in SPC, which resulted in the introduction during the 1970s of a range of new exchange systems incorporating various degrees of computer-control technology.

"which resulted in the introduction during the 1970s of a range of new exchange systems incorporating various degrees of computer-control technology."是一个定语从句,用来修饰 historic event,对它引起的后果进行了进一步的说明。"incorporating various degrees of computer-control technology."是分词短语作定语,修饰 new exchange systems,翻译的时候需前置,或单独成句。

全句可译为:这次历史事件引发了全世界对存储程序控制的兴趣,它导致了大量的具有不同程度计算机控技术的新交换系统 19 世纪 70 年代被引入(到电话网中)。

[3] The second obstacle was the inability of the available semiconductor devices to handle the high voltages and ringing currents required by the conventional telephone.

"required by the conventional telephone"是过去分词短语充当后置定语,修饰 voltages and ringing currents。

全句可译为:第二个障碍是现有的半导体设备处理不了传统电话所要求的高电压和铃流。

[4] The shift towards digital technology, and the overcoming of the two obstacles, was influenced by the introduction of digital transmission into the PSTNs and developments in semiconductor integrated-circuit (IC) devices.

本句是一个较为复杂的简单句。"The shift towards digital technology, and the overcoming of the two obstacles"是本句的两个并列主语。"the introduction of digital transmission into the PSTNs 和 developments in semiconductor integrated-circuit（IC）devices"是 by 的两个并列宾语。

全句可译为：数字传输技术引入到公众电话网以及半导体集成电路设备的发展影响了（模拟技术）向数字技术的转换和（对这）两个障碍的克服。

[5] A key advantage of digital switching is the elimination of the multiplexing equipment normally associated with the PCM digital-transmission systems terminating at the exchange.

"the elimination of the multiplexing equipment normally associated with the PCM digital-transmission systems terminating at the exchange"作整个句子的表语。

"normally associated with the PCM digital-transmission systems terminating at the exchange"作 multiplexing equipment 的后置分词定语；terminating at the exchange 是现在分词短语作定语修饰 systems。

全句可译为：数字交换的主要优势在于，它去除了复用设备。这些复用设备通常是和 PCM 数字传输系统联系在一起并终止于交换机。

[6] One was an analogue reed, relay unit which terminated the subscriber lines and concentrated their traffic on to internal highly loaded trunks that could economically be connected to analogue-to-digital convertors.

"which terminated the subscriber lines and…"是用来修饰 relay unit 的定语从句。"that could economically be connected to analogue-to-digital convertors"是修饰 trunks 的非限定性定语从句。

全句可译为：一种形式是模拟簧片、中继单元。中继单元用来终止用户线，并把用户线的业务汇集到内部高负载中继线上，这些中继线可以把模拟-数字转换器经济地连接在一起。

[7] The advent, in the early 1980s, of generally available integrated-circuit devices, that provided cheap analogue-to-digital conversion, enabled the cost of subscriber-line interfaces to decrease sufficiently for all-digital switching systems to be competitive with the analogue-digital hybrids.

"that provided cheap analogue-to-digital conversion"是一个非限定性定语从句，用来修饰 devices。

全句可译为：20 世纪 80 年代早期，能提供廉价模数转换的通用集成电路设备的出现，有效地降低了用户线接口的成本，使得全数字交换系统能跟模数混合系统得以竞争。

EXERCISES

一、将下述词组译成中文

SPC(Stored-program control)　　　　electromechanical switching device
reed relay　　　　　　　　　　　　　crosstalk
integrated digital network（IDN）　　　labour-intensive
public telephone switched network（PSTN）

二、将下述短文译成中文

An important aspect of the long-term flexibility provided by SPC systems is the ability for established exchanges to be upgraded without disruption to the service. This enables new capabilities and facilities not known or specified earlier to be incorporated during the life of an exchange system. Some of these enhancements may be achieved merely by the incorporation of new software, e. g. the introduction of a closed user-group facility for a certain class of subscriber. Other enhancements such as the introduction of digital data switching, also require the addition of new hardware. SPC offers short-term flexibility due to its ability to alter the status of exchange equipment simply by changes to data. Thus, the operation of an exchange can be made to react rapidly to network conditions. For example, routing algorithms may be changed so that calls are re-routed to avoid congestion in the network. The short-term flexibility of SPC enables a wide range of administration and subscriber facilities to be provided economically and with ease of operation.

Unit 18

Bluetooth

TEXT

Bluetooth wireless technology is a short-range communications technology in intended to replace the cables connecting portable and fixed devices while maintaining high levels of security. The key features of Bluetooth technology are robustness, low power, and low cost. The Bluetooth specification defines a uniform structure for a wide range of devices to connect and communicate with each other.

Bluetooth technology has achieved global acceptance such that any Bluetooth enabled device, almost everywhere in the world, can connect to other Bluetooth enabled devices in proximity. Bluetooth enabled electronic devices connect and communicate wirelessly through short-range, ad hoc networks known as piconets. Each device can simultaneously communicate with up to seven other devices within a single piconet. Each device can also belong to several piconets simultaneously. Piconets are established dynamically and automatically as Bluetooth enabled devices enter and leave radio proximity.

A fundamental Bluetooth wireless technology strength is the ability to simultaneously handle both data and voice transmissions. This enables users to enjoy variety of innovative solutions such as a hands-free headset for voice calls, printing and fax capabilities, synchronizing PDA, laptop, and mobile phone applications to name a few.

1. Core system

The Bluetooth core system, defined by Bluetooth specification, is a common service layer protocol which covers four lower layers in seven layer protocol. Service Discovery Protocol (SDP) and the overall profile requirements are defined by Generic Access Profile (GAP)[1]. A complete Bluetooth application requires a number of additional services and higher layer protocols that are defined in the Bluetooth specification.

The lowest three layers are sometimes grouped into a subsystem known as the Bluetooth controller. This is a common implementation involving a standard physical communications interface between the Bluetooth controller and remainder of the Bluetooth system including the L2CAP, service layers and higher layers (known as the Bluetooth host). Although this interface is optional, the architecture is designed to allow for its existence and characteristics. The Bluetooth specification enables interoperability between independent Bluetooth enabled systems by defining the protocol messages exchanged between equivalent layers, and also interoperability between independent Bluetooth sub-systems by defining a common interface between Bluetooth controllers and Bluetooth hosts.

A number of functional blocks are shown and the path of services and data between these. The functional blocks shown in the diagram are informative; in general the Bluetooth specification does not define the details of implementations except where this is required for interoperability.

Standard interactions are defined for all inter-device operation, where Bluetooth devices exchange protocol signaling according to the Bluetooth specification. The Bluetooth core system protocols are the radio frequency (RF) protocol, link control (LC) protocol, link manager (LM) protocol and logical link control and adaptation protocol (L2CAP), all of which are fully defined in subsequent parts of the Bluetooth specification [2]. In addition, the service discovery protocol (SDP) is a service layer protocol required by all Bluetooth applications.

The Bluetooth core system offers services through a number of service access points that are shown in the diagram as ellipses. These services consist of the basic primitives that control the Bluetooth core system. The services can be split into three types. There are device control services that modify the behavior and modes of a Bluetooth device, transport control services that create, modify and release traffic bearers (channels and links), and data services that are used to submit data for transmission over traffic bearers [3]. It is common to consider the first two as belonging to the C-plane and the last as belonging to the U-plane.

A service interface to the Bluetooth controller sub-system is defined such that the Bluetooth controller may be considered a standard part. In this configuration the Bluetooth controller operates the lowest three layers and the L2CAP layer is contained with the rest of the Bluetooth application in a host system. The standard interface is called the host to controller interface (HCI). Implementation of this standard service interface is optional.

As the Bluetooth architecture is defined with the possibility of a separate host and controller communicating through an HCI, a number of general assumptions are made. The Bluetooth controller is assumed to have limited data buffering capabilities in comparison with the host. Therefore the L2CAP layer is expected to carry out some simple resource management when submitting L2CAP PDUs to the controller for transport to a peer device. This includes segmentation of L2CAP SDUs into more manageable PDUs and then the fragmentation of PDUs into start and continuation packets of a size suitable for the controller buffers, and management of the use of controller buffers to ensure availability for channels with quality of service (QoS) commitments [4].

The baseband layer provides the basic ARQ protocol in Bluetooth technology. The L2CAP layer can optionally provide a further error detection and retransmission to the L2CAP PDUs. This feature is recommended for applications with requirements for a low probability of undetected errors in the user data. A further optional feature of L2CAP is a window-based flow control that can be used to manage buffer allocation in the receiving device. Both of these optional features augment the QoS performance in certain scenarios.

Although these assumptions may not be required for embedded Bluetooth technology implementations that combine all layers in a single system, the general architectural and QoS models are defined with these assumptions in mind, in effect a lowest common denominator.

Automated conformance testing of implementations of the Bluetooth core system is required. This is achieved by allowing the tester to control the implementation through the RF interface, Which is common to all Bluetooth systems, and through the test control interface (TCI), which is only required for conformance testing.

The tester uses exchanges with the implementation under test (IUT) through the RF interface to ensure the correct responses to requests from remote devices. The tester controls the IUT through the TCI to cause the IUT to originate exchanges through the RF interface so that these can also be verified as conformant.

The TCI uses a different command-set (service interface) for the testing of each architectural layer and protocol. A subset of the HCI command-set is issued as the TCI service interface for each of the layers and protocols within the Bluetooth controller subsystem. A separate interface is used for testing the L2CAP layer and protocol. As an L2CAP service interface is not defined in the Bluetooth core specification it is defined separately in the TCI specification. Implementation of the L2CAP service interface is only required for conformance testing.

2. Why Choose Bluetooth wireless technology?

Bluetooth wireless technology is the simple choice for convenient, wire-free, short-range communication between devices. It is a globally available standard that wirelessly connects mobile phones, portable computers, cars, stereo headsets, MP3 players, and more Thanks to the unique concept of "profiles", Bluetooth enabled products do not need to install driver software. The technology is now available in its fourth version of the specification and continues to develop, building on its inherent strengths — small-form factor radio, low power, low cost, built-in security, robustness, ease-of-use, and ad hoc networking abilities[5]. Bluetooth wireless technology is the leading and only proven short-range wireless technology on the market today shipping over five million units every week with an installed base of over 500 million units at the end of 2005.

3. Globally Available

The Bluetooth wireless technology specification is available free-of-charge to our member companies around the globe. Manufacturers from many industries are busy implementing technology in their products to reduce the clutter of wires, make seamless connections, stream stereo audio, transfer data or carry voice communications. Bluetooth technology operates in 2.4 GHz, one of the unlicensed industrial, scientific, medical (ISM) radio bands. As such, there is no cost for the use of Bluetooth technology. While you must subscribe to a cellular provider to use GSM or CDMA, with Bluetooth technology there is no cost associated with the use beyond the cost of your device.

4. Range of Devices

Bluetooth technology is available in an unprecedented range of applications from mobile phones to automobiles to medical devices for use by consumers, industrial markets, enterprises and more. The low power consumption, small size and low cost of the chipset solution enables Bluetooth technology to be used in the tiniest of devices. Have a look at the wide range products made available by our members in the Bluetooth product directory and the component product listing.

5. Ease of Use

Bluetooth technology is an ad hoc technology that requires no fixed infrastructure and is simple to install and set up. You don't need wires to get connected. The process for a new user is easy—you get a Bluetooth branded product, check the profiles available and connect it to another Bluetooth device with the same profiles. The subsequent PIN code process is as easy as when you identify yourself at the ATM machine. When out-and-about, you carry your personal area network (PAN) with you and can even connect to others.

6. Globally Accepted Specification

Bluetooth wireless technology is the most widely supported, versatile, and secure wireless standard on the market today. The globally available qualification program tests member products as to their accordance with the standard. Since the first release of the Bluetooth specification in 1999, over 4000 companies have become members in the Bluetooth Special Interest Group (SIG). Meanwhile, the number of Bluetooth products on the market is multiplying rapidly. Volumes have doubled for the fourth consecutive year and are likely to reach an installed base of 500 million units by the close of 2005.

7. Secure Connections

From the start, Bluetooth technology was designed with security needs in mind. Since it is globally available in the open 2.4 GHz ISM band, robustness was built in from the beginning. With adaptive frequency hopping (AFH), the signal "hops" and thus limits interference from other signals. Further, Bluetooth technology has built-in security such as 128 bit encryption and PIN code authentication. When Bluetooth products identify themselves, they use the PIN code the first time they connect. Once connected, always securely connected.

NEW WORDS AND PHRASES

proximity	n.	接近,临近
piconet	n.	微微网(是由采用蓝牙技术的设备以特定方式组成的网络)
ad hoc	adj.	特别的;变通的,非正式的
innovative	adj.	新发明的,新引进的;革新的

core	n.	核心，精髓，要点
laptop		膝上型轻便电脑
interoperability	n.	互用性，协同工作的能力
ellipse	n.	椭圆
RF(Radio Frequency)		射频
primitive	n.	[计]原语;原始事物
peer	adj	对等的
submit	vt.	提交，呈递
segmentation	n.	分割
fragmentation	n.	分区输入程序;碎片
continuation	n.	延长部分
commitment	n.	行为;委托;义务
baseband	n.	基带
scenario	n.	剧情说明书,电影剧本
denominator	n	[数]分母;共同的要素,共同的性质
conformance	n.	相似;相符;一致
clutter	n.	混乱
seamless	adj.	无缝的
chipset	n.	[计]芯片集
PDU(Protocol Data Unit)		协议数据单元
flow control		流量控制
stereo headsets		立体声耳机
encryption	n.	加密
authentication	n.	认证
versatile	adj.	多用途的，多功能的
logical link control and adaptation protocol（L2CAP）		逻辑链路控制适配协议

NOTES

[1] The Bluetooth core system, defined by Bluetooth specification, is a common service layer Protocol which covers four lower layers in seven layer protocol. Service Discovery Protocol(SDP) and the overall Profile requirements are defined by Generic Access Profile (GAP).

defined by Bluetooth specification 修饰前面的 The Bluetooth core system；which covers four lower layers in seven layer protocol 是后置定语从句,修饰前面的 common service layer Protocol。

SDP:Service Discovery Protocol(服务发现协议),蓝牙中定义的一个协议,主要用来提供一个方式,通过它能够让应用程序发现和使用有关服务,并且能够知晓这些服务的特点。

GAP:Generic Access Profile(通用接入框架),该应用描述了一种设备发现和访问另外一种设备的机制,而此时,这两种设备不共享普通的应用程序。

本句可译为:蓝牙规范将蓝牙核心系统定义为一个普通的服务层协议,这个服务层覆盖了七层协议的下四层,通用接入框架(GAP)定义了服务发现层协议(SDP)和所需要的通用协议子集。

[2] The Bluetooth core system protocols are the radio frequency (RF) Protocol, link control (LC) protocol, link manager (LM) protocol and logical link control and adaptation protocol (L2CAP), all of which are fully defined in subsequent parts of the Bluetooth specification.

LC:Link control(链路控制),链接控制器管理对其他蓝牙设备的链接。它是低层的基带协议管理者。

LM:Link Manager(链路管理),链路管理软件实体负责管理建立链接、鉴定、链路配置,以及实现其他协议等事务。

L2CAP:Logical Link Control and Adaptation Protocol(逻辑信道控制和适配协议),该协议支持高层协议多路复用技术,包括分割和重组装技术,以及保证传达服务信息的质量。

本句可译为:蓝牙核心系统协议包括射频协议、链路控制协议、连接管理协议、逻辑链路控制应用协议,所有这些协议在蓝牙规范的随后几个部分都有定义。

[3] There are device control services that modify the behavior and modes of a Bluetooth device, transport control services that create, modify and release traffic bearers (channels and links), and data services that are used to submit data for transmission over traffic bearers.

本句是一个 there be 结构,真正的主语是 device control services, transport control services,data services。

主语后的…that modify the behavior and modes of a Bluetooth device;…that create, modify and release traffic bearers (channels and links);…that are used to submit data for transmission over traffic bearers是修饰它们的非限定性定语从句。

本句可译为:设备控制服务用于改善蓝牙设备的性能和模式,传输控制服务用于创建、修改、释放(信道和链路上的)承载业务,数据服务则为承载业务的传输提交数据。

[4] This includes segmentation of L2CAP SDUs into more manageable PDUs and then the fragmentation of PDUs into start and continuation packets of a size suitable for the controller buffers, and management of the use of controller buffers to ensure availability for channels with quality of service (QoS) commitments.

本句是一个简单句,句中 this 是主语,指代的是前一句的 some simple resource management。segmentation of L2CAP SDUs into more manageable PDUs and then the fragmentation of PDUs into start and continuation packets of a size suitable for the controller buffers, and management of the use of controller buffers to ensure availability for channels with quality of service (QoS) commitments 是 includes 的并列宾语。segmentation…into:把……分割为。

本句可译为:这包括了把 L2CAP 层业务数据单元(SDU)分割为更容易管理的协议数据单元(PDU),然后把协议数据单元分成适合控制缓存器大小的开始和中间数据分组,以及为了保证对有业务质量承诺信道的可用性的控制缓存器的管理。

[5] The technology is now available in its fourth version of the specification and continues to develop, building on its inherent strengths — small-form factor radio, low power, low cost, built-in security, robustness, ease-of-use, and ad hoc networking abilities.

building on its inherent strengths 可译为"基于其与生俱来的特性（力量）"。small-form factor radio, low power, low cost, built-in security, robustness, ease-of-use, and ad hoc networking abilities 是对前面的 its inherent strengths 的具体解释。

本句可译为：现在，第四版的蓝牙规范已经定义了该技术，鉴于其与生俱来的特性，诸如尺寸小、低功耗、低成本、高安全性、生命力强、易操作、具备 ad hoc 网络能力等，该技术发展前景广阔。

EXERCISES

一、将下述词组译成英文

蓝牙规范　　　　　　　　免提电话
通用接入框架　　　　　　接入控制协议
业务发现协议　　　　　　立体声耳机

二、将下述短文译成中文

1. Although these assumptions may not be required for embedded Bluetooth technology implementations that combine all layers in a single system, the general architectural and QoS models are defined with these assumptions in mind, in effect a lowest common denominator.

2. The Bluetooth specification enables interoperability between independent Bluetooth enabled systems by defining the protocol messages exchanged between equivalent layers, and also interoperability between independent Bluetooth sub-systems by defining a common interface between Bluetooth controllers and Bluetooth hosts.

3. With adaptive frequency hopping (AFH), the signal "hops" and thus limits interference from other signals. Further, Bluetooth technology has built-in security such as 128 bit encryption and PIN code authentication. When Bluetooth products identify themselves, they use the PIN code the first time they connect. Once connected, always securely connected.

Unit 19

Integrating RFID on Event-based Hemispheric Imaging for Internet of Things Assistive Applications

TEXT

1. INTRODUCTION

The remote activity monitoring across large environments, such as government facilities, public buildings or industrial environments in real time, is a prerequisite for various monitoring applications. Such activities can also prove a useful addition in assistive environments in smaller size spaces, like houses and offices. Modern video-based surveillance systems, which employ powerful real time analysis techniques, are widely deployed. Additionally, the use of multiple cameras to provide surveillance coverage over a wider area while ensuring object visibility over a large range of depths, introduces the need to coordinate the cameras in order to detect events of interest, something which increases system complexity.

Radio Frequency Identification (RFID) technology is arguably the ideal solution for object identification. It has successfully been used in a large variety of applications, like enterprise supply chain management for inventorying, tracking and of course objects identification. RFID may also prove useful for pervasive computing, for providing identity to virtually everything. It is not accidental that RFID, along with wireless sensor and nanotechnologies have been combined to form what is known as the Internet of Things.

For nearly every pervasive computing application, another vital requirement is real time locating, which emanates from the inherent need for just-in-time actionable information. Over the years, many systems have addressed the problem of automatic location sensing with various techniques. In this paper we elaborate on the feasibility of developing a hybrid system by combining video surveillance feed and RFID, in order to provide a solid system for automatic identification and tracking of objects in the output of a video camera. The use of hemispheric imaging cameras that maximize the area coverage of a surveillance system is examined, in order to eliminate the need for multiple cameras and the factors that influence the purpose of such a system are identified[1].

The rest of this paper is organized as follows: In Section 2 we provide an overview of RFID and video processing technologies along with other competitive or complementary technologies. In Section 3 related research pertaining surveillance that uses RFID sensors, video cameras and their combination is provided. Section 4 describes the necessary components in terms of hardware and software that are necessary for such a system and discusses its advantages, disadvantages and possible implementation issues. Section 5 describes possible applications of this integration.

2. UNDERLYING TECHNOLOGIES

(1) RFID Overview

One of the pivotal technologies of pervasive and ubiquitous computing is RFID. Grouped under the broad category of automatic identification technologies, RFID is used as a generic term to describe a system where the identity (in the form of a unique serial number) of an object is transmitted wirelessly, using radio waves. A typical RFID system is composed of: (a) the RFID tag, which contains a digital number associated with the physical object that it is attached to and (b) the RFID reader (also known as interrogator) which is usually connected to a backend database. The reader is also equipped with an antenna, a transceiver and a processor that broadcasts a radio signal in order to query the tag and read its contents.

Two are the most important characteristics of an RFID system each encapsulating differences in range, data transfer and transmission under certain environmental conditions: (a) the energy resources and computational capabilities of RFID tags and (b) its operating frequency. According to the first characteristic, RFID tags are distinguished into passive and active, as well as their combinations. Active tags incorporate a battery and can transmit signals autonomously, over a long operation range with high performance but they are expensive and usually have a large size. On the other hand, passive tags require an external source to provoke signal transmission, which is acquired using either inductive coupling or electromagnetic capture and they communicate with the reader by utilizing load modulation or electromagnetic backscatter. Passive tags are widely used and in many cases they are preferred over the active due to their low cost, small size, and practically unlimited life time. Additionally, RFID systems can be categorized into four operating frequencies: (a) Low, (b) High, (c) Ultra High, and (d) Super High Frequency (or Microwave). As the frequency increases, range and data transfer rates also increase, but penetration through water and materials such as metal decreases.

The necessity of establishing uniform engineering criteria, methods, process and practices for the defining characteristics of RFID systems, led to the proposal of various standards, two of which are more prominent. EPC global defines a combined method of classifying tags that specifies unique identification numbers (Electronic Product Codes), frequencies, coupling methods, types of keying and modulation, information storage capacity and modes of interoperability among others. Similarly ISO (jointly with IEC) developed standards for identification, communication between the reader and the tag, data protocols for the middleware and testing, compliance and safety.

① Identification and RFID

A fundamental requirement of pervasive systems in general, is the ability to uniquely identify things and/or entities. RFID satisfies this requirement by nature. There are also several other technologies that serve this purpose, each having advantages and disadvantages, but steadily being replaced in most application areas with RFID.

The barcode, still the most widely used product tracking method in supply chain management and the cheapest identification solution, is an optical, machine readable write-once representation of an object category. The most important weaknesses of barcode technology are the inability to provide extra information regarding a single object (two-dimensional symbologies deal with this issue however) and the requirement of the bar-coded object to be in a line-of-sight (LOS).

Card technologies, is another category for identification of objects and entities that include magnetic cards, smart cards and optical cards. Usually embedded in a credit card-sized plastic card they encompass either a magnetic stripe or an integrated circuit and they have greater storage capacities. In case they incorporate a microprocessor, they also have increased processing capabilities, something which allows them to be used in demanding applications such as security (with great limitations however). On the downside, most cards either require contact or to be in a very close distance with the reader. The costs also increase significantly in proportion to the features of the card in use. RFID balances between efficiency and cost-effectiveness, while it alleviates the need of the tag being in a LOS. This is the reason why RFID is widely used in access control, anti-counterfeiting and tracking and tracing among others.

② Real time locating and RFID

RFID is primarily made for identification, over the last decade research efforts focused on the use of RFID for real time locating. There are plenty of competitive and/or complementary real time locating technologies to RFID, each of which differs in accuracy, precision, complexity and cost among other factors.

Wi-Fi (also referred to as IEEE 802.11), the technology used for wireless device interconnection, is probably the ideal solution for locating devices equipped with Wi-Fi tags, like laptops and PDAs, already connected in a wireless network. Wi-Fi real time locating however is highly dependent on network infrastructure, it has serious scalability issues and it may introduce some burden on the network, let aside the affection by various environmental conditions like obstacles, temperature and humidity, commonly met in most wireless technologies.

Another real time locating technology similar to Wi-Fi is Bluetooth, the wireless networking standard designed for low power consumption and communication in a personal area network. Bluetooth is standardized, widely adopted, multipurpose and relatively accurate. Nevertheless, the range of Bluetooth access points is rather short and because of the inquiry process, the positioning delay is relatively high. Along with Wi-Fi, Bluetooth tags are not suited for very small objects.

Ultra Wideband (UWB) is another radio technology that can be used at low energy levels for short-range high bandwidth communications. UWB systems provide high accuracy that can be reduced to a few centimeters, however UWB signals interference through metallic and liquid materials is a constant problem and their cost is prohibitive at least for small scale applications[2].

ZigBee is a low-cost, low-power, wireless mesh networking proprietary standard. Since it is standardized, interoperability of equipment from different manufacturers is guaranteed. Also it is has excellent performance in low signal to noise ratio environments and it is fault tolerant. Nonetheless, ZigBee routers have short range and their signal has low penetration through walls, and other obstacles.

As far as RFID, both passive and active tags can be used for real time locating. Passive tags can be acquired at a very low cost and can be attached to almost everything. They also facilitate higher read rates (approx. 1 500 tags per second). However they have also low tolerance on harsh environmental conditions and they require the presence of multiple readers and antennas in order to cover wider areas. Active tags on the other hand, improve the accuracy and tolerance but they pose serious maintenance challenges since they have limited lifetime. Currently, there is no best real time location sensing technique. Each technology has its own distinct characteristics when applied in real environments and the choice is clearly a matter of tradeoff between accuracy, precision, system complexity and suitability in a given environment[3].

(2) Video Surveillance

Video cameras, in the form of a closed circuit television (CCTV), have been widely used in surveillance applications, where a human operator evaluates the captured events to provide alert. These systems are installed mainly in public spaces, where security is the major concern. However, the human factor involved in the procedure greatly influences surveillance effectiveness, due to fatigue or lack of concentration.

Intelligent Surveillance (IS) systems have been developed, to automatically detect objects, track a person and recognize an event in order to react upon any abnormal behavior taking place in a scene. The IS systems are being extensively researched in literature and solutions have been proposed for a number of applications, especially in the case where a human operator can not be offered. Recently, these systems have been considered for pervasive applications, including ambient home, e-health and e-care systems.

However, IS systems still present certain limitation. Several cameras are required to cover a large space, even if they are equipped with wide angle lenses. In this case, extensive installation modifications limit acceptance of video surveillance by a wide audience, despite the fact that in some cases installing cameras can be proven useful, such as a home-assisting environments for the elderly.

Furthermore, the image processing modules of these systems are sensitive to complex environmental changes and object occlusions, that is, when a targeted object hides behind another. Additionally, video cameras that usually have a lower resolution than still cameras, can not robustly detect small or distant objects.

The Charged Coupled Device (CCD) that video cameras are equipped with also presents noise, by design, which in turn hinders the object location performance. Finally, multi camera environments and the storage capabilities they require lead to extra cost for the acquisition of a high-end pc and storage arrays.

Therefore, other solutions should be considered that would limit the cost of these systems and increase their effectiveness in order to become more appealing for wider audiences.

NEW WORDS AND PHRASES

prerequisite	n.	先决条件
surveillance	n.	监视,监督
arguably	adv.	可论证地,正如可提出证据加以证明的那样
inventory	n.	详细目录,存货,财产清册,总量
pervasive	adj.	普遍深入的
accidental	adj.	意外的,非主要的,附属的
nanotechnology	n.	纳米技术
emanate	vi.	散发,发出,发源
actionable	adj.	可控告的
elaborate	v.	详细描述
hemispheric	adj.	半球形状的
pivotal	adj.	枢轴的,中枢的,关键的
ubiquitous	adj.	到处存在的,(同时)普遍存在的
interrogator	n.	讯问者,质问者
backend database		后端数据库
inductive	adj.	诱导的,感应的
backscatter	n.	反向散射(背反射)
Internet of Things	vt.	物联网
penetration	n.	穿过,渗透,突破
interoperability	n.	互用性,协同工作的能力
bar-code	n.	条形码
laptop	n.	膝上型电脑
prohibitive	adj.	(费用等)高得负担不起的,过分昂贵的
fatigue	n.	疲乏,疲劳,累活

NOTES

[1] The use of hemispheric imaging cameras that maximize the area coverage of a

surveillance system is examined, in order to eliminate the need for multiple cameras and the factors that influence the purpose of such a system are identified.

"that maximize the area coverage of a surveillance system is examined"是后置定语从句,修饰前面的 cameras。"in order to eliminate the need for multiple cameras and the factors that influence the purpose of such a system are identified"是为了说明为什么讨论使用半球形摄像机。

本句可译为:为了减少对多个摄像机的使用需求讨论了半球形成像摄像机,该摄像机可以使监控系统的覆盖范围最大化,并且明确了影响系统目的的一些因素。

[2] UWB systems provide high accuracy that can be reduced to a few centimeters, however UWB signals interference through metallic and liquid materials is a constant problem and their cost is prohibitive at least for small scale applications.

"that can be reduced to a few centimeters"是后置定语从句,用来修饰 high accuracy。这里的 prohibitive 的意思是"昂贵的,不可承受的"。

本句可译为:UWB 系统能够提供小到几个厘米的高精确度,但是 UWB 信号通过金属和液态物质时的干扰一直是常态问题,并且其系统成本至少对小规模应用来说是过分昂贵了。

[3] Each technology has its own distinct characteristics when applied in real environments and the choice is clearly a matter of tradeoff between accuracy, precision, system complexity and suitability in a given environment.

本句是一个复杂的并列句。

本句可译为:当应用到真实的环境中时每种技术都有自己独特的性能。(在这之中的)选择显然是在准确度、精确度、系统复杂度和对特定环境的适应能力之间的平衡折中。

EXERCISES

一、翻译下列词组

Internet of Things	locating technology
Radio Frequency Identification	license plate
line-of-sight	Charged Coupled Device (CCD)
anti-counterfeiting	普适计算
视频监控	RFID

二、将下述短文译成中文

1. Radio Frequency Identification (RFID) technology is arguably the ideal solution for object identification. It has successfully been used in a large variety of applications, like enterprise supply chain management for inventorying, tracking and of course objects identification. RFID may also prove useful for pervasive computing, for providing identity to virtually everything. It is not accidental that RFID, along with wireless sensor and nanotechnologies have been combined to form what is known as the Internet of Things.

2. Video cameras, in the form of a closed circuit television (CCTV), have been widely used in surveillance applications, where a human operator evaluates the captured events to provide alert. These systems are installed mainly in public spaces, where security is the

major concern. However, the human factor involved in the procedure greatly influences surveillance effectiveness, due to fatigue or lack of concentration.

3. Video surveillance has been successfully applied on a number of situations. First of all, cameras have been installed to serve as image sensors and act as a non-intrusive means of increased security. Secondly, video processing methods have been extensively used for industrial applications. The industry inspection systems include, among others, quality textile production, metal product finishing, glass manufacturing, machine parts, printing products and many others. Another field in which video surveillance has been successfully applied is the development of Intelligent Transportation Systems. These include automatic lane finding and license plate recognition systems. Video surveillance has found recently increased usability in behavioral analysis. Finally, many e-health and e-care applications have been benefited from the use of video cameras.

Unit 20

Image & Video

TEXT

1. Video

The human eye has the property that when an image is flashed on the retina, it is retained for some number of milliseconds, before decaying. If a sequence of images is flashed at 50 or more images/sec, the eye does not notice that it is looking at discrete images. All video(i.e, television) systems exploit this principle to produce moving pictures.

To understand video systems, it is best to start with simple, old-fashioned black-and-white television. To represent the two-dimensional image in front of it as a one-dimensional voltage as a function of time, the camera scans an electron beam rapidly across the image and slowly down it, recording the light intensity as it goes. At the end of the scan, called a frame, the beam retraces. This intensity as a function of time is broadcast, and receivers repeat the scanning process to reconstruct the image. The scanning pattern used by both the cameras and the receiver is shown in Fig. 1. (As an aside, CCD cameras integrate rather than scan, but some cameras and all monitors do scan.)

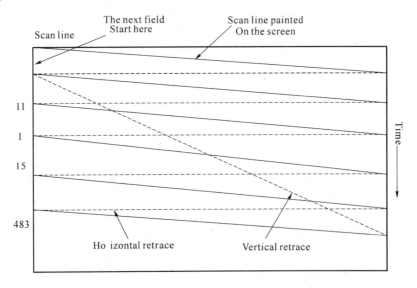

Fig. 1 The scanning pattern used for NTSC video and television

The exact scanning parameters vary from country to country. The system used in North and South America and Japan has 525 scan lines, a horizontal to vertical aspect ratio of 4∶3, and 30 frames/sec. The European system has 625 scan lines, the same aspect ratio of 4∶3, and 25 frames/sec. In both systems, the top few and bottom few lines are not displayed(to approximate a rectangular image on the original round CRTs). Only 483 of the 525 NTSC scan lines (and 576 of the 625 PAL/SECAM scan lines) are displayed. The beam is turned off during the vertical retrace, so many stations (especially in Europe) use this interval to broadcast Tele Text (text pages containing news, weather, sports, stock prices,etc.).

While 25 frames/sec is enough to capture smooth motion, at that frame rate many people, especially older ones, will perceive the image to flicker (because the old image has faded off the retina before the new one appears). Rather than increase the frame rate, which would require using more scarce bandwidth, a different approach is taken. Instead of displaying the scan lines in order, first all the odd scan lines are displayed, then the even ones are displayed. Each of these half frames is called a field. Experiments have shown that although people notice flicker at 25 frames/sec, they do not notice it at 50 fields/sec. This technique is called interlacing. Noninterlaced television or video is said to be progressive.

Color video uses the same scanning pattern as monochrome (black and white), except that instead of displaying the image with one moving beam, three beams moving in unison are used. One beam is used for each of the three additive primary colors: red, green, and blue (RGB). This technique works because any color can be constructed from a linear superposition of red, green, and blue with the appropriate intensities [1]. However, for transmission on a single channel, the three color signals must be combined into a single composite signal.

When color television was invented, various methods for displaying color were technically possible, and different countries made different choices, leading to systems that are still incompatible. (Note that these choices have nothing to do with VHS versus Betamax versus P2000, which are recording methods.) In all countries, a political requirement was that programs transmitted in color had to be receivable on existing black-and-white television sets. Consequently, the simplest scheme, just encoding the RGB signals separately, was not acceptable. RGB is also not the most efficient scheme.

The first color system was standardized in the United States by the National Television Standards Committee, which lent its acronym to the standard: NTSC. Color television was introduced in Europe several years later, by which time the technology had improved substantially, leading to systems with greater noise immunity and better colors. These are called SECAM (SEquentiel Couleur Avec Memoire), which is used in France and Eastern Europe, and PAL (Phase Alternating Line) is used in the rest of Europe. The difference in color quality between the NTSC and PAL/SECAM has led to an industry joke that NTSC really stands for Never Twice the Same Color.

To allow color transmissions to be viewed on black-and-white receivers, all three systems linearly combine the RGB signals into a luminance (brightness) signal, and two chrominance (color) signals, although they all use different coefficients for constructing these signals from the RGB signals[2]. Interestingly enough, the eye is much more sensitive to the luminance signal than to the chrominance signals, so the latter need not be transmitted as accurately. Consequently, the luminance signal can be broadcast at the same frequency as the old black-and-white signal, so it can be received on black-and-white television sets. The two chrominance signals are broadcast in narrow bands at higher frequencies. Some televisions sets have controls labeled brightness, hue, and saturation(or brightness, tint and color) for controlling these three signals separately. Understanding luminance and chrominance is necessary for understanding how video compression works.

In the past few years, there has been considerable interest in HDTV (High Definition Television), which produces sharper images by roughly doubling the number of scan lines. The United States, Europe, and Japan have all developed HDTV systems, all different and all mutually incompatible. The basic principles of HDTV in terms of scanning, luminance, chrominance, and so on, are similar to the existing systems. However, all three formats have a common aspect ratio of 4:3 to match them better to the format used for movies (which are recorded on 35 mm film).

2. Video on Demand

Video on demand is sometimes compared to an electronic video rental store. The user (customer) selects any one of a large number of available videos and takes it home to view. Only with video on demand, the selection is made at home using the television set's remote control, and the video starts immediately. No trip to the store is needed. Needless to say, implementing video on demand is a wee bit more complicated than describing it. In this section, we will give an overview of the basic ideas and their implementation. A description of one real implementation can be found in (Nelson and Linton. 1995). A more general treatment of interactive television is in (Hodge, 1995). Other relevant references are (Chang et al., 1994; Hodge et al., 1993; and Little and Venkatesh, 1994).

Is video on demand really like renting a video, or is it more like picking a movie to watch from a 500- or 5 000-channel cable system? The answer has important technical implications. In particular, video rental users are used to the idea of being able to stop a video, make a quick trip to the kitchen or bathroom, and then resume from where the video stopped. Television viewers do not expect to put programs on pause.

If video on demand is going to compete successfully with video rental stores, it may be necessary to allow users to stop, start, and rewind videos at will. Giving users this ability virtually forces the video provider to transmit a separate copy to each one.

On the other hand, if video on demand is seen more as advanced television, then it may be sufficient to have the video provider start each popular video, say, every 10 minutes, and run these nonstop. A user wanting to see a popular video may have to wait up to 10 minutes for it to start. Although pause/resume is not possible here, a viewer returning to the living room after a short break can switch to another channel showing the same video but 10 minutes behind. Some material will be repeated, but nothing will be missed. This scheme is called near video on demand. It offers the potential for much lower cost, because the same feed from the video server can go to many users at once. The difference between video on demand and near video on demand is similar to the difference between driving your own car and taking the bus.

Watching movies on (near) demand is but one of a vast array of potential new services possible once wideband networking is available. Here we see a high-bandwidth, (national or international) wide area backbone network at the center of the system. Connected to it are thousands of local distribution networks, such as cable TV or telephone company distribution systems. The local distribution systems reach into people's houses, where they terminate in set-top boxes, which are, in fact, powerful, specialized personal computers[3].

Attached to the backbone by high-bandwidth optical fibers are thousands of information providers. Some of these will offer pay-per-view video or pay-per-hear audio CDs. Others will offer specialized services, such as home shopping (with the ability to rotate a can of soup and zoom in on the list of ingredients or view a video clip on how to drive a gasoline-powered lawn mower). Sports, news, returns of "I Love Lucy," WWW access, and innumerable other possibilities will no doubt quickly become available.

Also included in the system are local spooling servers that allow videos to be prepositioned closer to the users, to save bandwidth during peak hours. How these pieces will fit together and who will own what are matters of vigorous debate within the industry. Below we will examine the design, one of the main pieces of the system: the video servers.

3. Video Servers

To have (near) video on demand, we need video servers capable of storing and outputting a large number of movies simultaneously. The total number of movies ever made is estimated at 65 000 (Minoli, 1995). When compressed in MPEG-2, a normal movie occupies roughly 4 GB of storage, so 65 000 of them would require something like 260 terabytes. Add to this all the old television programs ever made, sports films, newsreels, talking shopping catalogs, etc, and it is clear that we have an industrial-strength storage problem on our hands.

The cheapest way to store large volumes of information is on magnetic tape. This has always been the case and probably always will be. A DAT tape can store 8 GB (two movies) at a cost of about 5 dollars/gigabyte. Large mechanical tape servers that hold thousands of tapes and have a robot arm for fetching any tape and inserting it into a tape drive are commercially available now[4]. The problem with these systems is the access time (especially for the second movie on a tape), the transfer rate, and the limited number of tape drives (to serve n movies at once, the unit would need n drives).

Fortunately, experience with video rental stores, public libraries, and other such organizations shows that not all items are equally popular. Experimentally, when there are N movies available, the fraction of all requests being for the kth most popular one is approximately C/k (Chervenak, 1994). Here C is computed to normalize the sum to

1, namely

$$C = 1/(1 + 1/2 + 1/3 + 1/4 + 1/5 + \cdots + 1/N)$$

Thus the most popular movie is seven times as popular as the number seven movie. This result is known as Zipf's law (Zipf, 1949).

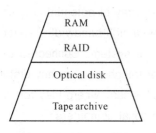

Fig. 2　A video server storage hierarchy

The fact that some movies are much more popular than others suggests a possible solution in the form of a storage hierarchy, as shown in Fig. 2. Here, the performance increases as one moves up the hierarchy.

Now let us take a brief look at video server software. The CPUs are used for accepting user requests, locating movies, moving data between devices, customer billing, and many other functions. Some of these are not time critical, but many others are. So some, if not all, of the CPUs will have to run a real-time operating system, such as a real-time microkernel. These systems normally break work up into smaller tasks, each with a known deadline. The scheduler can then run an algorithm such as nearest deadline next of the rate monotonic algorithm.

NEW WORDS AND PHRASES

retina	n.	视网膜
millisecond	n.	毫秒
discrete	adj.	分离的,不相关联的,离散的
frame	n.	帧
retrace	vt.	折回;回忆,回顾,追溯
beam	n.	束,柱
reconstruct	vt.	重建
scan	vt.	[计]扫描
horizontal	adj.	水平的,与地平线平行的
vertical	adj.	垂直的,竖的
flicker	vt.	闪烁,摇曳
perceive	vt.	感觉,察觉,理解
scarce	adj.	缺乏的,罕见的
monochrome	n.	单色画,单色照片,黑白照片
unison	n.	一致,同时
acronym	n.	只取首字母的缩写词
immunity	n.	免除;豁免
luminance	n.	[计]亮度
chrominance	n.	[物]色度
saturation	n.	饱和度,饱和(状态)

compression	n.	浓缩,压缩
rental	n.	租费,租金额
wee	adj.	很少的,微小的,很早的
hue	n.	色彩,色调
microkernel	n.	微核
deadline	n.	最后期限
monotonic	adj.	单调的,无变化的
scheduler	n.	[计]调度程序,日程安排程序
algorithm	n.	算法
coefficient	n.	系数
two-dimensional image		二维图像
PAL(Phase Alteration Line)		逐行倒相(一种电视制式)
HDTV (High Definition Television)		高清晰度电视
MPEG(Moving Picture Experts Group)		运动图像专家组
NTSC/SECAM(National Television Standards Community/Sequentiel Couleur Avec Memorie)		国家电视标准委员会/顺序传送,彩色与存储(一种欧洲电视制式)

NOTES

[1] This technique works because any color can be constructed from a linear superposition of red, green, and blue with the appropriate intensities.

superposition:重叠,重合,叠合。

全句可译为:之所以采用这种技术,是因为任何一种颜色都可以表示为红、绿、蓝三种颜色适当浓度的线性组合。

[2] To allow color transmissions to be viewed on black-and-white receivers, all three systems linearly combine the RGB signals into a luminance (brightness) signal, and two chrominance (color) signals, although they all use different coefficients for constructing these signals from the RGB signals.

To allow color transmissions to be viewed on black-and-white receivers 是目的状语从句,译为:为了……。although they all use different coefficients for constructing these signals from the RGB signals 是条件状语从句,译为:尽管……

全句可译为:为了使黑白接收机能接收到以彩色传输的信号,尽管从 RGB 信号得到亮度和色度信号时它们使用了不同的系数,这三种系统都从 RGB 信号线性组合出了一个亮度信号和两个色度信号。

[3] The local distribution systems reach into people's houses, where they terminate in set-top boxes, which are, in fact, powerful, specialized personal computers.

set-top boxes:机顶盒;distribution systems:分发系统。

本句可译为:本地分发系统到达(被接入)人们家里,终止于机顶盒。事实上,机顶盒是功能强大的特种个人计算机。

[4] Large mechanical tape servers that hold thousands of tapes and have a robot arm for

fetching any tape and inserting it into a tape drive are commercially available now.

…that hold thousands of tapes and have a robot arm for fetching any tape and inserting it into a tape drive…是非限定性定语从句,修饰前面的servers。fetching…and…inserting…是并列的目的状语,作for的目的状语。

全句可译为:大型的机械磁带服务器可容纳上千盒录像带,它的机械手可以取到任意一盒录像带,并把它塞入录像驱动器,这种服务器现在在商业上是可行的。

EXERCISES

一、将下述词组译成英文

逐行倒相　　　　　　　　视频点播
高清晰度电视　　　　　　机顶盒
运动图像专家组　　　　　国家电视标准委员会

二、将下述短文译成中文

1. When color television was invented, various methods for displaying color were technically possible, and different countries made different choices, leading to systems that are still incompatible.

2. Some of these will offer pay-per-view video or pay-per-hear audio CDs. Others will offer specialized services, such as home shopping (with the ability to rotate a can of soup and zoom in on the list of ingredients or view a video clip on how to drive a gasoline-powered lawn mower).

3. The total number of movies ever made is estimated at 65 000 (Minoli, 1995). When compressed in MPEG-2, a normal movie occupies roughly 4 GB of storage, so 65 000 of them would require something like 260 terabytes. Add to this all the old television programs ever made, sports films, newsreels, talking shopping catalogs, etc., and it is clear that we have an industrial-strength storage problem on our hands.

第三部分

英文文献阅读

READING 1

Lightwave System Components

TEXT

For a fiber-optic communication system, the communication channel is an optical fiber cable. The other two components, the optical transmitter and the optical receiver, are designed to meet the needs of such a specific communication channel. In this section we discuss the general issues related to the role of optical fiber as a communication channel and to the design of transmitters and receivers. The objective is to provide an introductory overview.

1. Optical Fibers as a Communication Channel

The role of a communication channel is to transport the optical signal from transmitter to receiver without distorting it. Most lightwave systems use optical fibers as the communication channel because silica fibers can transmit light with losses as small as 0.2-dB/km. Even then, optical power reduces to only 1% after 100 km. For this reason, fiber losses remain an important design issue and determine the repeater or amplifier spacing of a long-haul lightwave system. Another important design issue is fiber dispersion, which leads to broadening of individual optical pulses with propagation. If optical pulses spread significantly outside their allocated bit slot, the transmitted signal is severely degraded. Eventually, it becomes impossible to recover the original signal with high accuracy. The problem is most severe in the case of multimode fibers, since pulses spread rapidly (typically at a rate of 10 ns/km) because of different speeds associated with different fiber modes. It is for this reason that most optical communication systems use single-mode fibers. Materials dispersion (related to the frequency dependence of the refractive index) still leads to pulse broadening (typically < 0.1 ns/km), but it is small enough to be acceptable for most applications and can be reduced further by controlling the spectral width of the optical source. Nevertheless, material dispersion sets the ultimate limit on the bit rate and the transmission distance of fiber-optic communication systems.

2. Optical Transmitters

The role of an optical transmitter is to convert the electrical signal into optical form and to launch the resulting optical signal into the optical fiber. Fig. 1 shows the block diagram of an optical transmitter. It consists of an optical source, a modulator, and a channel coupler. Semiconductor lasers or light-emitting diodes are used as optical sources because of their compatibility with the optical-fiber communication channel. The optical signal is generated by modulating the optical carrier wave. Although an external modulator is sometimes used, it can be dispensed with in some cases, since the output of a semiconductor optical source can be modulated directly by varying the injection current. Such a scheme simplifiers the transmitter design and is generally cost-effective. The coupler is typically a microlens that focused the optical signal onto the entrance plane of an optical fiber with the maximum possible efficiency.

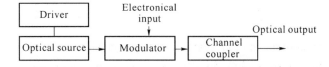

Fig. 1 Components of an optical transmitter

The launched power is an important design parameter. One can increase the amplifier (or repeater) spacing by increasing it, but the onset of various nonlinear effects limits how much the input power can be increased. The launched power is often expressed in "dBm" units with 1mW as the reference level. The general definition is

$$\text{power}(\text{dBm}) = 10\log_{10}\left(\frac{\text{power}}{1 \text{ mW}}\right)$$

Thus, 1 mW is 0 dBm, but 1 μW corresponds to -30 dBm. The launched power is rather low (<-10 dBm) for light-emitting diodes but semiconductor lasers can launch power ~ 10 dBm. As light-emitting diodes are also limited in their modulation capacities, most lightwave systems use semiconductor lasers as optical sources. The bit rate of optical transmitters is often limited by electronics rather than by the semiconductor laser itself. With proper design, optical transmitters can be made to operate at a bit rate of up to 40 Gbit/s.

3. Optical Receivers

An optical receiver converts the optical signal received at the output end of the optical fiber back into the original electrical signal. Fig. 2 shows the block diagram of an optical receiver. It consists of a coupler, a photodetector, and a demodulator. The coupler focuses the received optical signal onto the photodetector. Semiconductor photodiodes are used as photodetectors because of their compatibility with the whole system. The design of the demodulator depends on the modulation format used by the lightwave system. The use of FSK and PSK formats employ a scheme referred to as "intensity modulation with direct detection" (IM/DD). Demodulation in this case is done by a decision circuit that identifies bits as 1 or 0, depending on the amplitude of the electric signal. The accuracy of the decision circuit depends on the SNR of the electrical signal generated at the photodetector.

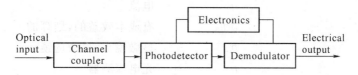

Fig. 2 Components of an optical receiver

The performance of a digital lightwave system is characterized through the bit error rate (BER). Although the BER can be defined as the number of errors made per second, such a definition makes the BER bit-rate dependent. It is customary to define the BER as the average probability of incorrect bit identification. Therefore, a BER of 10^{-6} corresponds to on average one error per million bits. Most lightwave systems specify a BER of 10^{-9} as the operating requirement; some even require a BER as small as 10^{-10}. The error-correction codes are sometimes used to improve the raw BER of a lightwave system.

An important parameter for any receiver is the receiver sensitivity. It is usually defined as the minimum average optical power required to realize a BER of 10^{-9}. Receiver sensitivity depends on the SNR, which in turn depends on various noise sources that corrupt the signal received. Even for a perfect receiver, some noise is introduced by the process of photodetection itself. This is referred to as the quantum noise or the shot noise, as it has its origin in the particle nature of electrons. Optical receiver operates at the shot-noise limit are called quantum-noise-limited receivers. No practical receiver operates at the quantum-noise limit because of the presence of several other noise sources. Some of the noise sources such as thermal noise are internal to the receiver. Others originate at the transmitter or during propagation along the fiber link. For instance, any amplification of the optical signal along the transmission line with the help of optical amplifiers introduces the so-called amplifier noise that has its origin in the fundamental process of spontaneous emission. Chromatic dispersion in optical fibers can add additional noise through phenomena such as intersymbol interference and mode-partition noise. The receiver sensitivity is determined by a cumulative effect of all possible noise mechanisms that degrade the SNR at the decision circuit. In general, it also depends on the bit rate as the contribution of some noise sources (e. g., shot noise) increases in proportion to the signal bandwidth.

Technical Words and Expressions

silica	n.	硅石,二氧化硅
propagation	n.	(声波,电磁辐射等)传播

refractive index		折射率
modulator	n.	调制器
coupler	n.	耦合器
diode	n.	二极管
compatibility	n.	一致(性)
dispense with		免除,省却,无须
current	n.	电流
cost-effective	adj.	有成本效益的,划算的
microlens	n.	显微镜头,显微透镜
photodetector	n.	光电探测器
demodulator	n.	解调器
photodiode	n.	光电二极管
sensitivity	n.	敏感
corrupt	vt.	使恶化
quantum noise		量子噪声
shot noise		散粒噪声
electron	n.	电子
thermal		热噪声
spontaneous	adj.	自发的

EXERCISES

一、将下述词组译成英文

通信信道　　光发送机　　光接收机　　光脉冲　　光源
非线性效应　　信噪比　　误码率　　强度调制直接检测

二、将下述词组译成中文

1. semiconductor lasers
2. light-emitting diode
3. semiconductor photodiodes
4. intensity modulation with direct detection
5. error-correction codes
6. receiver sensitivity

READING 2

Fiber to the Home

Fiber to the Home (FTTH) is a residential communications infrastructure where fiber optic cables run all the way to the subscriber premises. After years of anticipation, various deployments of fiber to the Home are finally emerging in communities across the U. S. Although Fiber to the Home is just a technology, it has interesting implications for the dynamics of competition in the local access market. Fiber to the Home networks can provide many times more bandwidth than currently available with existing broadband technologies. Today it seems that everyone wants high-speed data, dependable voice service, and high-quality video. Whether these services are delivered by Digital Subscriber Line (DSL), cable modems, or wireless architectures is insignificant as long as the service is fast and dependable.

FTTH enables carriers to offer a variety of communications and entertainment services, including high-speed Internet access, broadcast cable television, Direct Broadcast Satellite (DBS) television, and interactive two-way video-based services. All of these services are provided over network via a single optical fiber to the home. In addition, an FTTH solution based on Wavelength Division Multiplexing (WDM), allows for additional flexibility and adaptability to support further services.

In a FTTH system, equipment at the head end or CO is interfaced into the Public Switched Telephone Networks (PSTN) sing DS-1 and is connected to ATM or Ethernet interfaces. Video services enter the system from the Cable Television (CATV) head end or from a satellite feed.

All of these signals are then combined into a single fiber using WDM techniques and transmitted to the end user via a passive optical splitter. the splitter is typically placed approximately 3 000 feet from the Center Office (CO). The split ratio may range from 2 to 32 users and is done without using any active components in the network. The signal is then delivered another 3 000 feet to the home over a single fiber. An ideal FTTH system would have the ability to provide all of the services users are currently paying for, such as circuit-switched telephony, high-speed data and broadcast video services.

At the home, the optical signal is converted into an electrical signal using an Optical Electrical Converter (OEC). The OEC then splits the signal into the services required by the end user. Ideally, the OEC will have standard user interfaces so that special set-up boxes are not needed to provide services. These interfaces would include RJ11 jacks for telephony,

RJ45 jacks to high-speed data, and 75 ohm coax ports for CATV and DBS service.

There are several advantages associated with FTTH, as following:
- It is a passive network, so there are no active components from the CO to the end user. This dramatically minimizes the network maintenance cost and requirements, as well as eliminating the need for a DC power network.
- It is a single fiber to the end user, providing a variety of services with industry standard user interfaces, including voice, high-speed data, analog or digital CATV, DBS, and video.
- FTTH features local battery backup and low-power consumption.
- FTTH is reliable, scalable, and secure.
- The FTTH network is a fixture-proof architecture.

With consumer demand for high-speed bundled services, FTTH has been recognized as the ultimate solution for providing these services to the end user. Twisted pair, coax, and Hybrid Fiber/Coax (HFC) networks are not as robust or future-proof as FTTH architecture. And with the continued declining costs of optical equipment, FTTH is getting more and more feasible.

The desire for two-way, video-based services such as interactive television, distance learning, motion picture-quality videoconferencing, and videophones is expected to continuously increase. In fact, some observers believe that there is already a worldwide demand for these futuristic services today. The capability to meet this demand and continuously add new services at mouse-click speed is creating enormous competitive pressures in the area of communication.

Such capability also offers tremendous potential. Carriers who are able to offer these services to an ever-growing customer base can double or even triple their revenue in a short period of time.

As a result, demands for fiber technologies such as FTTH are on the rise. Technology advancements in the area of WDM are expected to further refine and enhance the technology, enabling more carriers to justify the investment in FTTH.

Technical Words and Expressions

architecture	n.	建筑,建筑学,体系机构
interactive	adj.	交互式的
distribution	n.	分配,分发
adaptability	n.	适应性
splitter	n.	分裂机,分路器
approximately	adv.	近似地,大约
telephony	n.	电话学,电话,电话制造
videoconference	n.	视频会议

Comprehension

1. Fiber to the Home networks can provide many times more _____ than currently available with existing broadband technologies.

    A. accuracy   B. time   C. speed   D. bandwidth

2. FTTH enables carriers to offer a variety of communication services, which of the following is not including. _____

    A. high-speed Internet access

    B. broadcast cable television

    C. Direct Broadcast Satellite (DBS) television

    D. interactive three-way video-based services

3. The splitter is typically placed approximately _____ feet from the Central Office (CO).

    A. 300   B. 3 000   C. 30 000   D. 300 000

4. At the home, the optical signal is converted into an electrical signal using _____.

    A. an Optical Electrical Converter (OEC)

    B. an Electrical Optical Converter (EOC)

    C. an Optical Image (OVC)

    D. an Optical Voice Converter (OVC)

5. With consumer demand for high-speed bundled services, _____ has been recognized as the ultimate solution for providing these services to the end user.

    A. coax   B. HFC   C. FTTH   D. Twisted pair

READING 3

Technologies on Fourth-Generation Mobile Communication

Fourth-generation mobile communications involves a mix of concepts and technologies in the making. Some can be recognized as deriving from 3G, and are called evolutionary (e. g. evolution of WCDMA and CDMA2000), while others involve new approached to wireless mobile, and are sometimes labeled revolutionary. What is important, though, is the common understanding that technologies beyond 3G are of fundamental relevance in the movement toward a wireless world, a term introduced by the WWRF, all of these terms are meant to signify fundamentally better wireless mobile communications future.

Fourth-generation mobile includes concepts and technologies for innovations in spectrum allocation and utilization, radio communication, networks, and services and applications. These four major areas are intertwined, and innovations in one will inevitably call for changes in the others. In all cases, it is the interplay of these approaches, technologies, and services/applications with the market, user needs and desires, and even unrecognized future uses that could drive a major technological movement and provides the potential for revolutionary, or very rapid and profound change. IT is the belief that we are at the beginning of that process, and that the rest of the first decade of the 21st century will provide the underlying basis for making wireless as useful and ubiquitous in the future as computers are today. These four major areas are providing innovations that will drive the process.

Spectrum allocation and utilization are just at the beginning of a possible paradigm change. Research in adaptive spectrum and bandwidth allocation is underway, as is research in dynamic utilization of spectral resources. The idea of having a spectral resource allocated, assigned, or used in a way that is not fixed is under investigation in Europe, Asia, and the United States, and is beginning to be considered as a possibility by regulators. Spectrum is too precious a resource for us not to do the best we can. Advances in understanding spectral needs and usage, along with physical, MAC link, and network layer approaches to optimize the use of that spectrum, and also including the processing resources to control them, can be used to provide the right services and QoS. Regulatory and system changes will also be necessary.

Radio communications technology innovations will truly be the engine of any major change. The ability to provide large data rates, up to 100 Mbit/s or 1 Gbit/s, has been mentioned. This is largely determined by the ability of the multiple access, modulation and coding, and radio resource technologies to provide these data rates efficiently in a mobile wireless environment. Going to higher-speeds means that the channels are truly wideband, and the waveform processing must thus account for the larger number resolvable but random, multiple paths. Improved multiple access and channel coding are also needed. MC-CDMA and OFDM are under investigation as are improved coding schemes, as well as combinations of various multiple access multi-user modulations and coding schemes. Also included is space-division multiple access, smart, antennas, and space-time coding techniques. In all cases, fast adaptation to the channel and traffic conditions is key to providing the needed QoS.

Two additional aspects of the radio access area are also critical, as is the network area. One is reconfigurable radio access points and technologies. Those are needed to allow the hardware and software to adopt the beat radio access technique suited to each case (i. e. to adapt to the available spectrum channel conditions, and network). Fortunately, there are software reconfigurable radio technologies under investigation, and in some cases, in very rudimentary form, deployed. More will be needed. But more than reconfigurable radios are needed; reconfigurable networks are also required, since the convergence of the various access technologies will require the networks to provide access to a number of radio technologies, and in fact to be a part of the adaptation process.

The network changes will be apparent in two major aspects. One is the almost certain evolution toward more of an IP, or packet switch, approach, and away from circuit switching, or even a packet switch overlay on circuit switch technology as is the case in 3G. Thus, physical layer techniques for fast acquisition and other needs of burst-type communications will be needed. Also needed are the MAC/link and network layer technologies to implement all IP networks, and to control and optimize radio and network operation in a highly variable environment. A second and related aspect, requiring major network changes, involves the possible convergence of various technologies and services, such as WLAN and mobile. As these strive toward serving users who wish to communicate data, voice, and possibly video and other applications for a variety of services, there will be both a drive for convergence as well as a need for new technologies.

In the end it will be whether these, and possibly other technologies, can meet the challenge of providing new and effective services and applications to a future wireless market that wants more, but is not quit sure what it wants, that will determine what the wireless world will look like. Research in fourth-generation mobile is one key toward this.

New words and Technical Terms

evolutionary	adj.	进化的
intertwine	v.	(使)纠缠,(使)缠绕
underlying	adj.	根本的,优先的
ubiquitous	adj.	普遍存在的
paradigm	n.	范例

resolvable	adj.	可分解的
rudimentary	adj.	基本的；初步的，未来发展的
overlay	n.	覆盖，覆盖图

Exercise

根据课文内容回答下列问题

1. Is fourth-generation mobile communications a mix of new concepts and technologies? Give your reasons.

2. Please look at the second sentence in the second paragraph, what does "These four major areas" refer to?

3. Why do we need reconfigurable networks in the radio access area?

READING 4

Polarization Mode Dispersion of Installed Fibers

Fiber optics revolutionized telecommunications over two decades ago, spurred by the promise of a low-loss transmission medium with seemingly infinite bandwidth. However, as the bandwidths of transported signals rapidly increased in the late 1980s, birefringence, which is a dependence of refractive index on the state of polarization (SOP), became recognized as a new impairment. Essentially, if the transit times for an optical fiber pulse were different for the x and y polarizations, for example, then an optical pulse launched in an arbitrary SOP would create two time-displaced replicas at the receiver, introducing distortion errors. As pulse widths became shorter with higher bandwidths, this differential time displacement, called differential group delay (DGD, defined later), became more injurious. Even more troubling was the recognition that this impairment varied from fiber-to-fiber (even in the same lot), from wavelength to wavelength for a given fiber at any given time, and even at each wavelength over time. For carriers, this randomness begs the question of how to assess the likelihood that any given fiber will suffer an outage for a given system. Since billions of dollars of fiber were installed before these problems surfaced, and transmission rates are likely to increase, it is clear that this problem has enduring economic implications.

Early views of these issues were fleshed out in the late 1980s and early 1990s, the impairment became known as "polarization mode dispersion" (PMD), and research has continued to the present (the term PMD is also used to quantify the phenomenon by the introduction of a PMD vector, to be defined in Section II). As a measure of the maturity of the field, there have been several reviews since the earliest work of Poole and Wagner as well as two recent books concerned with PMD; the theoretical foundations are well established.

During the telecom bubble, the temporary overbuild of fiber routes with low-PMD fibers allowed the widespread deployment of 10 Gbit/s systems, mitigating the need for immediate PMD compensation. For a while, most carriers seemed to have enough recent vintage fiber to satisfy the increasing demand of their customers using multiple wavelength-division multiplexed channels to form terabit per second links. However, as the telecommunications industry comes out from a long downturn, there is a renewed interest in PMD as "good" fibers have been cherry picked on existing routes and even better fiber is needed for the worldwide deployment of 40 Gbit/s systems that has already begun.

PMD-related research can be roughly divided in seven overlapping subfields, each involving both theoretical and experimental work.

(1) Development of low-PMD fiber. The PMD coefficient of the fiber, having units of picosecond per square root kilometer, is roughly proportional to the fiber birefringence and inversely proportional to the birefringence correlation length. The former parameter has been improved by better control over the drawing process, and the latter was shortened dramatically by the introduction of so-called spun fibers. By twisting the fiber in the drawing process, one dramatically increases the rate at which the birefringence axis changes its orientation along the fiber. That leads to a faster randomization and to significantly lower PMD coefficients, down to $0.01 \text{ ps/km}^{1/2}$.

(2) Faithful emulation of PMD. For system testing purposes, it is highly impractical to wait for a rare instance of high PMD in a fiber. Therefore, PMD emulators, for which any value of PMD may be programmed at will, are used for testing single-channel systems. For multi-channel testing, it is important that the PMD correlation among the channels be close enough to that in the real fiber. It remains an open question of whether emulators are adequate to study the interaction of nonlinear and polarization effects.

(3) Modulation formats and receiver impact. From the earliest days, it was clear that the return-to-zero (RZ) modulation format would be more robust to uncompensated PMD links than non-return-to-zero (NRZ) formats. Later, the robustness of other formats such as carrier-suppressed RZ and duo-binary formats was studied. The interaction of PMD with nonlinearities adds another dimension to the problem.

(4) In-service monitoring of PMD and PMD-induced penalties. The evolution of the magnitude and direction of the PMD vector is driven by temperature variation indoors, as well as outdoors, changes in the stress level in cables, and technical crew activities. When the bit error rate in a system increases, it is therefore desirable to be able to tell whether the system performance degradation is caused by PMD or other deleterious effects. Several methods have been developed for in-service estimation of the PMD-induced penalty. Various measurable quantities can be used for that purpose, including eye opening, synchronous and asynchronous histograms, degree of polarization, various frequency components, and frequency resolved SOP traces.

(5) PMD compensation by optical and electronic means. PMD compensation techniques can be categorized by the location of the device (input, output, distributed), its tracking speed, and the number of degrees of freedom. Optical techniques have been developed that introduce a compensating PMD (with only a few degrees of freedom) to cancel a large measure of a link's PMD at a given wavelength, but the problem for multiple wavelengths is still an issue. Electronic methods center on tapped delay lines and delayed decision techniques at the receiver to infer the transmitted signal. While it must be implemented at each receiver, this approach uses integrated electronics, whose speed and processing power keep increasing. PMD compensation has gone a long way to reach a status where it is quite well developed in terms of understanding the requirements, laboratory demonstrations, and some field tests. However, at present, there seems to be no commercially viable multi-

channel solution.

(6) System aspects of PMD: calculation and measurement of outage statistics, development of optimal PMD avoidance strategies, etc. Historically, there have been three distinct system approaches to PMD mitigation. If the PMD is low, it can be ignored. For a medium severity of PMD, the problem can be avoided either by cherry picking good fiber among the available fiber strands in a cable or letting higher logical levels of the communication system worry about it. Finally, if the system has high PMD, it needs to be actively mitigated.

(7) Study of PMD statistics and dynamics of installed fiber plant. Unless PMD is so low that it can be ignored, it is obvious that the single most important piece of information, which is crucial to formulating outage probabilities, evaluating mitigation strategies, and developing compensation techniques, is the full understanding of PMD dynamics.

Existing theoretical tools and developments have been successful in predicting the statistical properties of an infinite ensemble of statistically equivalent fibers, and thus, a carrier might reliably estimate the number of transmission systems that can be expected to suffer an outage due to PMD. But the prediction of what will happen to a particular traffic-bearing field-installed fiber is a more difficult theoretical issue and also provides more valuable operational knowledge: is this fiber-optic transmission system (currently operational, creating revenue, and subject to service level agreements) likely to fail in the future, and if so, when and for how long? Much of the discussion to date has made implicit use of what might be called the "fast mixing assumption" that, from moment to moment, the fiber's state randomly samples the statistical ensemble and is equally likely to evolve into any of the other ensemble elements. In this view, the outage time per year would be calculated from the appropriate cumulative distribution function. While complete mixing undoubtedly occurs over long enough time scales, we will present evidence, gathered by groups on all continents, that the fast mixing assumption is generally not valid in field installed (buried) fibers over practical time scales, and we will give an interpretation that has evolved over the last few years.

This paper is organized as follows: Section II contains an overview of birefringence and PMD, briefly reviews early field measurements, and introduces a "hinge" model for viewing such results. Since the model has slightly different emphases than the conventional model, this section's review is aimed at elucidating the terminology and concepts that we will use later in the text. Our development uses what has become the conventional notation. The next two sections deal with long-term measurements of installed fibers that were not carrying live traffic, i.e., "dark" fibers. In Section III, we review our measurements of urban and suburban routes that were performed with the traditional interferometric technique and compare them to measurements by other groups. In the Appendix, we also discuss uncertainties in estimates of the magnitude of PMD associated with this technique and relate them to the nature of links composed of long stretches of buried fiber. Analysis of the measurement statistics gives evidence that fast mixing is not taking place. A more detailed measurement technique using wavelength-resolved measurements of dark fibers gives greater insight into the dynamics of buried fibers and is discussed in Section IV. By comparing experimental PMD measurements with the ambient temperature, we show that it is possible to establish upper bounds on the variability of buried sections of the fiber. While such dark fiber experiments are useful in developing an understanding of the underlying processes, deployed systems are much more complex. Section V deals with measurements on a live system. We discuss the consequences of optical components in offices and huts, as well as the presence of active components in the optical path, and describe them as another class of polarization-rotating "hinges." The last two sections describe how the experimental results developed in Sections III-V change the view of how outages arise and persist. In Section VI, temporal DGD statistics is reviewed, and the fact that outage probabilities can be expected to vary as a function of communication frequency is addressed. Finally, in Section VII, we explore several numerical and analytical approaches that might be taken to exploit the properties of these channel-specific outages. We conclude with open questions that might be addressed in future studies.

Technical Words and Expressions

birefringence	n.	双折射
replica	n.	复制品，拷贝，一模一样的东西
polarization	n.	偏振（现象），极化（作用）
mitigate	v.	减轻
downturn	n.	低迷时期
faithful	adj.	守信的，忠实的，详确的，可靠的
asynchronous	adj.	不同时的，异步的
interferometric	adj.	干涉测量（法）的，干涉仪的，用干涉仪测量的

Exercise

将下列词汇翻译成中文

1. state of polarization
2. pulse width
3. differential group delay
4. polarization mode dispersion
5. wavelength-division multiplex
6. birefringence correlation length

READING 5

High-Bandwidth Plastic Optical Fiber

1. HISTORY OF POF

The biggest challenge in information technology will be how to install gigabit optical fibers to local area networks at homes, offices, and buildings.

It is estimated that the peripheral component of the communications network, which is referred to as "the last 1 mile," accounts for approximately 95% of the overall network, for which copper wire [unshielded twisted pair wire (UTP)] has chiefly been used to date. However, limits exist for both transmission bandwidth and transmission distance, and especially when 100m is exceeded inside a building, handling communication speeds enabling transfers on the order of gigabits is difficult. On the other hand, silica-based single-mode (SM) fibers used for the backbone system can sufficiently respond to high speeds. However, due to its minute diameter of less than 10 μm, precision techniques are demanded for connection and branching, which necessitate high costs for peripheral systems where a substantial number of connection points exist. In contrast, plastic optic fiber (POF), which employs as its base material a very soft polymer of high flexibility compared to glass fibers, exhibits characteristics which easily enable a larger core diameter (100~1000 μm) despite its ease of bending (i.e., comparable to UTP), and presents the advantage that elaborate connection techniques and high installation costs are unnecessary. In this paper, the current status and outlook of POFs as a communications medium capable of achieving broadband service in recent years is reviewed. The POFs developed for high-speed data communication are classified into four types: SM POF, multilayer (ML) step-index (SI) POF, multicore (MC) SI POF, and graded-index (GI) POF.

An SM POF was prepared by the interfacial-gel polymerization technique by forming a small core, and then, the SM condition was satisfied for the first time. On the other hand, other three types of POF have large cores, because of which huge number of modes (more than 50 000) is propagated. Therefore, reduction of modal dispersion has been a key issue in such multimode POFs. In ML POFs, the core region is composed of several layers with a different refractive index. This concentric ML structure decreases modal dispersion compared to a conventional SI-type POF, and a data rate as high as 500 Mbit/s for 50 m transmission is achieved experimentally. On the other hand, MC POF has a core region composed of a bundle of tens of small core. By reducing the core diameter, not only modal dispersion but also bending loss is decreased. A data transmission at 500 Mbit/s for 50 m is also achieved by the MC POF. Although a data rate of 500 Mbit/s seems high enough for existing applications such as Web browsing and text-based communications, a 1 Gbit/s data port is already equipped, even on some personal computers. For the backbone networks, switches and other equipment that cover the 10 Gbit/s Ethernet are commercially available. The gigabit and 10 Gbit/s Ethernet standards specify the use of multimode fibers and inexpensive vertical cavity surface emitting lasers (VCSELs). However, the dispersion of existing multimode fibers was the serious problem, particularly in the 10 Gbit/s transmission systems, and then, new-generation multimode fiber has been developed to cover such a high data rate. On the other hand, a data rate of 1~2.5 Gbit/s has been already required for an interface of high-resolution digital display: digital video interface (DVI, 1.65 Gbit/s/channel, display resolution: ultra extended graphics array). Thus, much higher data rate will be required in the area of consumer electronic appliances. It has been demonstrated that the optimum refractive index profile enables GI POFs to transmit a data rate of 10 Gbit/s and beyond. A low-loss perfluorinated (PF) polymer-based GI POF has been developed, and a PF polymer-based GI POF can also support such a high data rate because of its lowmaterial dispersion property. In addition, the attenuation of the current PF polymer-based GI POF is decreased to 10 dB/km over the 800~1 300 nm wavelength range.

Hence, we believe that GI POF is the only POF that can cover such a high data rate and that can seamlessly connect the backbone fiber-optic communication networks and electronic appliance in the home. Therefore, in the following sections, we focus on the characteristics and prospected applications of GI POFs.

2. HISTORY OF POF DEVELOPMENT

A. Development in Attenuation of POF

The first idea of POF goes back to the 1960s before Corning demonstrated silica optical fibers with attenuation lower than 20 dB/km. In 1966, Du Pont invented the first POF named "Crofon" that was of SI-type composed of PMMA core surrounded by a partially fluorinated-polymer cladding. Because of the rapid progress made in silica optical fiber technologies, fiber optics have become the backbones of long-distance telephone networks around the world. On the other hand, POFs have proved more practical for communications in very-shortreach (VSR) networks or for light guide and illumination applications, because of their advantages such as large diameter with great mechanical flexibility and high numerical aperture (NA). Particularly, the potential of polymer materials such as great mechanical flexibility and easy handling can reduce not only the cost of the fiber itself but also the cost of fiber installation. Therefore, great interest has been focused on such POF applications as the transmission media in VSR networks.

In 1975, Mitsubishi Rayon commercialized the first SI POF whose trade name was "Eska". Then, Asahi Chemical and Toray soon followed in 1970s. The POF market was originally dominated by these three-major Japanese companies who have been manufacturing SI-type POFs composed of PMMA core. Experimental analyses of the loss reduction in

PMMA-core SI POF were conducted mainly in the 1980s. Kaino et al. reported in 1984 that very low-loss SI POF was experimentally obtained by employing perdeuterated PMMA.

An impressive analysis was made at the end of 1980s. Groh theoretically calculated the overtone absorption loss due to carbon-hydrogen stretching vibration in PMMA and other polymers by introducing Morse's potential energy theory. Actually, the calculated peak positions and the attenuation of the overtone absorption spectrum of PMMA agreed well with that experimentally obtained. Thus, the calculation process of the attenuation limit of POFs was developed. These reports set off a competition to make better POFs among the three major Japanese companies aforementioned, and almost the lowest level of the attenuation was achieved even by the commercialbased SI POFs in late 1980s. The development in the attenuation of SI POFs is summarized in Fig. 1 compared to that of GI POFs.

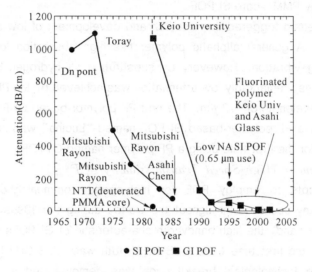

Fig. 1 Development in the attenuation of POFs

In terms of GI-type POF, the first report of PMMA-core GI POFs was presented from Keio University in 1976. A nearparabolic refractive index profile in the first GI POF was formed by copolymerizing methyl methacrylate (MMA) monomer (as M_1 monomer) with the other M_2 monomer with a refractive index higher than MMA. During the copolymerization process, the composition ratio of two polymers was gradually varied in the radial direction utilizing the difference of monomer reactivity between M_1 and M_2 monomers. Actually, the attenuation first measured for GI POF composed of MMA and vinyl benzoate was 1 000 dB/km, which was approximately ten times higher than that of SI POF. However, it is revealed in this process that the resulting copolymer composition is mainly divided into two compositions, i.e., M_1 rich copolymer and M_2 rich copolymer, which largely increases the inherent excess scattering loss.

In order to decrease such an excess scattering loss caused by the difference of monomer reactivity, a new interfacial copolymerization process based on random copolymerization was developed. The attenuation of an MMA-benzyl methacrylate copolymer GI POF by this random copolymerization process is remarkably decreased to about 200 from 1 000 dB/km. However, the excess scattering loss of about 100 dB/km due to heterogeneous structure in "copolymer" still remained. Based on the fundamental research on the relationship between scattering loss and heterogeneous structure in polymer materials, we could break through the high-attenuation problem mentioned above. Instead of the copolymerization process, we invented the process of doping low-molecular weight compound. The refractive index profile of the new GI POF is formed by the radial concentration distribution of the dopant. There were more freedoms in selecting the dopant materials compared to M_2 monomer selection. By designing the dopant structure to have a compatibility with PMMA, we could decrease the size of the heterogeneous structure in the polymer, and remarkable progress was made by the new GI POF in decreasing the attenuation to be as low as the value which had been already achieved by PMMA-core SI POF.

The doping method triggered the research and development of low-attenuation polymer materials as well. A general aliphatic polymer has high absorption loss due to carbon-hydrogen stretching vibration. However, by substituting all hydrogen bonding in polymer molecules for fluorine, remarkably low attenuation was achieved by the PF polymer-based GI POF, even at a wavelength of 1.3 μm. The first PF polymer-based GI POF was reported in 1994, and in 2000, a PF polymer-based GI POF named "Lucina" was commercialized from Asahi Glass Co., for the first time using a PF polymer named CYTOP.

B. Development in High-Speed Transmission by POF

Several attempts to employ POF for high-speed communication were advanced concurrently by many countries throughout the world, during the 1990s, mainly on SI-type POFs. On the other hand, the high-bandwidth characteristic of GI POFs was experimentally verified in 1990 for the first time (The 3 dB bandwidth was 17.3 GHz for 15 m at 670 nm wavelength.). The technological breakthrough was demonstrated in 1994 as shown in Fig. 2, following the successive development of the semiconductor edge-emitting red laser (NEC) and VCSELs emitting at 670 nm wavelength (by IBM) in Japan and the United States, respectively.

After 1994, gigabit-transmission experiments employing POF began to be actively conducted worldwide, by combining GI POF with one of these light sources for high-speed modulation. We reported the first 2.5 Gbit/s transmission demonstration by 100 m PMMA-core GI POF as a cooperative work with NEC in 1994.

The successful experimental transmission of 11 Gbit/s for 100m in 1999 by Asahi Glass Co., Ltd. and Bell Laboratories in the United States was an extremely significant result, which demonstrated the high-bandwidth performance, surpassing that of silica-glass multimode optical fibers. The high-bandwidth and low-loss characteristics of the PF GI POF have been advanced further in the 2000s, and the successful experimental transmission of 1 Gbit/s 1 km was reported. Based on these experiments, it was demonstrated for the first time that PF GI POFs could cover broadband fields, from the areas of VSR networks to the access networks. The POF entered into actual use in various networks in the 2000s, when

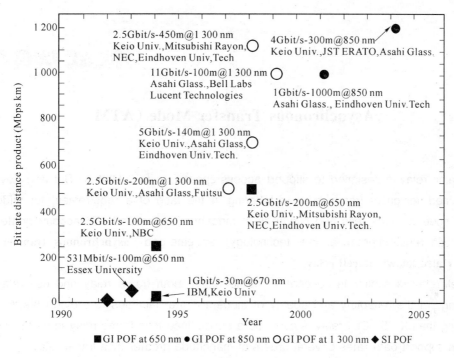

Fig. 2 Development of data rate achieved by POF links

the high-bandwidth PF polymer-based GI POF also became commercially available. A 1 Gbit/s campus LAN utilizing PF GI POF was constructed at Keio University in 2000. Subsequently, the GI POF has been used in Tokyo in housing complexes, hospitals, medical conference halls, etc.

Technical Words and Expressions

peripheral	adj., n.	外围的,外围设备
polymer	n.	聚合物,多聚物
multicore	adj.	多芯的
perfluorinated	adj.	全氟化合物的
attenuation	n.	减少,减弱,衰减
copolymerizing methyl methacrylate	n.	聚甲基丙烯酸酯
dopant	n.	掺杂物,掺杂剂

Exercise

将下列词汇翻译成中文
1. silica-based single-mode fibers
2. backbone system
3. plastic optic fiber
4. modal dispersion
5. vertical cavity surface emitting lasers

READING 6

Asynchronous Transfer Mode (ATM)

Frame relay is designed to support access speeds up to 2 Mbit/s. But now, even the streamlined design of frame relay is faltering in the face of a requirement for wide area access speeds in the tens and hundreds of megabits per second. To accommodate these gargantuan requirements, a new technology has emerged: **asynchronous transfer mode (ATM)**, also known as **cell relay**.

Cell relay is similar in concept to frame relay. Both frame relay and cell relay take advantage of the reliability and fidelity of modern digital facilities to provide faster packet switching than X.25. Cell relay is even more streamlined than frame relay in its functionality and can support data rates several orders of magnitude greater than frame relay.

1. Virtual Channels and Virtual Paths

ATM is a packet-oriented transfer mode. Like frame relay and X.25, it allows multiple logical connections to be multiplexed over a single physical interface. The information flow on each logical connection is organized into fixed-size packet, called **cells**. As with frame relay, there is no link-by-link error control or flow control.

Logical connections in ATM are referred to as **virtual channels**. A virtual channel is analogous to a virtual circuit in X.25 or a frame relay data link connection. It is the basic unit of switching in an ATM network. A virtual channel is set up between two end users through the network and a variable-rate, full-duplex flow of fixed-size cells is exchanged over the connection. Virtual channels are also used for user network exchange (control signaling) and network-network exchange (network management and routing).

For ATM, a second sublayer of processing has been introduced that creates and manages virtual paths. **A virtual path** is a bundle of virtual channels that have the same endpoints. Thus, all of the cells flowing over all of the virtual channels in a single virtual path are switched together.

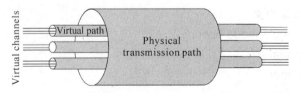

Fig. 1　ATM Connection Relationship

The types of traffic parameters that can be negotiated include average rate, peak rate, burstiness, and peak duration. The network may need a number of strategies to deal with congestion and manage existing and requested virtual channels. At the crudest level, the network may simply deny new requests for virtual channels to prevent congestion. Additionally, cells may be discarded if negotiated parameters are violated or if congestion becomes severe. In an extreme situation, existing connecting connections might be terminated.

I. 150 also lists characteristics of virtual paths. The first four characteristics listed are identical to those for virtual channels. That is, quality of service, switched and semi permanent virtual paths, cell sequence integrity, and traffic parameter negotiation and usage monitoring are characteristics of a virtual path. There are a number of reasons for this duplication. First, this provides some flexibility in how the network manages the requirements placed upon it. Second, the network must be concerned with the overall requirements for a virtual path, and within a virtual path may negotiate the establishment of virtual circuits with given characteristics. Finally, once a virtual path is set up, it is possible for the end users to negotiate the creation of new virtual channels. The virtual path characteristics impose a discipline on the choice that the end user may make.

2. Control signaling

In ATM, a mechanism is needed for the establishment and release of virtual paths and virtual channels. The exchange of information involved in this process is referred to as control signaling and takes place on separate connections from those that are being managed.

For virtual channels, I. 150 specifies four methods for providing an establishment/release facility. One or a combination of these methods will be used in any particular network:

(1) **Semipermanent virtual channels** may be used for user-to-user exchange. In this case, no control signaling is required.

(2) If there is no preestablished call control signaling channel, one must be set up. For that purpose, a control signaling exchange must take place between the user and the network on some channel. Hence we need a permanent channel, probably of low data rate, that can be used to set up a virtual channel that can be used for call control. Such a channel is called a meta-signaling channel, because the channel is used to set up signaling channels.

(3) The meta-signaling channel can be used to set up a virtual channel between the user and the network for call control signaling. This user-to-network signaling virtual channel can then be used to set up virtual channels to carry user data.

(4) The meta-signaling channel can also be used to set up a user-to-user signaling virtual channel. Such a channel must be set up within a preestablished virtual path. It can then be used to allow the two end user, without network intervention, to establish and release user-to-user virtual channels to carry user data.

For virtual path, three methods are defined in I. 150:

(1) A virtual path can be established on a semipermanent basis by prior agreement. In this case, no control signaling is required.

(2) Virtual path establishment/release may be customer controlled. In this case, the customer use a signaling virtual channel to request the virtual path from the network.

(3) Virtual path establishment/release may be network controlled. In this case, the network establishes.

A virtual path for its own convenience. The path may be network, user to network, or user to user.

3. ATM Cells

The asynchronous transfer mode makes use of fixed-size cells, consisting of a 5-octet header and a 48-octet information field. There are several advantages to the use of small, fixed-size cells. First, the use of small cells may reduce queuing delay for a high-priority cell, because it waits less if it arrives slightly behind a lower-priority cell that has gained access to a resource (e.g., the transmitter). Second, it appears that fixed-size cells can be switched more efficiently, which is important for the very high data rates of ATM. With fixed-size cells, it is easier to implement to the network.

Figure.2a shows the header format at the user-network interface. Figure.2b shows the cell header format internal to the network.

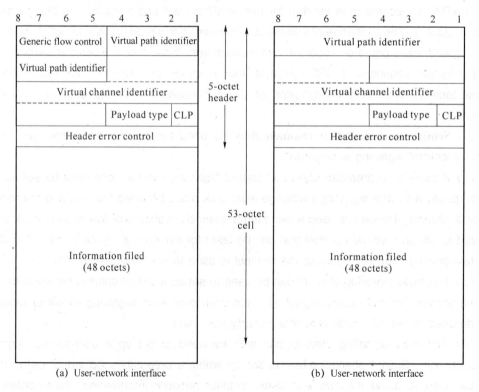

Fig. 2 ATM cell Format

The Generic Flow Control (GFC) field does not appear in the cell header internal to the network, but only at the user-network interface. Hence, it can be used for control of cell flow only at the local user-network interface. The field could be used to assist the customer in controlling the flow of traffic for different qualities of service. In any case, the GFC mechanism is used to alleviate short-term overload conditions in the network.

I. 150 lists as a requirement for the GFC mechanism that all terminals be able to get access to their assured capacities. This include all constant-bit-rate (CBR) terminals as well as the variable-bit-rate (VBR) terminals that have an element of guaranteed capacity (CBR and VBR are explained subsequently).

The Virtual Path Identifier (VPI) field constitutes a routing field for the network. It is 8 bits at the user-network interface and 12 bits at the network-network interface, allowing for more virtual paths to be supported within the network. The Virtual Channel Identifier (VCI) field is used for routing to and the end user. Thus, it functions much as a service access point.

The cell loss priority (CLP) bit is used to provide guidance to the network in the event of congestion. A value of 0 indicates a cell of relatively higher priority, which should not to be discarded unless no other alternative is available. A value of 1 indicates that this cell is subject to discard within the network. The user might employ this field so that extra cells (beyond the negotiated rate) may be inserted into the network, with a CLP of 1, and delivered to the destination if the network is not congested. The network may set this field to 1 for any data cell that is in violation of the agreement concerning traffic parameters between the user and the network. In this case, the switch that does the setting realizes that the cell exceed the agreed traffic parameters but that the switch is capable of handing the cell. At a later point in the network, if congestion is encountered, this cell has been marked for discard in preference to cells that fall within agreed traffic limits.

The Header Error Control (HEC) field is an 8-bit error code that can be used to correct single-bit errors in the header and to detect double-bit errors. In the case of most existing data link layer protocols, such as LAPD and HDLC, the data field that serves as input to the error code calculation is in general much longer than the size of the resulting error code. This allows for error detection. In the case of ATM, the input to the calculation is only 32 bits, compared to 8 bits for the code. The fact that the input is relatively short allows the code to be used not only for error detection but also, in some cases, for actual error correction. This is because there is sufficient redundancy in the code to recover from certain error patterns.

The error protection function provides both recovery from single-bit header errors and a low probability of the delivery of cells with errored headers under bursty error conditions. The error characteristics of fiber-based transmission systems appear to be a mix of single-bit errors and relatively large burst errors. For some transmission systems, the error correction capability, which is more time-consuming, might not be invoked.

4. ATM Service Categories

An ATM network is designed to be able to transfer many different types of traffic simultaneously, including real-time flows such as voice, video, and bursty TCP flows. Although each such traffic flow is handed as a stream of 53-octet cells traveling through a virtual channel, the way in which each data flow is handed within the network depends on the characteristics of the traffic flow and QoS requirement of the application. For example, real-time video traffic must be delivered within minimum variation in delay.

In this subsection, we summarize ATM service categories, which are used by an end system to identify the type of service required. The following service categories have been defined by the ATM Forum:

Real-Time Service

- Constant bit rate (CBR)
- Real-time variable bit rate (rt-VBR)

Non-Real-Time Service

- Non-real-time variable bit rate (nrt-VBR)
- Available bit rate (ABR)
- Unspecified bit rate (UBR)
- Guaranteed frame rate (GFR)

Real-Time Service The most important distinction among applications concerns the amount of delay and the variability of delay, referred to as jitter, that the application can tolerate. Real-time applications typically involve a flow of information to a user that is intended to reproduce that flow at a source. For example, a user expects a flow of audio or video information to be presented in a continuous, smooth fashion. A lack of continuity or excessive loss results in significant loss of quality. Applications that involve interaction between people have tight constraints on delay. Typically, any delay above a few hundred milliseconds becomes noticeable and annoying. Accordingly, the demands in the ATM network for switching and delivery of real-time data are high.

The **Constant Bit Rate (CBR)** service is perhaps the simplest service to define. It is used by applications that require a fixed data rate that is continuously available during the connection lifetime and a relatively tight upper bound on transfer delay. CBR is commonly used for uncompressed audio and video information. Examples of CBR applications include the following:

- Videoconferencing
- Interactive audio (e.g., telephony)
- Audio/video distribution (e.g., television, distance learning, pay per view)
- Audio/video retrieval retrieval (e.g., video on demand, audio library)

The **Real-Time Variable Bit Rate (rt-VBR)** category is intended for time-sensitive applications; that is, those requiring tightly constrained delay and delay variation. The principal difference between applications appropriates for rt-VBR and those appropriate for CBR is that rt-VBR applications transmit at a rate that varies with time. Equivalently, an rt-VBR source can be characterized as somewhat bursty. For example, the standard approach to video compression results in a sequence of image frames of varying sizes. Because real-time video requires a uniform frame transmission rate, the actual data varies.

The rt-VBR service allows the network more flexibility than CBR. The network is able to statistically multiplex a number of connections over the same dedicated capacity and still provide the required service to each connection.

Non-Real-Time Service non-real-time services are intended for applications that have bursty traffic characteristics and do not have tight constraints on delay and delay variation. Accordingly, the network has greater flexibility in handling such traffic flows and make greater use of statistical multiplexing to increase network efficiency.

For some non-real-time applications, it is possible to characterize the expected traffic flow so that the network can provide substantially improved quality of service (QoS) in the areas of loss and delay. Such applications can use the **Non-Real-Time Variable Bit Rate (nrt-VBR)** service. With this service, the end system specifies a peak cell rate, a sustainable or average cell rate, and a measure of how bursty or clumped the cells may be. With this information, the network can allocate resources to provide relatively low delay and minimal cell loss.

The nrt-VBR service can be used for data transfers that have critical response-time requirements. Examples include airline reservations, banking transactions, and process monitoring.

At any given time, a certain amount of the capacity of an ATM network is consumed in carrying CBR and the two types of VBR traffic. Additional capacity is available for one on both of the following reasons: ① Not all of the total resources have been committed to CBR and VBR traffic, and ② the bursty nature of VBR traffic means that at some times less than the committed capacity is being used. All of this unused capacity could be made available for the **Unspecified Bit Rate (UBR)** service. This service is suitable for applications that can tolerate variable delays and some cell losses, which is typically true of TCP-based traffic. With UBR, cells are forwarded on a first-in, first-out (FIFO) basis using the capacity not consumed by other services; both delays and variable losses are possible. No initial commitment is made to a UBR source and no feedback concerning congestion is provided; this is referred to as a **best-effort service**. Examples of UBR applications include the following:

- Text/data/image transfer, message, distribution, retrieval
- Remote terminal (e.g., telecommuting)

Bursty applications that use a reliable end-to-end protocol such as TCP can detect congestion in a network by means of increased round-trip delays and packet discarding. However, TCP has no mechanism for causing the resources within the network to be fairly among many TCP connections. Further, TCP does not minimize congestion as efficiently as is possible using explicit information from congested nodes within the network.

To improve the service provided to bursty sources that would otherwise use UBR, the **Available Bit Rate (ABR)** service has been defined. An application using ABR specifies a peak cell rate (PCR) that it will use and a minimum cell rate (MCR) that it requires. The network allocates so that all ABR applications receive at least their MCR capacity. Any unused capacity is then shared in a fair and controlled fashion among all ABR sources. The ABR mechanism users explicit feedback to sources to assure that capacity is fairly allocated. Any capacity not used by ABR sources remains available for UBR traffic.

An example of an application using ABR is LAN interconnection. In this case, the end systems attached to the ATM network are routers.

The most recent addition to the set of ATM service categories is **Guaranteed Frame Rate (GFR)**, which is designed specifically to support IP backbone subnet-works. GFR provides better service than UBR for frame-based traffic, including IP and Ethernet. A major goal of GFR is to optimize the handing of frame-based traffic that passes from a LAN through a router onto an ATM backbone network. Such ATM networks are increasingly being used in large enterprise, carrier, and Internet service provider networks to consolidate and extend IP services over the wide area. While ABR is also an ATM service meant to provide a greater measure of guaranteed packet performance over ATM backbones, ABR is relatively difficult to implement between routers over an ATM network. With the increased emphasis on using ATM to support IP-based traffic, especially traffic that originates on Ethernet LANs, GFR may offer the most attractive alternative for providing ATM service.

One of the techniques used by GFR to provide improved performance compared to UBR is to require that network elements be aware of frame or packet boundaries. Thus, when congestion requires the discard of cells, network elements must discard all of the cells that comprise a single frame. GFR also allows a user to reserve capacity for each GFR VC. The user is guaranteed that this minimum capacity will be supported. Additional frames may be transmitted if the network is not congested.

Technical Words and Expressions

streamlined	adj.	最新型的，改进的
analogous to	adj.	类似的，相似的，可比拟的
crude	adj.	天然的，未加工的，粗糙的
	n.	天然的物质
semipermanent	adj.	非永久(性)的，暂时的
violate	vt.	冒犯，干扰，违反，侵犯
meta-signaling channel		元信令信道
jitter	vi.	抖动
interactive	adj.	交互式的

Exercises

一、阅读理解题

1. What are the advantages to the use of small, fixed-size cells in ATM?
2. What services can be provided by ATM?
3. What application can use the nrt-VBR service? List some examples.
4. In addition to carrying CBR and the two types of VBR traffic, the additional capacity is available for some services, why?

二、将下述短文译成中文

The Header Error Control (HEC) field is an 8-bit error code that can be used to correct single-bit errors in the header and to detect double-bit errors. In the case of most existing data link layer protocols, such as LAPD and HDLC, the data field that serves as input to the error code calculation is in general much longer than the size of the resulting error code. This allows for error detection. In the case of ATM, the input to the calculation is only 32 bits, compared to 8 bits for the code. The fact that the input is relatively short allows the code to be used not only for error detection but also, in some cases, for actual error correction. This is because there is sufficient redundancy in the code to recover from certain error patterns.

READING 7

Embedded Systems and Applications

1. What are embedded systems?

A completely new branch of computer engineering is that of embedded systems. It is the development of specialized computer equipment that is not programmable by the user, but is dedicated to drive or control a piece of equipment, such as medical equipment or machinery. The skill of embedded systems is marrying the computer technology with the mechanical engineering design.

An embedded system is a special purpose computer that is used inside of a device. For example, a microwave contains an embedded system that accepts input from the panel, controls the LCD display, and turns on and off the heating elements that cook the food. Embedded systems generally use micro-controllers that contain many functions of a computer on a single device. Motorola and Intel make some of the most popular micro-controllers.

The embedded systems market is getting wider all the time as engineers think of other engineering projects that can benefit from the embedded systems technology. We now have embedded systems in everything from food processors to cars and beyond. Living in the computer age means that in all likelihood, before this decade is out, we will be hard put to find a mechanical device that has not been subjected to embedded systems of some sort.

There are different grades of embedded systems. Computerized toys and kitchen implements are a very simple form of embedded systems. Many of the more complicated medical machines actually benefit from the use of more than one embedded system. Although this means that the machines we use as a matter of course in daily life are a lot more effective in general, it does also mean that the repair process of embedded systems machinery can be difficult and costly. But it does also mean that our time is freed up by embedded systems machinery so that we can spend more time doing what we love. We all use washing machines with embedded systems, for example. More and more, the cars we buy have embedded system.

Even the tools we use for manufacturing are the result of embedded systems. It stands to reason that there are companies that specialize in the development of embedded systems, either independently, or in tandem with the machinery with which they're to be used. More and more, engineering firms are calling on this kind of expertise to upgrade their products in every way imaginable.

2. Without embedded systems…

You get into your car and turn the key on. You take a 3.5' floppy disk from the glove compartment, insert it into a slot on the dashboard, and drum your fingers on the steering wheel until the operating system prompt appears on the dashboard LCD. Using the cursor keys on the center console you select the program for electronic ignition, then turn the key to start the engine. On the way to work you want to listen to some music, so you insert the program CD into the player, wait for the green light to flash indicating that the digital signal processor in the player is ready, then put in your music CD.

3. With embedded systems…

- You don't need a traditional user interface to decide which programs should be running the car's electronic ignition program will respond to the car key.
- You don't need to load programs into your devices—the ones needed to make it work should already be loaded (although in some new mobile phones you can download extra programs).
- You don't need to waste time waiting for the O/S to load—if one is needed, then it doesn't have baggage that make it slow to load.
- You don't need to load programs or data from a slow disk drive—most information needed will be in fast ROM.

Embedded systems can be roughly defined as "a system that is not primarily a computer but contains a processor". But rather than focusing on a definition, it is useful to consider aspects that most embedded systems share, at least to some degree.

(1) Embedded systems are frequently price and size sensitive.

Many embedded systems such as PDAs or cell-phones are high-volume, low-cost and low-margin. This requires use of the cheapest components possible, which typically means simple processors and small memory (RAM and NVRAM/flash). This causes embedded systems software to trade off maintainability aspects such as portability, clarity, or modularity for performance optimization aspects such as a small boot image footprint, a small RAM footprint, and small cycle requirements. The increased up-front software development costs and periodic maintenance costs are amortized by the high-volume sales, and outweighed by the continuous hardware cost savings of cheaper components.

Many other embedded systems, though not so price-sensitive, have physical constraints on form factor or weight to use the smallest components possible. Again, this favors performance optimization at the cost of maintainability.

In addition to trading off portability, clarity, or modularity, embedded systems may also require optimization by using a low-level language, e.g. assembly rather than C, or C rather than code automatically generated from a UML model. However, this hand tuning is typically only applied to small portions of the software identified by the "90/10" guideline as being the major performance bottlenecks.

(2) Embedded systems often have power limitations.

Many embedded systems run from a battery, either continually or during emergencies. Therefore, power consumption performance is favored in many embedded systems at the cost of complexity and maintainability.

(3) Embedded systems are frequently real-time.

By nature, most embedded systems are built to react in real-time to data flowing to and through the system. The real-time constraints again favor performance aspects (particularly cycles usage) over maintainability aspects. There are generally both hard real-time constraints, which require an event to be handled by a fixed time, and soft real-time constraints, which set limits on the average event response time. Real-time operating systems use preemptive prioritized scheduling to help ensure that real-time deadlines are met, but careful thought is required to divide processing into execution contexts (threads), set the relative priorities of the execution contexts, and manage control/data flow between the contexts.

(4) Embedded systems frequently use custom hardware.

Embedded systems are frequently comprised of off-the-shelf processors combined with off-the-shelf peripherals. Even though the components may be standard, the custom mixing and matching requires a high degree of cohesion between the hardware and the software — a significant portion of the software for an embedded system is operating system and device driver software. Though this low-level software is often available for purchase, license, or free use, frequently a large portion of the operating system for an embedded system is custom-developed in-house, either to precisely match the hardware system at hand, or to glue together off-the-shelf software in a custom configuration.

Often the functionality of an embedded system is distributed between multiple peer processors and/or a hierarchy of master/slave processors. Careful thought is required regarding the distribution of processing tasks across processors, and the extent, method, and timing of communication between processors.

Furthermore, many embedded systems make use of specialized FPGAs or ASICs, and thus require low-level software to interact with the custom hardware.

(5) Embedded systems are predominantly hidden from view.

By nature, embedded systems typically have a limited interface with their "user"(real user or another component of the super-system). Thus, much of the system is developed to meet the software functional specifications developed during architecture and high-level design, rather than the user requirements.

(6) Embedded systems frequently have monolithic functionality.

Most embedded systems are built for a single primary purpose. They can be decomposed into components, and potentially the components could have low cross-cohesion and cross-coupling. That is, each component could serve a distinct purpose, and the interactions between components could be restricted to a few well-defined points.

Nevertheless, the system as a whole will not function unless most or all of the components are operational. A system that requires all components to function before the system as a whole achieves useful functionality is a "monolithic system". This non-linear jump in system functionality as a function of component functionality is in contrast to some other types of software, where the system may be 50% functional (or more) when the software is 50% complete.

For example, a space probe is built to travel by or to other planets and send back information about them. Though there are many lower-level responsibilities of the space probe components, such as targeting, landing, deploying sensors, deploying solar panels, and communications. Each of these lower-level responsibilities is an indispensable component of the over-arching functionality. The space probe will fail if any of these vital components is missing, even if all other components are completely functional.

Another example is a cell phone, in which all the sub-features such as the user interface, the cellular base station selection, the vocoder, and the communications protocols are all vital aspects of the over-arching goal to transfer bi-directional audio information between the user and specific remote nodes.

These are in contrast to other software regimes, such as web services or desktop tools, in which lower-level responsibilities are more likely to contribute independently to the aggregate system functionality rather than serving as indispensable parts of a monolithic whole.

Though the software components of an embedded system are combined into a monolithic functionality, the components themselves are often very distinct. Embedded systems will frequently combine software components that perform signal processing, low-level device driver I/O, communications protocols, guidance and control, and user interfaces. Each of these specialized components requires a distinct developer skill set.

(7) Embedded systems frequently have limited development tools.

Though some software regimes have a whole host of tools to assist with software development, embedded systems software development are more limited, and frequently use only basic compiler tools. This is in part because embedded systems often use custom hardware, which may not have tool support, and because embedded systems are often real-time and performance constrained, making it difficult to freeze the entire execution context under the control of a debugger or transfer control and data between the embedded target and a host-based tool, or capture extensive execution-tracing logs.

Because of the limited choices of commercial tools for embedded systems software development, many embedded system projects create their own tools to use for debugging and testing, or at least augment commercial tools with in-house tools.

(8) Embedded systems frequently have stringent robustness requirements.

Embedded systems are often used in harsh environments and for mission-critical or medical purposes. Therefore, requirements for reliability, correct exception handling, and mean time between failures are typically more stringent for embedded systems than for many other types of software. This translates into rigorous development processes and testing requirements. In turn, this increases the overhead needed to make a release of software.

Some types of embedded systems are subject to regulatory requirements that purport to reduce fault rates by mandating the software development process, or at least specifying what documentation must accompany the embedded systems product.

Furthermore, for several types of embedded systems, it is difficult or even impossible to upgrade firmware, which emphasizes the need to "get it right" in the system's initial commercial release.

(9) Embedded systems are frequently very long-lived.

Embedded systems often stay in use for many years. Frequently the duration of support for an embedded system is far greater than the turnover rate of the original software developers. This makes it paramount to have good documentation to explain the embedded systems software, particularly since the source code itself may have its self-documentation quality compromised due to performance trade-offs.

Technical Words and Expressions

embedded system		嵌入式系统
microwave	n.	微波炉
micro-controller	n.	微控制器
console	n.	控制台
a matter of course		理所当然的事,必然的结果
in tandem with		同……串联,同……合作
roughly	adv.	概略地,粗糙地
form factor		外形因素
real-time	adj.	实时的
off-the-shelf		从商店可以直接购买的,非顾客定制的
PDA		数字助理
trade off		交替换位,交替使用,卖掉
portability	n.	可携带,轻便
clarity	n.	清楚,透明
modularity	n.	[计]模块性
up-front	adv.	在前面,在最前面
Amortize	v.	分期清偿
peripheral	adj.	外围的
stringent		严厉的,迫切的
harsh	adj.	粗糙的,荒芜的,苛刻的
robustness	n.	健壮性
preemptive	adj.	有先买权的,有强制收购权的,抢先的

execution context		[计]执行文本
FPGA	abbr.	可编程器件
ASIC	abbr.	[电]特定用途集成电路
predominantly	adv.	支配性地,主要地,有影响地
monolithic	n.	单片电路,单块集成电路
architecture	n.	建筑,建筑学,体系机构
cohesion	n.	结合,凝聚
cross-coupling		交叉耦合
non-linear	adj.	非线性的
solar panels		太阳电池板
vital	adj.	生死攸关的,重大的,生命的,生机的
compiler	n.	编辑者,[计]编译器
rigorous	adj.	严格的,严厉的,严酷的,严峻的
be subject to		受支配
paramount	adj.	极为重要的
compromise	n.v.	妥协,折中
stands to reason		显而易见

Exercises

一、将下述词组译成英文

嵌入式系统　　　特定用途集成电路　　　数字助理　　　交替使用

通信协议　　　　微控制器　　　　　　　微波炉　　　　实时系统

二、将下述短文译成中文

　　By nature, most embedded systems are built to react in real-time to data flowing to and through the system. The real-time constraints again favor performance aspects (particularly cycles usage) over maintainability aspects. There are generally both hard real-time constraints, which require an event to be handled by a fixed time, and soft real-time constraints, which set limits on the average event response time. Real-time operating systems use preemptive prioritized scheduling to help ensure that real-time deadlines are met, but careful thought is required to divide processing into execution contexts (threads), set the relative priorities of the execution contexts, and manage control/data flow between the contexts.

READING 8

The Added Advantages of Digital Technology

The use of digital (rather than analogue) switching within SPC exchanges adds the following features.

(1) Speed of call set-up. The electronic hardware of the control element of SPC exchanges operates at high speed and at low-voltage levels (typically 5 V DC). Thus, for SPC exchanges with electromechanical switches, which are by their nature slow and require relatively heavy operating voltages and currents, there is a significant mismatch in speed and power between the control and switching systems, and this must be overcome by appropriate buffering equipment. However, digital switches are entirely composed of semiconductor gates and stores, in integrated-circuit form, which operate at speeds and voltages compatible with the control systems, thus forming a fully electronic SPC exchange.

Connections can be established across digital switching systems very quickly (e.g. 250 μs). This, together with their economical high capacities and near-nonblocking characteristics, enables system-design economies to be gained by using the digital switches for sequential path set-up between the various exchange subsystems (serial trunking) during the call-connection phase. In addition, automatic repeat attempts across the switches (e.g. to avoid congestion or outages in the network) can be made without incurring perceptible increases in post-dialing delay. The result is that digital switching with SPC enables complex call connections within an exchange to be established using relatively cheap and simple switch designs.

(2) Accommodation savings. Digital switching systems are significantly smaller than analogue exchanges of equivalent capacity. This is due to both the miniaturization achieved by the integrated circuitry and the large-scale time-division multiplexing used throughout a digital exchange. The latter is possible because of the high speeds of operation of the semiconductor technology used.

However, the savings in accommodation can be significantly reduced by the presence of analogue-to-digital interworking equipment required to terminate analogue lines. The need for such equipment, and hence the accommodation space, can be minimized by appropriate planning to maximize the proportion of digital circuits terminating at the exchange. The potentially high accommodation savings may also be reduced, to some extent, by the need to provide air-conditioning and a controlled environment for the exchanges. In some cases, additional power-supply equipment is required when SPC digital systems are installed in an existing exchange. Despite these additions, the overall space required for a digital SPC exchange is typically less than 25% of that for step-by. step or crossbar exchanges, and 50% of that for analogue SPC systems.

(3) Ease of maintenance. The equipment used in digital SPC exchanges has a lower fault rate than that used in analogue SPC exchanges because of the absence of moving parts and the inherent reliability of semiconductor technology. In addition, unlike step-by-step and crossbar exchanges, digital systems do not require any routine adjustments. Diagnostic programs within the exchange-control system usually enable hardware faults to be located quickly to a particular module or plug-in unit. Where appropriate, the use of hardware redundancy enables the control system to restore service rapidly by automatic reconfiguration of the use of the equipment, replacing a faulty unit with a spare one. The exchange-control system then provides the necessary information for the maintenance staff to replace the faulty unit later, in a planned way. Faulty units are usually sent to specialist repair centre. Therefore, the hardware maintenance load is low in comparison with that for analogue exchanges.

(4) Quality of connection. There are three important transmission advantages with networks using digital switching and transmission (i. e. integrated digital networks). First, the overall transmission loss of a call connection through the network is independent of the number of digital switching units and transmission links. Furthermore, the overall loss is set by the analogue-to-digital conversion processes at each end of the connection. This enables the loudness to be optimized, taking into account preferred listening levels. consistent with adequate stability and echo control. Secondly, because noise does not accumulate over digital transmission systems, users perceive significantly lower noise levels than with connections over analogue networks. Thirdly, digital local exchanges have line-interface cards permanently connected to 2-wire local lines. This enables improved impedance matching within the 2-to-4 wire conversion equipment, resulting in fewer instability problems compared to 2-wire-switched analogue networks. (Such improved impedance control is particularly important because, compared to analogue networks, digital networks tend to have lower end-to-end losses, but with increased delay, thus potentially worsening the echo performance.)

(5) Potential for non-voice services. Digital transmission is an ideal medium for conveying the outputs from data terminals, computers, etc. , which originate in digital format. Transmission of data, particularly at speeds above 4.8kbit/s, is cheaper and more efficient over digital systems than over analogue systems, because the signals can be carried directly, without the need for voice-frequency modems, with their attendant high cost and restriction on throughput. Digitally encoded analogue signals (e. g. speech and video) can be freely mixed with digitally-sourced traffic and carried over a common bearer without the power-spectrum constraints that exist when such a variety of signals is carried over analogue-transmission systems. Thus, digital exchanges, when associated with digital transmission, have the potential for the economic provision of a range of services in addition

to telephony.

(6) Cost. In general, digital SPC exchange systems are economical to run compared with their analogue equivalents, and their capital costs can be significantly lower. However, the cost aspects of running telephone exchanges are varied and complex. As well as the capital cost of the switching equipment, the initial investment involves costs resulting from accommodation, power, operation-and-maintenance support systems, spares holding, documentation, staff training, interconnection with the existing network. etc. When deciding on the choice of switching systems, administrations also need to consider the consequential running costs. These result from software support (provided by the manufacturer and the administration), operational management, maintenance, billing, etc. The ease of upgrading the system with new facilities may also be reflected in the cost evaluation. All these factors contribute to the "whole-life cost" of an exchange system.

(7) Installation time. The time to install digital SPC exchanges is less than that for analogue exchanges of equivalent capacity. This is due to the smaller physical volume and the modularization of the digital equipment. Speedy installation is also attributable to the factory pre-testing and simple plug-in-unit construction of the equipment now employed in modern SPC exchanges.

Technical Words and Expressions

SPC(Stored-Program Control)		存储程序控制
integrated-circuit(IC)		集成电路
PCM-encoding		PCM 编码
reed	n.	芦苇,芦笛,簧片,管乐器
subscriber-line		用户线
analogue-to-digital		模数转换
tandem	n.	汇接局
crosstalk	n.	串话
semiconductor	n.	半导体
multifrequency		多频的
interexchange	v.	互换,交换
extension	n.	分机
labour-intensive	adj.	劳动密集的
miniaturization	n.	小型化
man-machine-interface		人机界面
operations-command		操作命令

Exercises

一、将下述词组译成英文
集成电路　　　汇接局　　　半导体　　　　　　用户线
人机界面　　　操作命令　　存储程序控制　　　PCM 编码

二、将下述短文译成中文

As well as the capital cost of the switching equipment, the initial investment involves costs resulting from accommodation, power, operation-and-maintenance support systems, spares holding, documentation, staff training, interconnection with the existing network. etc. When deciding on the choice of switching systems, administrations also need to consider the consequential running costs. These result from software support (provided by the manufacturer and the administration), operational management, maintenance, billing, etc. The ease of upgrading the system with new facilities may also be reflected in the cost evaluation. All these factors contribute to the "whole-life cost" of an exchange system.

READING 9

Open Systems Interconnection Reference Model

During the 1960s and 1970s, companies such as Burroughs, Digital Equipment Corporation (DEC), Honeywell, and IBM defined network communications protocols for their computer products. Because of the proprietary nature of the protocols, however, the interconnection of computers from different manufacturers, or even between different product lines from the same manufacturer, was very difficult.

In the late 1970s, the International Organization for Standardization (ISO) developed the Reference Model for Open Systems Interconnection. The OSI model comprises a seven-layer architecture, which is the basis for open network systems allowing computer from any vendor to communicate with each other.

The goals of OSI model are to expedite communication between equipment built by different manufacturers. The layering of the OSI model provides transparency; that operation of a single layer of the model is independent of the other layers.

The OSI model is described here because it provides an excellent reference with which to compare and contrast different protocols and functionality. Implementations of OSI are few and far between, however, and it could be argued that Transmission Control Protocol/Internet protocol (TCP/IP) is the best implementation so far of an open systems protocol suite.

The OSI model specifies seven functional protocol layers (Fig. 1). Peer layers across the network communicate according to protocols; adjacent layers in the same system communicate across an interface. Network architectures (such as ISDN and B-ISDN) specify the function of the layers, the protocol procedures for peer-to-peer communication, and the communication across the interface between adjacent protocol layers. Actual implementations and algorithms are not typically specified.

The lower three layers of the OSI model are:

(1) *Physical Layer* (layer 1).

The physical layer covers the physical interface between devices and rules by which bits are passed from one to another. The physical layer has four important characteristics:

Mechanical. Relates to the physical properties of interface to a transmission medium. Typically, the specification is of a pluggable connector that joins one or more signal conductors, called circuits.

Electrical. Relates to the representation of bits (e.g., in terms of voltage levels) and

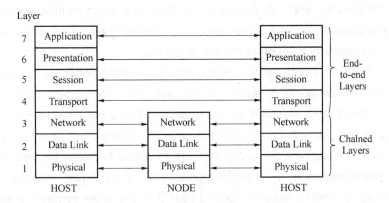

Fig. 1　Reference model for OSI

the data transmission rate of bits.

Functional. Specifies the functions performed by individual circuits of physical interface between a system and the transmission medium.

Procedural. Specifies the sequence of events by which bit streams are exchanged across the physical medium.

Common example include EIA-232-E (for merely RS-232-C), EIA-530, High-Speed Serial Interface (HSSI), V.24, V.28, and V.35.

(2) *Data Link layer* (layer 2).

Whereas the physical layer provides only a raw bit-stream service, the data link layer attempts to make the physical link reliable while providing the means to activate, Maintain, and deactivate the link. The principal service provided by the data link layer to higher layers is that of error detection and control. Thus, with a fully functional data-layer protocol, the next higher layer may assume error-free transmission over the link. However, if communication is between two systems that are not directly connected, the connection will comprise a number of data links in tandem, each functioning independently. Thus, the higher layers are not relieved of any error control responsibility.

Common examples include IBM's Binary Synchronous Communications (BISYNC) and Synchronous Data Link Control (SDLC) protocols, DEC's Digital Data Communication Message Protocol (DDCMP), ISO's High-level Data Link Control (HDLC), and ITU-Ts Link Access Procedures Balanced (LAPB), Link Access Procedures on the D-channel (LAPD), and Link Access Procedures to Frame Mode Bearer Services (LAPF).

(3) *Network Layer* (layer 3).

The network layer provides for the transfer of information between end systems across some sort of communications network. It relieves higher layers of the need to know anything about the underlying data transmission and switching technologies used to connect systems. At this layer, the computer system engages in a dialogue with the network to specify the destination address and to request certain network facilities, such as priority.

There is a spectrum of possibilities for intervening communications facilities to be managed by the network layer. At one extreme, there is a direct point-to-point link between stations. In this case, there may be no need for a network layer because the data link layer can perform the necessary function of managing the link.

Next, the systems could be connected across a single network, such as a circuit-switching or packet-switching network. As an example, the packet level of the X.25 standard is a network layer standard for this situation. The lower three layers are concerned with attaching to and communicating with the network. The packet created by the system pass through one or more network nodes that act as relays between the two end systems. The network nodes implement 1~3 of the architecture. In the figure, two end systems are connected through a single, network node. Layer 3 in the node performs a switching and routing function. Within the node, there are two data link layers and two physical layers, corresponding to the two end system. Each data link (and physical) layer operates independently to provide service to the network layer over its respective link.

This layer specifies protocols for such functions as routing, congestion control, accounting, call setup and termination, and user-network communications. Examples include ISO's Connections Network Protocol (CLNP), and ISDN's call control procedures (Q.931 and Q.2931).

There three layers are called the chained layer and comprise procedures for host-to-node and node-to-node communication. End users (hosts), as well as all switching devices (nodes) along the route between the hosts, must implement these protocol layers.

The upper four layer of the OSI model are:

(1) *Transport Layer* (layer 4).

The transport layer provides a mechanism for exchange of data between end system. The connection-oriented transport service ensures that data are delivered error-free, in sequence, with no losses or duplications. The transport layer may also be concerned with optimizing the use of network services and with providing a requested quality of service to session entities. For example, the session entity may specify acceptable error rates, maximum delay, priority, and security.

The size and complexity of a transport protocol depend on how reliable or unreliable the underlying network and network and network layer services are. Accordingly, ISO has developed a family of five transport protocol standards, each oriented toward a different underlying service. In the TCP/IP protocol suite, there are two common transport-layer protocols: the connection-oriented TCP (transmission control protocol) and the connectionless UDP (user datagram protocol). Examples include TCP and ISO's Transport Protocol (TP).

(2) *Session Layer* (layer 5).

The lowest four layers of OSI model provide the means for the reliable exchange of data and of provide an expedited data service. For many applications, this basic service is insufficient. For example, a remote terminal access application might require a half-duplex dialogue. A transaction-processing application might require checkpoints in the data-transfer stream to permit backup and recovery. A message-processing application might require the ability to interrupt a dialogue in order to prepare a new portion of a massage and later to resume the dialogue where it was left off.

All these capabilities could be embedded in specific applications at layer 7. However, because these types of dialogue-structuring tools have widespread applicability, it makes sense to organize them into a separate layer: the session layer.

The session layer provides the mechanism for controlling the dialogue between applications in end system. In many cases, there will be little or no need for session-layer services, but for some applications, such services are used. The key services provided by the session layer include:

Dialogue discipline. This can be two-way simultaneous (full duplex) or two-way alternate (half duplex).

Grouping. The flow of data can be marked to define groups of data. For example, if a retail store is transmitting sales data to a regional office, the data can be marked to indicate the end of the sales data for each department; this would signal the host computer to finalize running totals for that department and start new running counts for the next department.

Recovery. The session layer can provide a check-pointing mechanism, so that if a failure of some sort occurs between checkpoints, the session entity can retransmit all data since the last checkpoint. Mainly specifies process-to-process communication, error recovery, and session synchronization.

(3) *Presentation layer* (layer 6).

The presentation layer defines the format of the data to be exchanged between applications and offers applications programs a set of data transformation services. The presentation layer also defines the syntax used between application entities and provides for the selection and subsequent modification of the representation used. Examples of specific services that may be performed at this layer include data compression and encryption.

(4) *Application Layer* (layer 7).

The application layer provides a means for application programs to access the OSI environment. This layer contains management functions and generally useful mechanisms that support distributed applications. In addition, general-purpose applications such as file transfer, electronic mail, and terminal access to remote computers are considered to reside at this layer. Sample applications and protocols include TCP/IP's Simple Mail Transfer Protocol (SMTP) and ITU-T X.400 for e-mail, X.500 for directory service, TCP/IP's Telnet and ISO's VT protocol for remote login and terminals, TCP/IP's File Transfer Protocol (FTP) and ISO's File Transfer Access Method (FTAM).

These four layers are called the end-to-end layer since they are implemented only in hosts. End-to-end information is transparent to the chained layer. The network nodes that deal with the chained layers generate higher-layer protocol traffic specific to their applications. A switching node, for example, could generate network management traffic using the SNMP protocol, but this would not affect the operation of the chained layers or the network nodes.

The ITU-T standard ISDN protocols define a user-network interface that comprises only the chained layers. While an ISDN itself can provide many types of services using many types of protocols. These protocols are discussed in pore detail in Chaos. 4 though 7.

New words and Expressions

proprietary	adj.	所有的,私人拥有的
	n.	所有者,所有权
protocol suite		协议族
pluggable connector		可插拔式连接器
underlying	adj.	在下面的,根本的,潜在的
checkpoint	n.	检查点,检查站
syntax	n.	[语]语法,有秩序的排列,句子构造,句法
representation	n.	表示法,表现,陈述,请求,扮演,画像,继承,代表
ITU-T(International Telecommunication Union-Telecommunication)		国际电信联合会-电信分部
FTP (File Transfer Protocol)		文件传输协议
TCP/IP (Transmission Control Protocol/Internet Protocol)		传输控制协议/网络协议
LAPB (Link Access Procedures Balanced)		平衡链接规程
LAPD (Link Access Procedures on the D-channel)		D 信道链接规程
HDLC (High-level Data Link Control)		高级数据链路控制
ISO (International Organization for Standardization)		国际标准化组织
OSI-RM(Open Systems Interconnection Reference Model)		开放系统互联参考模型

Exercise

一、理解题

1. Explain the reason that ISO developed the Reference Model for Open Systems Interconnection.

2. According to the text, which layer can provide the data compression function?

3. According to the text, how many layers are implemented in the network nodes? why?

二、将下述短文译成中文

Next, the systems could be connected across a single network, such as a circuit-switching or packet-switching network. As an example, the packet level of the X. 25 standard is a network layer standard for this situation. The lower three layers are concerned with attaching to and communicating with the network. The packet created by the system pass through one or more network nodes that act as relays between the two end systems. The network nodes implement 1~3 of the architecture. In the figure, two end systems are connected through a single, network node. Layer 3 in the node performs a switching and routing function. Within the node, there are two data link layers and two physical layers, corresponding to the two end system. Each data link (and physical) layer operates independently to provide service to the network layer over its respective link.

READING 10

Computer Security

1. Computer Virus

(1) What is a virus?

Just as human viruses invade a living cell and then turn it into a factory for manufacturing viruses, computer viruses are small programs that replicate by attaching a copy of themselves to another program.

Once attached to the host program, the viruses then look for other programs to "infect". In this way, the virus can spread quickly throughout a hard disk or an entire organization if it infects a Local Area Network or a multi-user system.

Skillfully written viruses can infect and multiply for weeks or months without being detected. During that time, system backups duplicate the viruses, or copies of data or programs are made and passed to other systems to infect. At some point—determined by how the virus was programmed the virus attacks. The timing of the attack call be linked to a number of situations, including: a certain time or data; the presence of a particular user ID; the use or presence of a particular file; the security privilege level of the user; and the number of times a file is used.

Likewise, the mode of attack varies. So-called "begin" viruses might simply display a message, like the one that infected IBM's main computer system last Christmas with a season's greeting.

Malignant viruses, on the other hand, are designed to damage your systems. One common attack is to wipe out data, to delete files, or to perform a format of your hard disk.

(2) What kind of viruses are there?

There are four main types of viruses: shell, intrusive operating system, and source code.

Shell viruses wrap themselves around a host program and do not modify the original program. Shell programs are easy to write, which is why about half of all viruses are of this type. In addition, shell viruses are easy for programs like Data Physician to remove.

Intrusive viruses invade an existing program and actually insert a portion of themselves into the host program. Intrusive viruses are hard to write and very difficult to remove without damaging the host file.

Shell and intrusive viruses most commonly attack executable program files those with a .COM or .EXE extension—although data files are also at some risk.

Operating system viruses work by replacing parts of the operating system with their own logic. Very difficult to write, these viruses have the ability, once booted up, to take total control of your system. According to Digital Dispatch, known versions of operating system viruses have hidden large amounts of attack logic in falsely marked bad disk sectors. Others install RAM—resident programs or device drivers to perform infection or attack functions invisibly from memory.

Source code viruses are intrusive programs that are inserted into a source program such as those written in Pascal prior to the program being compiled. These are the least common viruses because they are not only hard to write, but also have a limited number of hosts compared to the other types.

2. What's in password?

The ideal password is one that people will not be tempted to write down. It will permit correct keying-in on the first try and will not be difficult to use. Otherwise, the users can expect to make so many typing mistakes that the almost correct password entries will start showing up in security logs.

Seven simple rules will eliminate most of the easy methods for discovering a password:

—Never tell anyone else what password is being used. The bad habit of sharing a password might be broken by choosing passwords that would create embarrassment if told to anyone else.

—Never write down a password. If the password is for a group of people (e. g., a system or program password) use a mnemonic device to make the password more memorable.

—Avoid the obvious choices. Select passwords that have nothing to do with you personally. Avoid selecting anything that someone could look up or guess.

—Make them work for it. Testing all possible password combinations gets expensive, and a reasonable password guesser would take several shortcuts such as all the words in a dictionary. Combinations of words, misspelled Words, or made-up words plus a digit here and there will make this difficult.

—Use longer passwords. A password should be at least six characters long and double that if the individual can comfortable type it in.

—Change passwords. Choose a new password every month, more often if it is a privileged account. Do not reuse passwords.

—Use different passwords for different systems. The most secure approach is for each password to bear no relation to any other. The easy way involves using an algorithmic password with a fixed part and a part that changes from system to system.

Be alert to programs that steal or trap passwords. Keep track of failed log on attempts, and make sure the count of these matches the system's log-on failure count. If they do not match, either an error has been made in the count or a password grabber is at work. Change the password immediately and start looking for the culprit.

An effective password policy takes into consideration the limitations of a system's users as well as the overall information security policy of the organization. Make users feel personally involved in implementing the password policy. Convey the idea that protection their password is more in their own interest than anyone else's but that password policy is not working, take the time to determine why before attempting to force the issue.

Tips for selecting passwords:

—variations on titles, slogans, and phrases;

—misspelled words;

—misplaced fingers on the keyboard, shifting up or down for parts of the password;

—foreign words and those with a different alphabet from the Roman;

—made up words by stringing a few syllables together;

—mathematical formulas which leave out the operators but do not reduce it just numbers.

3. Network security

Corporate America's local area networks are full of security gaps. Distributed networks virtually beg for intruders. An examination of PC LAN security products reveals products designed to close different holes, depending on vendor philosophies; a potential security breach that seems dangerous to one vendor may be of little importance to anther. The same inconsistency is for user organizations.

For many companies, tightening up security begins with protecting PCs-a LAN's weakest link. Several packages take over the desktop upon power-up, forcing users authentication. Most security products supply some sort of password control, but multiple systems beget multiple passwords, and users have begun to object. In response, vendors are developing something called "single sign-on"—a single password that takes a user anywhere he or she is allowed to go.

But single sign-on poses an obvious threat. Companies offering single sign on routinely encrypt the password, among other security measures. Should you endorse the idea of single sing-on, keep in mind that, as no real security standards are widely accepted, no company has yet been able to implement single sing-on for incompatible LANs.

Most LAN security software builds walls around operating systems to keep users form altering DOS CONFIG . SYS and AUTOEXEC . BAT files. In environments where server resources are critical, administrators may not want to rely solely on the network operating system for server protection.

Remove dial-in is a dangerous vulnerability. One user uses NET/DACS to protect NetWare LANs, backing up the full-featured product with sophisticated security policies that allow for central administration but local implementation of security controls.

What is needed to improve the security of remote dial-in is an as yet unavailable handshake protocol. The server only knows the authorization exists to get data, not how or if the workstation requesting the data will protect it. Vendors are making progress toward providing such handshakes.

Finally, there is encryption. The US government has standardized on the Data Encryption Standard (DES) algorithm, but some vendors are urging the adoption of Rivest Shamir-Adleman (RSA) public key encryption as a standard. To date, there is no worldwide encryption standard, making international security cumbersome. People communication via outside networks—particularly store-and-forward systems, such as the Internet—should be wary of sending unencrypted data.

4. Encryption and its standards

Encryption and decryption of data are performed by complex mathematical algorithms that use an encryption key in application and hardware to cloak data.

Another cryptographic alterative is so-called hashing algorithms, which create a mathematical model of file contents and ship it with the file.

The hash acts as a file seal; recipients create their own hash of a file upon receiving the data and compare it to the sender's version. If the file hasn't been tampered with, the two hashes will match. Hashing can be performed with either public-or private-key encryption.

Private-key systems require sender and recipient of an encrypted document to exchange a shared cryptographic key directly and secretly.

Public-key systems offer an additional feature over private key: The user can sign a document electronically with a digital signature that can be checked by the intended recipient using the sender's public key.

Public-key technology, pioneered 10 years ago by scientists at the Massachusetts Institute of Technology and Stanford University, only recently began appearing in products and finding acceptance among users.

The current ANSI private-key standard, the Data Encryption Standard (DES), is the government standard set by the National Institute and Technology (NIST) for the protection of no classified but sensitive government data.

U. S. corporations must obtain special permission to export DES compliant products outside of the country to support network operations.

The use of DES is ubiquitous for many applications. Every major bank credit card network encrypts its transaction with DES to protect data.

Virtually every private-key encryption device on the market is DES-based, and public-key systems also typically use DES as the private-key part of the dual-key system.

After years of promising Congress and industry participants it would establish a public-key standard, NIST officials in July 1991 finally unveiled the specification it would back: the Digital Signature standard (DSS).

But DSS, which does not provide for actual document encryption, only performs the digital signature and hasting functions founding public-key technology.

Network and computer vendors, many of whom have licensed public-key encryption algorithms from RSA Data Security Ins. Attacked DSS for being only half a standard. RSA's algorithms are considered a de facto standard.

Vendors also criticized DSS for being slower than RSA's digital signature algorithm in verifying digital signatures. But NIST promised that products adhering to DSS could be exported freely, while products based on RSA technology cannot.

Technical Words and Expressions

authenticate	vt.	认证,鉴定,证实
authentication	n.	证明,文电鉴别
beget	vt.	招致,引起,孕育
benign	adj.	良性的,慈祥的,温和的
breach	n.	缺口,裂口,破坏,违反
cloak	vt.	掩护,掩饰,隐蔽,假装
culprit	n.	罪人,罪犯
cumbersome	adj.	麻烦的,侧重的,繁重的
cryptographic	a.	密码的,密码方式
cryptograph	n.	密码,密码通信法
decryption	n.	解密
de facto	adj.	事实上的
encrypt	vt.	加密
encryption	n.	加密
endorse	vt.	背书,同意,赞成,支持
malignant	adj.	恶意的,恶性的,有害的
tandem	n. adj.	前后直排的,串联的,纵列的
in tandem		纵列地,密切地,协力地
unencrypted	adj.	未加密的
unveil	v.	揭露,初次公开,新发售
vulnerability	n.	易受伤,脆弱性,弱点
wary	adj.	谨慎的,小心的,周到的
boot up		得手,引导
Digital Dispatch		公司名
digital signature		数字签名
dual-key system		双密钥系统
handshake protocol		握手协议
hashing algorithm		散列(又译杂凑)算法
made-up		编造的,自造的
security privilege level		安全保密等级
smartcard	n.	灵巧卡(一种安全控制卡)

Exercises

一、将下述词组译成英文

数字签名 双密钥系统 握手协议 安全保密等级

二、将下述短文译成中文

An effective password policy takes into consideration the limitations of a system's users as well as the overall information security policy of the organization. Make users feel personally involved in implementing the password policy. Convey the idea that protection their password is more in their own interest than anyone else's but that password policy is not working, take the time to determine why before attempting to force the issue.

第四部分

参考译文

第1单元 通信理论的进化

多年以来,从传输和有效性的角度来说,已经用多种方式研究过各种组织机构中的通信,Shannon(香农)和 Weaver 的通信传输模型为后来分析通信方式的许多见解提供了基础。但是这个模型却被用于且继续被用于偏离其设计本意的应用。本质上,它是一个数据传输模型,而不是宣称的一个通信理论:在该理论中,为了分析组织通信,它一定要包括更广泛的考虑因素,诸如语言、记号语言、社会测量和文化。另外,可用传输信道的增加使得通信的分析更为复杂,并成为组织计划所必不可少的任务。

Shannon 的过程模型由 Weaver 进一步改进(见图1),其本质上是一个数据传输模型。它基于 Hartley(哈特莱)和 Nyquist(奈奎斯特)提出的信息论,该理论后来并入 Shannon 的信道容量准则理论。

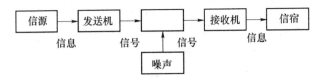

图1 基本通信系统

信息论基于信息的可预测性,即信息的信息量随其发生概率的增加而单调递减。公式(1)说明:信息的信息量 I 可通过对发生概率 p_m 取以2为底的对数得到的比特数来进行量化:

$$I_m = -\log_2 p_m \tag{1}$$

因而信息的信息量是其缺失性的一种度量。由此,一个确知信息是不含任何信息的,其信息量是0。信息量的一个重要方面是它衡量的不是消息本身的意义或语义。平均信息量的二进制表示被称为信源的熵 H,它与公式(1)中所定义的每条信息的信息量和发生概率有关。如公式(2)所示:

$$H = -\sum p_i \log_2 p_i \tag{2}$$

信号容量准则显示了以数字通信信道每秒的二进制位表示的最大传输容量 C 与传送信号的资源及传输环境之间的关系。在该模型中,信号用来表示消息,并采用最适合于传输媒介的形式。用于建模信源的实参包括信号功率 S、传输时间 T，以及信道带宽或容量 B。考虑环境因素，即信号的失真或信号干扰，将这些畸变建模为信道噪声功率谱密度，得到的噪声功率为噪声谱密度与信道带宽的乘积。则 Shannon 所得出的信道容量如式(3)：

$$C = B\log_2(1 + S/N) \tag{3}$$

传送消息的时间 T 如式(4)：

$$T = IC \tag{4}$$

为了减少消息传送时间，当然信道容量 C 尽可能越大越好。由式(3)可知，信道容量可以通过增加带宽 B 来实现最大化。但移动系统不可能这么做，因为带宽是宝贵的。在英国 3G 牌照拍卖中，五大移动运营商为提供其业务的带宽支付了 22.5 亿英镑。有线运营商利用有线系统提供电话、网络接入、广播无线电和电视业务，因此带宽决定了距离和技术成本。可是，带宽增加，噪声也会随之加大，所以带宽与噪声的权衡也是工程学中的一个效益悖反。原则上，噪声的增加能够通过增加信号功率 S 来补偿，但是有一个缺点：一个信道信号功率的增加意味着另一个信道干扰(噪声)的增加。对于移动设备而言，传输功率的增加有好的效应，同时也缩短了电池充电时间间隔(手机充电对于用户来说是一个极为不便的问题)。

从对 Shannon 信道容量准则的检验可以看出，它仅仅陈述了影响发送者与接收者间实际数据传输的各种原因，没有考虑接收者接收到信息的信息值。

因此，为了拓宽对通信的理解，引入了其他应考虑的方面：在基本模型中必须增加语义属性传输领域的发展。比方说，在考虑通信系统的熵值之前有必要区分数据与信息的不同。数据被认为是接收到的没有相关意思的信息，而信息要求接收者把意思和消息联系起来，因此接收方需要做一些积极的加工。因此这个信息与人的脑力模型关联到一起，并加入了人脑中的知识。Fiske 认为，描述和设计通信系统的概念模型可以被归类于过程模型或者记号语言模型。Shannon 1948 年提出的过程模型是从工程的角度出发，而记号语言模型则基于人类感知。

现在，基于人类认知力、理解力和语义属性的通信模型发展可被看成对通信工程认识的补充。下列通信模型举例说明了从不同角度拓宽对于通信的理解。

Berlo 在他关于通信涉及到元素的实验中提到："要理解通信，必须理解人的行为。"他构建了一个人体内通信模型，包含了影响通信保真度的如下 4 个部分：

信源——通信的发送方用作消息的调制器：交谈技巧、态度、知识、社会理解力以及通信发生的文化氛围。

消息——消息应该包含以下要素：内容、结构和编码。

信道——消息在信道中编码和解码。例如，会话、视频或者其他感官信道。

信宿——通信的接收方应该使用与信源相同的调制器。

然而，这些并非完全相同。

Berlo 据此在通信过程中加入了人文因素，有助于在通信过程中添加可预期、可理解的信息。通信的保真度指的是这些信息保持一致的程度。

Ross 建立了一个模型，具有很多 Berlo 模型的特征，但是又在收、发双方增加了情绪因素。这会影响属于接收机的信息。比方说愤怒或挫败感会引起通信的畸变。他将这些通信事件中的综合因素称之为"气候状况"。

Hellriegal 等人注意到,为了实现发信方要表达的信息与接收方对信息的理解一致的"理想状态",双方的语言必须相同。言下之意是,不仅需要英语、法语、德语这些语种必须相同,而且对这些语言的运用,比如特殊用法、方言、缩写等也必须完全一致。

"成功通信"的概念由 Myers 解释为"有说服力的通信"。也就是说,一个通信越有说服力,也就越接近成功通信。他定义了可影响通信说服力的一系列变量,比如交流者的可信度,传输信道的主动性和被动性。他发现信息内容可能受初始语言和最终语言不同所影响。Myers 将社会学维度引入了对通信的分析之中。

第 2 单元 数字通信系统

电信系统使用数字方法来传输模拟信号正变得越来越普遍。原因主要有两个:第一,如果传输的是数字信号(而不是模拟信号),只要噪声电平低于门限电平,系统就几乎不受影响。因为长距离传输的数字信号可以在再生器中重新生成,产生一个新的、无噪声的信号,所以噪声不会像在模拟系统中一样产生累积。第二,数字系统的部件更适合于使用大规模集成电路的集成应用。

但是,即使在数字传输系统里,许多被处理的信号通常本身是模拟信号。因此这些模拟信号需要被转换为数字形式。有多种调制方法可以完成这种转换,包括脉宽调制(PWM)、脉幅调制(PAM)和脉冲编码调制(PCM)。目前,数字电信系统中运用最广泛的调制方式是PCM。通过对模拟信号进行抽样、量化和编码就可以得到 PCM 信号。(调制后的)结果是二进制比特序列,即信号高低电平的交替变换,则这个数据流可适用于频率调制。

对模拟电压 $V(t)$ 的采样过程包括生成一个脉冲串,在这个脉冲串中,第 n 个脉冲的幅度等于 $V(t)$ 在 $t=nT$ 时的幅值。对于脉冲序列来说,为了能唯一表示包含在 $V(t)$ 中的信息,抽样频率 $f_c=1/T$ 至少是 $V(t)$ 频谱的最高频率的 2 倍,然后量化抽样信号的脉冲幅度,并且转换为一系列的比特,这些比特称为数字信号。

在实际的 PCM 电信系统中数字信号的传输通常使用时分复用(TDM)方式。时分复用系统中,来自不同信道的数字信号在同一条传输线上交织传输。因此,音频(电话)系统中,通常是 24 或 32 路话音信道复用在一对电缆上。国际电报电话咨询委员会(CCITT)建议了两种主要的体系结构(体制),现在许多全国性的 PCM 传输网络都采用它们(作为建设标准)。第一种如图 1 所示,主要应用在欧洲、非洲、澳大利亚和南美。在这种系统中,输入复用器(MUX)交织复用 32 路数字信号。其中的 30 路信息表示 30 个话音信道的幅值,而其余的 2 个时隙包含了信令和同步信息。第二种体系如图 2 所示,主要应用在美国、加拿大和日本。在这种系统中,24 路话音信道在输入端被复用在一起。

数字电信系统主要完成传输、交换两个任务。传输把数字编码的话音信号从一个地方发送到另一个地方,而交换建立两个话音信道间的有效连接,这两个信道是(用来)承载数字信号的。

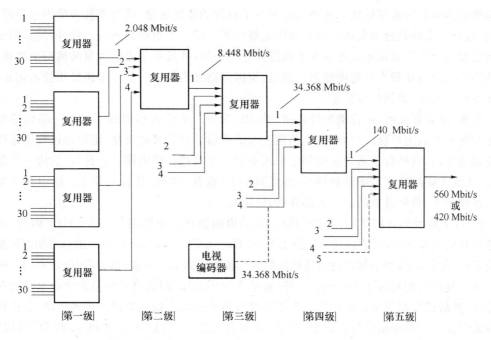

图 1　应用在欧洲、非洲、澳大利亚和南非的 PCM 体系

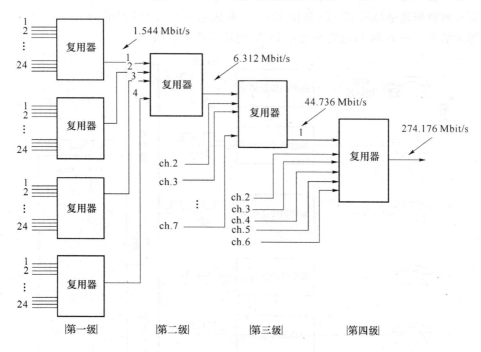

图 2　应用在美国、加拿大和日本的 PCM 体系

数字传输系统中完成脉冲编码调制和解调的单元称为编码器-解码器，或简称为编解码器。在早期的数字系统中，交换部分（的信号）是模拟形式的，所使用的是诸如机电纵横制机械此类的模拟设备。

那么，24 路或 30 路模拟话音信号信道被时分复用为一组。然后每组信号通过一个高速编解码器转换为数字形式。这种安排减少了器件的使用数量,线间串扰和噪声也足够低,但是,设计所需的高速全集成(各路)共用编解码器却是一个很难的问题。此外,编解码器的任何错误都可以导致该单元所服务的线路业务的丢失;并且系统需要大量的模拟交换机,而这些模拟交换机体积大且速度较慢。最后,模拟多路复用技术与数字多路复用技术相比,在实现上更为困难,灵活性也更差。

近来,随着低成本、高性能集成电路的运用,为每一个话音信道而不是为一组信道配置一个编解码器成为可能。因此,每个信道上的话音信号首先被数字化,随后通过数字系统进行交换和复用,这些数字系统使用的是低成本数字逻辑和存储电路。这种"每信道一个编解码器"系统大幅度减小了串话和噪声,并且减小了(设备)体积,节省了开支。原因在于减少了大量体积大、价格昂贵的机电式部件(的使用)。

CCITT 推荐的常用 300~3 400 Hz 话音信道的抽样频率标准是 8 000 Hz。因此,在每信道编解码器系统中,模拟信号每间隔 $1/8\ 000\ Hz=1.25\times10^{-4}\ s=125\ \mu s$,抽样的幅度值被转换为 8 bit 数字信息,然后被串行传送到复用器。转换用的 125 μs 长的时间间隔被称为一帧。

数字复用器把对应于 24 路或 30 路(依赖于所用的体制)各路采样值的全部比特放在一个帧中,然后传输结果串行比特流。为了在接收器处标志出每一帧的开头和结尾,会在传输比特流中加入一些标示信号。比如,在 AT&T 开发的 24 信道 8 比特 PCM 的 D2 系统中,在每一帧中会增加一个额外比特。因此,一个 D2 系统帧包含了 $24\times8+1=193$ bit。所以传输信号的数据速率是每 125 μs 传输 193 bit,对应速率为 1.544 Mbit/s。

图 3 给出了一个 24 信道时分复用 PCM 电话系统示意图。

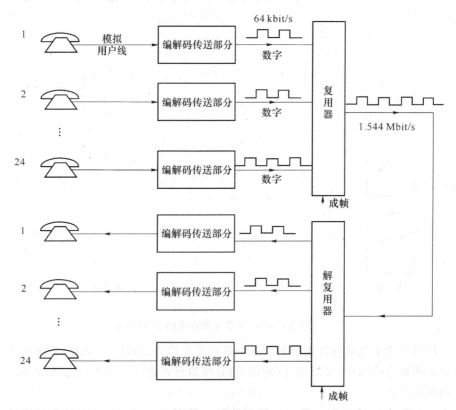

图 3　一个 24 信道时分复用 PCM 电话系统

典型的交换或传输路径的构成如图 4 所示。在发送方向，用户线连接到用户线接口电路上(SLIC)。用户接口电路完成 2/4 线转换、馈电、线路监视、提供振铃和过压保护功能。然后信号穿过发送方滤波器，(此处)滤波器把信号频谱限制到 3 400 Hz 左右。传输方滤波器能够去除超过 4 kHz 的频谱部分，从而在不引入混淆噪声的情况下使得 8 kHz 速度抽样成为可能。另外，信号频谱的低频部分(300 Hz 以下)也受到滤波器的抑制，以防止电力线频率(50 Hz 或 60 Hz)噪声被传输出去。

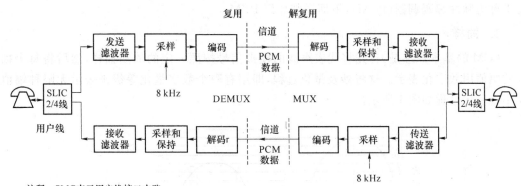

图 4　信号通过一个典型脉冲编码系统的过程

过滤过的信号，现在其波带被限制在 300～3 400 Hz 范围内，就可以以每秒 8 000 次的速率进行抽样，然后被转换(编码)为 8 比特 PCM 数据。这种转换是非线性的，也就是说(编码后)数字信号中小信号的分辨度比大信号的要好一些。

非线性 A/D 转换器的输出是一个特别编码的 8 比特数字信息。第一位表明了输入 x 的正负，其值为 1 表示 x 极性为正，为 0 表示 x 极性为负。其余 7 位表示了信号的幅度值。

回到图 4 中，编码器的数字输出和其他线路的输出被时分复用到一起，所得到的比特流随后通过信道传送出去。在接收端，输入数据被解复用(即被分发到不同的信道中)和解码(即 D/A 转换)。模拟输出被取样保持后送入接收端滤波器。接收端滤波器是一个低通平滑滤波器，它能去除信号频谱中的高频旁瓣，消除信号中的台阶噪声。低通滤波器也常常用来均衡由于取样保持而引入的正弦幅度失真。

经过 2/4 线转换后，话音信号被传送到用户电话的听筒中，这样一方通话就完成了。

第 3 单元　脉冲编码调制

1. 引言

话音信号在传输过程中会遇到这样的问题：传输距离增加时，传输电路中引入的噪声也会随之增加。然而,自从一个世纪前电话技术问世起,各种各样的电磁干扰与日俱增。单纯地使用信号放大技术并不能抑制噪声,因为信号放大的同时噪声也放大了。

1983 年,Alec Reeves 提出了一种解决话音长距离传输中噪声的方法,即将模拟话音信号转换为一组数字脉冲信号串。在识别前,假如这些脉冲信号在受损前被再生,理论上这些脉冲信号就可以无损(除了在模数、数模信号转换时固有的损坏)地传输很远的距离。这种信号的损坏称为量化噪声,将在后面的部分中进行讨论。将模拟信号转换为数字脉冲串的技术称为脉冲编码调制(PCM),下面详细介绍 PCM。

2. 抽样

PCM 的基本原理是:首先将代表声波的模拟信号按照一定的周期抽样,然后将每个抽样的幅值用数字化表示。这将涉及量化过程,即用有限个数字量化等级来表示无限种幅值大小。量化过程如图 1 所示。

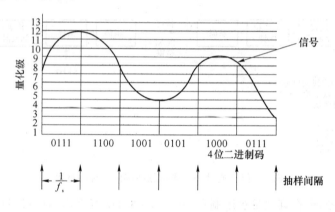

图 1 模拟信号的量化

抽样定理告诉我们,要想在接收端无损地重建模拟信号,抽样频率必须大于或等于要抽样信号最高频率的两倍。由于话音频带的带宽为 300~3 400 Hz,因此 PCM 的抽样频率取为 8 000 Hz。

3. 量化

接下来要解决的问题是:需要多少个量化等级才能足够准确地表示信号幅值呢?如果量化级差较粗,会由于量化噪声导致信号损坏。一方面,由于量化过程固有的原因,造成实际信号和再生信号的存在差别,从而导致了量化噪声。另一方面,表示量化等级需要多少个二进制数与量化过程中的等级数有关。这样,如果量化级差分得太细,则用于表示每个抽样幅值的二进制编码数量过多。通过实践发现,256 个幅值等级就足以达到可接受的话音质量,每个抽样需 $\log_2 256 = 8$ 个二进制数表示。然而,在信号的所有幅值范围内,量化级差并不是均匀的,信号幅值越大级差间隔越大。这将确保话音信号全动态范围内的量化误差为一个大体上的恒定值。

因为非线性量化等级的作用是在传输时压缩大的幅值信号,而在接收端扩展,这个过程称为"压缩扩展"。

4. 压缩扩展

为了实现对大幅值信号的压缩,可采用对数函数的特性。然而,如图 2 所示,函数 $y=$

$\log x$ 不能通过原点。因此必须将 x 的低值线性部分替换成曲线。大多数实际的压缩扩展系统都是基于 K. W. Cattermole 提出的 A 律实现的。

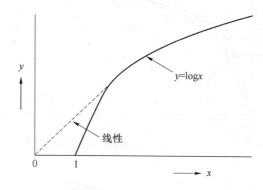

图 2　$y=\log x$ 函数

A 为压缩系数，曲线在 $x=1/A$ 处连续，如图 3 所示。

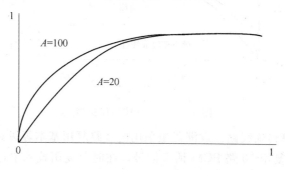

图 3　Cattermole 的压扩定律

在实际使用 A 律时，需要按照线性量化对非线性信号进行处理。非线性变换和在接收端进行的非线性反变换存在很多问题。因此，通常采用分段线性近似表示 A 律。常采用两段线性律。欧洲使用的是 CCITT 的 A 律压缩扩展。A 律压缩扩展的每一级由 8 段线性段组成，除最低的两段外，每一段的斜率都减半，如图 4 所示。用 3 比特表示段，段又分为 16 个线性级，用另外 4 比特表示；最后，用 1 比特定义信号的极性，这样共用 8 比特表示完整的一段。因为全部曲线共有 13 个线性段，A 律压缩扩展常被称为 13 段压缩扩展。A 律压缩扩展的压缩效率约为 87.6。美国使用的是 μ 律压缩扩展，与 A 律略有不同。如图 4 所示，μ 律 8 段的斜率又减半了，其他部分与 A 律近似。因为全部曲线共有 15 个线性段，μ 律压缩扩展常被称为 15 段压缩扩展。

在模数转换过程中，分段线性压缩扩展很容易实现。当信号抽样从一段到另一段，只需加倍模数转换器的级差大小。

5. PCM 帧结构

在每秒 8 000 次采样并用 8 bit 表示每个采样值的情况下，传输 PCM 语音信号的二进制数据速率为 64 kbit/s。该速率构成了所有 PCM 传输的基础，是公认的 PCM 国际标准。

PCM 在电话网中的汇接和中继传输中有着广泛的应用。在汇接和中继链路中，PCM 不是用来确定到每一个单一电话通话的传输路由。而是采用多路复用的方法，将多个话音

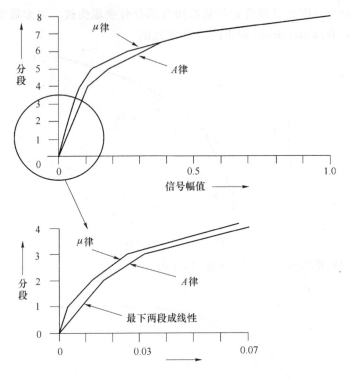

图 4　A 律与 μ 律压缩扩展

信道复用在一起，共享传输线路。欧洲普遍采用的多路复用基本等级是用时分复用(TDM)的方法在一条基带上复用 30 路 PCM 话音信号。在时分复用技术中，用一个 8 比特八位组代表一个采样值，这些八位组从每个信号采样值转换获得并按照顺序在信道中传输。除了表示语音信号的比特外，还必须传送用于指示采样值是按何种复用方式的信息，只有知道该信息，当传输完成后才能把复用信号解复用并分发给正确的接收端。

网络需要的信号路由信息也需要传送，这些信号分别为同步信号和信令数据。虽然只需要 30 路语音信道，但为了将这些信息统一复用到复用信号中，因此 PCM 提供了 32 个时隙。这 32 个时隙通常编号为 0～31。0 号时隙用于传输帧同步信息，16 号时隙用作传输信令信息。1～15 号和 17～31 号时隙用来传输话音信号。基本帧结构如图 5 所示。

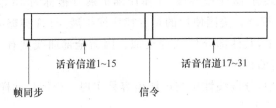

图 5　PCM 基本帧结构

每帧包含 32×8＝256 bit，传送每个话音信道中的一个采样。因此，所需的总传输速率为 256×8 k＝2.048 Mbit/s。该速率通常称为"一次群速率"，因为它代表同步数字体系(SDH)中所使用的第一个复用等级。

在北美和日本，复用的一次群包括 24 个语音信号和为每 24×8 k 比特帧同步的一个比特,故帧的大小为 193 比特。因此,所需的总传输速率为 $193 \times 8 \text{ k} = 1.544 \text{ Mbit/s}$。在该系统中,信令信息被整合入了信息载荷的八位组。英国早期也使用过 24 信道的系统,用每个八位字节的第八位传输信令和同步信息,其余七位仅用来表示信号的每一个 PCM 采样。因此,其量化噪声是采用 8 比特量化时的两倍。这种系统所需的总传输速率为 $24 \times 8 \times 8 \text{ k} = 1.536 \text{ Mbit/s}$。然而,现在英国所有的 24 信道系统都被符合 CCITT 标准的 30 信道系统所取代。

6. 信令和同步

现在我们详细考虑包含在 PCM 帧 30 个时隙中的第 0 和 16 时隙的信令和同步信号。包含在连续帧的间隔第 0 时隙的帧对准规律如图 6 所示。

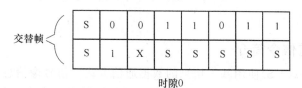

注:S=空闲的,可用来传递数据;
X=正常为0,用作远程告警时变换为1。

图 6 帧对准规律

在帧结构中,一些比特不属于特定规律的组成部分,(所以)这些比特位就可以用来承载数据。为了对远端站点告警表明(其)帧对准(信号)的丢失,在每个交替帧中有一位用来作为远程告警信号。

通常,包含在时隙 16 中的信道信令有两种不同的使用方法:最早的和目前应用最广泛的两种。目前应用最广泛的称为"信道相关信令"。信道相关信令被合并成一个 16 帧的复帧结构。这些帧从 0 到 15 顺序编号。0 号帧的时隙 16 的前 4 个比特包含了 4 个连续的 0 的复帧告警规律,如图 7(a) 所示。时隙 16 的另外 4 个比特中的 3 个比特是空闲的,可以用来传输用户数据,第 8 比特用来作复帧对准的信号远程丢失表示。

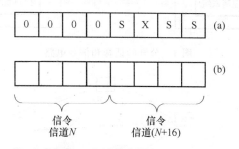

注:S=空闲的,可用来传递数据;
X=正常为0,用作复帧排列时为1。

图 7 时隙 16 的位排列

在帧 1~15,时隙 16 被划分为 2 个 4 比特的子域,如图 7 所示。前 4 个比特用来传输信道 N 的信令,后 4 个比特用来传输信道 $N+16$ 的信令。每个信道分配给 4 个比特的信令(容量),信令信息每隔 16 帧可以更新(一次),即每隔 2 ms 更新(一次)。每信道 4 比特信令有 15 种可能的状态。全 0 组合从不使用,因为这样有可能和复帧对准方式混淆。

利用现代数字交换系统，把信令信道仅仅作为信息传输工具使其利用率更高是可能的，信令信息的初始化是交换设备的功能。

这意味着某一特定信道对应的信令信息只有在那个信道的状态改变时才被需要（传送）。这样，就可以避免重复传送信令信息以及与信令相关的信道特性信息。这项技术称为公共信道信令。应用于数字交换网络的国际电联的公共信道信令称为7号信令系统。7号信令系统的操作是基于数据分组概念的。在我们完成学习数字交换网络的操作原理之前，暂缓详细学习7号信令系统。

第4单元 公共信道信令

1. 公共信道信令简介

公共信道信令（CCS）使用基于信息的数据通信方式。信号像信息一样在程控交换机的控制系统之间进行传送。信息数据字段的信息不仅仅可以用来表示信号，也可以用来识别与它有关的呼叫，所以公共信道信令就从话音通道中分离出来了（这也是其名字的来源）。所以，在两个交换机之间，多个话音信道的信令可以放在单个信令信道上，如图1所示。更进一步地，由于共路信令的处理速度依赖于计算机的处理速度，所以两个交换机之间直接的信令电路连接不是必需的。当然，一旦信令传输部分从话音传输系统中分离出来，则可能产生一个独立的信令网络。比如，图2就表示了7个交换机通过独立的话音和信令网络互联在一起。信令网络的尺寸计算不仅仅依靠承载容量和经济学的计算，也依赖于安全性等因素。

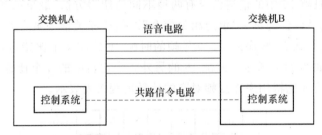

图1 分开的话音和信令电路

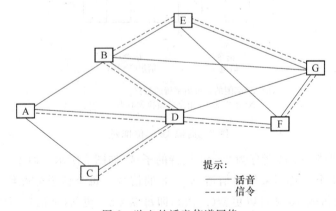

图2 独立的话音信道网络

公共信道信令克服了所有随路信令的不足。考虑到这些不足,共路信令的优点包括以下几点:

(i) 由于共路信令在处理器之间直接使用数字传输,所以速度很快。

(ii) 共路信令的信号指令系统由于仅仅依赖于数据字段的尺寸,所以可能很庞大。

(iii) 考虑到上面第二条,信号指令系统的扩充将不受限于技术约束,而仅仅受限于国际协议。

(iv) 指令系统将不仅为电话提供信令服务,也为所有的业务提供信令服务。

(v) 信令网的高速度和方便性便捷了网管信号的传送。

(vi) 由于信令信号链路独立于话音通道,所以信令信号可随时传送。

(vii) 由于信令信号不通过话音通道传送,所以信令信号对用户来说是不可见的。

(viii) 信息的传输依赖于同步的准确性,但是当有问题出现时可以很快地检测到错误并自动地纠正。单个信息内置的纠错能力可以实现检测,还可以通过网络自身的多个自检错机制实现。

(ix) 在共路信令系统中,由于几百比特的信息包括了建立一个呼叫所需的所有信息,所以一个单独的信令信道可以容纳下与许多个话音信道有关的信令信息。因此,信令信道得到了充分的利用;不像随路信令系统中没有为话音信道分配永久的信令信道。因此,共路信令系统中信令信道的容量计算是基于流量基础的。

除此之外,由于共路信令是直接在处理器之间进行传输的,信号由软件直接处理,所以不需要那些随路信令系统中必需的、大量的、昂贵的、占据大量空间的设备。

如上所述,相比早期的随路信令,共路信令具有很多的优点。重要的是,它避免了对大部分噪声抑制电路信令设备的使用,而这些设备对于随路信令来说是必需的,这也反过来降低了它的整个系统成本。共路信令系统的一个更重要的特点是它(具有)庞大的信令信息集。在早期的模拟随路信令系统中,能被传送的信号数量是有限的,传送速度也慢。比如,在多频信令系统中,其指令集只有 16 个指令码。在这个系统中一个信号相当于 4 bit 信息,并且,需要 100 ms 时间去传送它,比特率是 40 bit/s。在共路信令系统中用户线信令的速度典型地可达到每秒 64 kbit/s。

这种高速度(相当于一个非常高速的信令带宽)对于许多基于 ISDN 的新业务来说是非常重要的。在这些业务中,要使一个呼叫进行下去,节点间需要传输的信息量至少要在 1 000 bit 以上。如果这些信息以随路信令系统的速度传输,呼叫建立的延时将会过长,这对于用户来说是无法接受的。

对于电话信令的历史来说,共路信令的开发是一个巨大的突破。因为共路信令是跨处理器的系统,独立于交换或传输技术,所以不需要和电话系统的每个发展同步。这样就可以制定对所有应用保持不变的标准。因此,世界上第一次有了一个既可以应用在国内网络,又可以用在国际网络上的系统。实际上,国际电信联盟的 7 号信令就是一个既可以应用在国内网络,又可以应用于国际网络上的系统。它也常常被扩展从而为新业务和网络管理提供信令。共路信令也常常应用在用户和本地交换机之间,它使用的是综合业务数字网架构。

2. 国际电信联盟的公共信道信令 7 号信令

国际电联 7 号信令系统现在是国际上接受的、交换机间的共路信令系统,可以应用在国内网和国际网中。图 3 是一个交换机间 7 号信令链路的简化示意图。信令在交换机间的、

PCM 系统承载话音的信道中通过某一特定时隙进行传输。在 2 个 2 Mbit/s 系统中,承载 60 多个话音信道,其中一个 PCM 系统在第 16 时隙承载 7 号信令链路。信令被提取出来后通过交换机的交换模块插入到 2 Mbit/s 系统中,如图 3 所示。

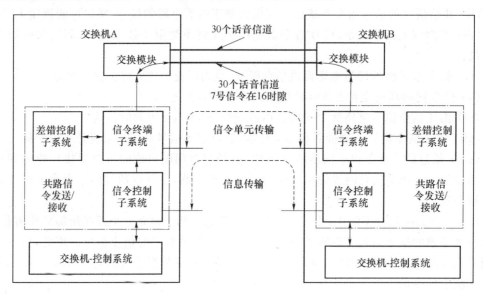

图 3　国际电联 7 号信令系统简化示意图

信令信息从一个交换机到另一个交换机的传送由交换机控制系统规划控制,然后传送到 7 号信令共路信令发送器/接收器(CCS S/R)。共路信令发送器/接收器包括 3 个子系统:信令控制子系统、信令终端子系统和差错控制子系统,所有这些子系统都是基于微处理器(控制的)。来自交换机控制系统的信息由信令控制子系统接收,在这里把信息组装成合适的格式。然后信息被缓存下来直到被发送出去。当没有信息要发送时,信令控制子系统产生填充信息以使得链路处于活动状态。图 3 中,虚线标记的信息传送标识了信令信息的源和目的。

然后信息被传送到信令终端子系统,在这里使用信息序号和由错误控制子系统产生的检测比特信息被组装成完整的 7 号信令单元。图 3 中,标记信令单元传输的虚线表明了信令单元的真实来源和目的地(与包含了基本信息的报文不同)。

在接收端,交换机执行与上述相反的流程。由于国际电联 7 号信令对于数字程控交换网络很重要,所以将在下面的几个部分对它的体系结构和操作进行讨论。

把一个系统模型化为协议栈是信令系统设计者使用的一种技术。这里,"协议"指的是通信双方需要遵守的一系列规则。协议栈使用了数据抽象的原理:栈中的每个协议层是从它的上层和下层中抽象出来的。因此,协议栈(这种形式)允许设计者把信令系统所需的功能划分成单独的模块,每个可管理部分和它的上、下层之间进行信息交换,所以可对每个模块进行单独开发。协议栈把设计划分成几个层,形成一个概念塔。上层的设计依据了这样一个假设:每个低层协议能无差错地执行一定的功能。例如,如果一个低层负责信息传输过程中错误纠正,则它的上层就会假设它通过低层传输或接收的信息是没有错误的。因此,每一层都依赖它下面的那些层,并且,当提到第 N 层时,第一层到第 N 层的功能也都假设包含在里面了。

图 4 是国际电联 7 号信令的传统协议栈结构。从图中可以看出:"level"被用来描述前面提到的"layer"的含义。传统模型有 4 个层。

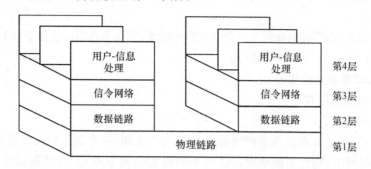

图 4 4 层协议栈体系结构

(1) 第 1 层:物理承载层

第 1 层位于协议栈的底层。概括来说,它是把信息比特流从物理连接上的一点送往另一点的手段。在这一层,对信息的结构形式没有定义或要求,也没有错误检测机制,除非传输设备能提供(这样的功能)。

(2) 第 2 层:数据链路层

第 2 层接受第 1 层的支持,提供基本的信令链路。具体地说,该层的功能是:差错控制、链路初始化、错误率监测、流量控制和信令信息的定界。

(3) 第 3 层:信令网络层

在一个国家电信网络内部有几千部公共交换机,信令信息必须能够在它们之间进行灵活、安全的传送。7 号信令系统的第 3 层提供了信令网络管理所需的功能。

(4) 第 4 层:用户层

在 7 号信令传统框架结构中,第 4 层称为用户部分。它包括了一些专门处理业务的过程,而这些业务受到信令系统的控制。在用户部分分别定义和设计了 3 个过程,目的是为了支持电话业务、数据业务和基于 ISDN 的业务,这 3 个过程是:电话用户部分(TUP)、数据用户部分(DUP)和综合业务数字网用户部分(ISDN-UP)。因此,信息传输部分(MTP)支持多方用户的能力是至关重要的。有了用户部分提供的灵活性和扩展性,7 号信令就能够(具有)处理一些新产生业务(的能力)。如果网络要演进到全 ISDN 网络,这个能力是必不可少的。的确,运用 7 号信令软件控制的新业务,只需要对交换机的硬件进行很少的改动就可以了,这降低了引入业务的成本和复杂性。这在早期的随路信令系统中是不可能的。早期的随路信令被调整到与它协同工作的传输和交换系统相匹配,并且它的信息指令系统还极度受限。

3. 共路信令网络

与随路信令不同,共路信令为网络管理者提供了开发一个单独信令网络的可能性。如图 2 所示,这来源于信令和相关业务信道的分离(现实)。一个信令网络包括了信令节点,这些节点位于交换机内部,是交换机系统的一部分,它们由传输网络提供的信令链路连接在一起。

开发一个单独的共路信令网络的优点在于它可以:

(i) 使共路信令的(强大)能力被完全开发出来;

(ii) 共路信令链路可以被优化使用从而更经济；

(iii) 使用共路信令系统的安全保障部分和线路组的可选路由可以获得较高的系统恢复能力。

信令节点(或者,在国际电联的 7 号信令系统中的术语"信令点")可能位于以下几个地方：

(i) 交换单元(本地、支局和国际局)；

(ii) 操作、管理和维护中心；

(iii) 智能网数据所在地；

(iv) 信号传输点。

一些情况下,某个节点是两个网络的公共节点。比如,一个国际网关交换机既连接国内网络也连接国际网络(则此交换机就是这两个网络的公共节点)。在共路信令系统中,所有的信令点都会被分配一个编码,信令点就是通过这个编码被寻址到的。在上面谈论到的情况中,国际交换机将会被分配给两个信令点编码,一个是国内网络的,一个是国际网络的。

共路信令系统的链路和相关业务信道有 3 种形式的关系,简单地,就是以下 3 种。

(i) 关联式。在关联方式中,与两交换机间相关业务电路有关的信息直接使用信令链路进行传输,这些信令链路位于两个交换机之间,如图 5(a)所示。

(ii) 非关联式。图 5(b)所示就是非关联式方式。A 和 B 之间的信令信息按照当时的网络状况通过几个信令链路进行路由,而业务信息在 A 和 B 之间直接进行路由。在不同的时间,共路信令系统的(信令)信息可能按照不同的路径进行路由转发。这种方法不常使用,因为在某一给定时间信令信息的确切路由的确定比较困难。

(iii) 半关联式。这是一种非关联式的受限情况,节点 A 和 B 之间的信令信息沿着事先确定好的路由线路进行传输(该路线链接了支局内的几个信令链路),如图 5(c)所示,而业务信息则在 A 和 B 之间直接进行传输。通常,共路信令和其相关业务链路使用不同的传输承载信道。

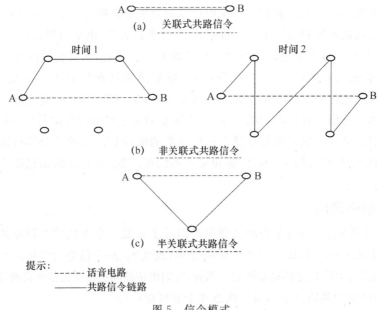

图 5　信令模式

关联式操作一般应用于交换机间的业务路由较大的情况下。比如,在两个交换机间有200个电路的情况下,需要7个2 Mbit/s数字传输系统,其中一个2 Mbit/s系统在第16时隙承载一个单独的共路信令链路。但是,在网络具有较小业务路由能力的情况下,为每个业务路由提供共路信令端口的开销(较大),只能降低(标准)到使用半关联式操作了。不过,半关联式操作的最重要使用场合是作为一种安全备份方式,下面将讨论这种使用方式。

在以上的例子中,承载共路信令链路的PCM系统的故障不但会导致30个业务电路的信息丢失,而且也会导致其余170个电路的信令信息的丢失,尽管这170个电路是没有故障的。为了把发生这种故障的风险降到可以接受的程度,使用了承载共路信令的链路替代方式。最常用的方法是:当主要的关联式路由链路发生故障时,可以在半关联式链路上重新路由共路信令(来弥补损失)。

除了重新路由(当主要的共路信令链路出现故障时,系统可通过程序自动触发重新路由机制)之外,还可以通过在两个或多个并行相关链路上持续发送共路信令信息来提高网络的恢复能力。这样,在以上例子中,200个业务电路的信令可以通过两个共路信令链路来传输,该信令链路位于2M系统的第16时隙。理想地,为了保证最大的安全性,这两个共路信令链路使用物理上分离的电路承载。

图6给出了一个共路信令系统网络恢复能力的例子,在图6中,节点A和B通过一个网状网连接在一起。正常情况下从A到B的共路信令是按照ACDB的顺序转发的,如果AC、CD、DB中的某一条出现了故障,则选择的替代链路可能是AEFB、ACFB或ACDFB。

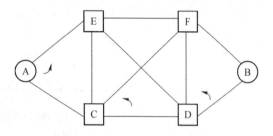

提示: ↙ 替代的共路信令链路路由
—— 主要的路由路径

图6 网状网的信令方式举例

第5单元 抽样定理

在一定的条件下,一个连续时间信号完全可以由该信号在时间等间隔点上的瞬时值或样本值来表示,并且能用这些样本值恢复出原信号来。这个有点奇特的性质是根据抽样定理的基本结论所得出的。这个定理极其重要且非常有用。例如,抽样定理在电影里得到了应用。电影由一组按时序排列的单个画面所组成,其中每一个画面都代表着连续变化景象中的一个瞬时画面(即时间样本)。当以极快的速度来顺次观察这些瞬时画面时,我们感觉到的就是对原来连续活动场景的一个准确再现。

抽样定理的重要性还很大程度上体现在:它起着连接连续时间信号和离散时间信号之间的桥梁作用。在一定的条件下,可用信号的时序样本值完全恢复出原连续时间信号的事实,提供了用一个离散时间信号来表示一个连续时间信号的机理。在许多方面,处理离散时间信号要更加灵活些,因此往往比处理连续时间(信号)更为可取。这主要归功于在过去几十年中高速发展的数字技术,使我们可以得到价格低廉、质量较轻、易于编程并且可重复使用的离散时间系统处理芯片。通过抽样,将连续时间信号转换为离散时间信号,再利用离散时间系统来处理离散时间信号,然后将其转换回连续时间信号。

抽样定理表述如下:设 $x(t)$ 是一个带宽受限信号,当 $|\omega|>\omega_m$,$X(j\omega)=0$,若 $\omega_s>2\omega_m$,其中 $\omega_s=2\pi/T$,则 $x(t)$ 可以被其抽样值 $x(nT)$ 唯一地确定,其中 $n=0,\pm 1,\pm 2,\cdots$

已知这些样本值,我们可以用以下方法重构 $x(t)$:产生一个周期的脉冲序列,其中脉冲的幅度等于依次而来的样本值。然后将脉冲序列通过一个增益为 T,截止频率大于 ω_m,而小于 $\omega_s-\omega_m$ 的理想低通滤波器,产生的输出信号将精确的等于 $x(t)$。

由抽样定理可知:抽样频率必须超过 $2\omega_m$。通常将 $2\omega_m$ 频率称为 Nyquist 抽样率。

在前面的讨论中,假设抽样频率足够高,从而满足抽样定理的条件。如图 1 所示,若 $\omega_s>2\omega_m$,取样(后的)信号的频谱就是对原信号 $x(t)$ 频谱的周期性延拓。这就构成了抽样定理的基础。当 $\omega_s<2\omega_m$ 时,$x(t)$ 的频谱 $X(j\omega)$,不再被 $X_P(j\omega)$ 所复制,也无法由低通滤波器恢复。重建的信号也不再等于 $x(t)$,这种现象称为频谱混叠。

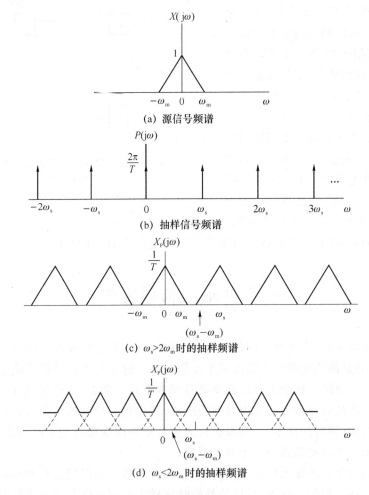

(a) 源信号频谱

(b) 抽样信号频谱

(c) $\omega_s>2\omega_m$ 时的抽样频谱

(d) $\omega_s<2\omega_m$ 时的抽样频谱

图 1 时域抽样在频域上的结果

抽样有许多重要的应用。一些特别重要的应用是利用微型计算机、微处理器,或任何一种专门用于离散时间信号处理的器件,通过抽样来处理连续时间信号。

第 6 单元　光波系统的发展变革

　　光纤通信系统的研究大约始于 1975 年。该系统从 1975 直到 2000 年这 25 年间的巨大发展可以划分为特点鲜明的数个技术发展阶段。图 1 显示了在这段时间内,不同实验室给出的 BL 乘积随时间的变化规律。图中直线表示 BL 乘积以每年增长一倍的趋势发展。在每个不同的技术阶段,BL 乘积最初呈增大趋势,然而随着技术的成熟,该阶段的 BL 值将会趋于饱和,增长速度变缓。每一代新技术将会对上一代技术带来根本性的变革,这些变革将会进一步提升系统的性能。

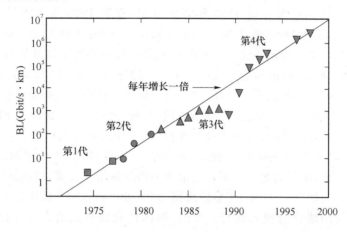

图 1　在 1975 年至 2000 年期间,BL 乘积随数代光波系统的增长。
不同的图形符号表示不同的技术发展阶段

　　第一代光波系统工作于 $0.8~\mu m$,采用的是 GaAs 半导体激光器。该系统通过 1977—1979 年几次现场实验后于 1980 年商用,其数据传输率为 45 Mbit/s,中继距离可达 10 km。该系统远长于同轴系统 1 km 的中继距离是设计者的一大动力,因为较长的中继距离意味着与每一中继器相关的安装、维护成本的降低。

　　在 20 世纪 70 年代,通过使光波系统工作在损耗低于 1 dB/km 的 $1.3~\mu m$ 附近的波长范围内可以显著增加中继距离,这一点是显而易见的。而且光纤在这一波段内还有较低的色散特性。因此这就激发了世界范围内对工作于 $1.3~\mu m$ 的 InGaAsP 半导体激光器和探测器的研制。在 20 世纪 80 年代,第二代光纤通信系统得以商用化,但由于模间色散的影响,该系统的传输速率被限制在 100 Mbit/s 以内。单模光纤可以克服这种限制。1981 年,实验验证了采用单模光纤实现 44 km,2 Gbit/s 速率的传输。随后就商用化了该系统。直到 1987 年,速率高达 1.7 Gbit/s,中继距离为 50 km 的第二代光波系统才商用化。

　　第二代光波系统的中继距离主要由其工作在 $1.3~\mu m$ 波段内的损耗所限制(典型损耗值为 0.5 dB/km)。石英光纤在 $1.55~\mu m$ 波段内的损耗最小。实际上,在 1979 年,在这一波段就实现了 0.2 dB/km 的损耗。然而,第三代光波系统由于在 $1.55~\mu m$ 波段内存在较大的色散,因此未能很快推广。常规的 InGaAsP 半导体激光器不能用于第三代光波系统,因为该激光器中多纵模的同时振荡会引起脉冲的展宽。色散问题可以通过设计在 $1.55~\mu m$ 波段内的色散位移光纤或采用单纵模激光器来解决。这两种方法在20世纪80年代相继出现。直到1985年，实验室完成了高达10 Gbit/s传输速率的实验。最佳工作状态是同时采用色散位移光纤和单纵模激光来实现的。

第三代1.55 μm光波系统的缺点是其信号每60～70 km就需要电中继器对其进行恢复。中继距离可以通过零差或外差检测方式来提高，因为这两种方式提高了接收机的灵敏度。这种类型的光波系统被称为相干光波系统。20世纪80年代，相干光波系统在世界范围内得到广泛研究，它们潜在优点在许多实验中都得到证实。尽管如此，该系统的商用化直到1989年随着光纤放大器的出现才得以实现。

第四代光波系统采用光放大器用以延长中继距离，利用波分复用系统来增加比特率。对于大部分波分复用系统，光纤损耗都是由间隔为60～80 km放置的掺铒光纤放大器来周期性地进行补偿。这些放大器是1985年开始研制，直到1990年才满足商用化的要求。1991年的实验利用环形结构装置实现了21 000 km, 2.5 Gbit/s和14 300 km, 5 Gbit/s的数据传输。这个性能指标表明基于光放大器的全光海底传输系统可用来进行洲际间的通信。到1996年，不仅可以用实际的海底光缆以5 Gbit/s的速率传播11 300 km，而且穿越大西洋和太平洋的光缆系统也开始商用。从那时起，就在世界范围内大量铺设海底光波系统。

1998年，连接亚洲和欧洲国家27 000 km的"环球"光纤链路（简称为FLAG）就已投入运行。另一个较大的光波系统，非洲1号系统在2000年正式投入运行，这个系统覆盖了非洲大陆，传输总距离可达35 000 km。在1998年至2001年期间，大西洋和太平洋区域铺设了多个波分复用系统，用于满足互联网对通信速率的急速增长需求，这些系统极大地提高了系统的通信容量。预期在2002年，传输距离高达250 000 km，速率高达2.56 Tbit/s的真正意义上的全球光波网络将会投入运行。显然，第四代光波系统给光纤通信带来技术上的革新。

第五代光波系统致力于扩展可用于波分复用系统的波段宽度。传统的波段窗口，也就是C波段，只包括1.53～1.57 μm的波长范围。向长波长和短波长扩展的波段，分别称为L波段和S波段。Raman放大技术可用以这3个波段的信号放大。同时，一种新型的光纤——无水光纤——也已开始铺设，这种光纤具有在1.30～1.65 μm整个波段内都有较小损耗的特性。这种光纤的使用以及新型放大技术的出现会成千上万地提高波分复用系统的信道数量。

同时，第五代光波系统也致力于提高波分复用系统中单个信道的比特率。从2000年开始，多个实验室就完成了单信道为40 Gbit/s的波分复用系统实验，可以预见160 Gbit/s的单信道速率也可实现。这些系统需要有非常好的色散管理技术。一个非常有趣的方法是采用光孤子技术，这种技术利用光纤的色散和其非线性效应相互抵消的特性，因而在无损光纤中可保持其特定波形进行传输。虽然早在1973年就提出了这一基本思想，但直到1988年在实验室中进行的一次试验才证明，通过拉曼放大来补偿光纤损耗，使数据传输4 000 km成为可能。1989年，推出了利用掺铒光纤放大器用以放大光孤子的技术。随后，许多试验验证了光孤子通信的可行性。1994年，实现了35 000 km, 10 Gbit/s以及24 000 km, 15 Gbit/s的光孤子传输。1996年，采用色散补偿技术，实现了波分复用与光孤子相结合的应用。2000年，利用混合放大技术，实现了单信道20 Gbit/s，传输距离超过9 000 km的27信道波分复用技术。

尽管光纤通信技术的发展只有短短的25年的时间（截至2000年），然而它发展飞速，且日臻完善。从 1995 年,大量刊发的光纤通信和波分复用网络的书籍也印证了该技术的飞速发展。

第 7 单元 光 纤

作为通信方式的一种变革,利用光纤进行信息传输已经发展成熟。光纤通信系统具有带宽极宽,抗干扰能力强,不易被捕获,保密性好,价格低廉等优点。可以说,硅是地球上含量最丰富的物质。

1. 光纤系统基础

光纤材料本身可以导引光线,因为当光线从一种介质进入另一种介质时会发生弯曲或者说改变方向。弯曲的原因是光在不同介质中的传播速度不同,这种现象称为折射。发生折射的一个最常见的例子是当你站在水池边看水底的物体,总是看起来比实际要远一些,除非你站在物体的正上方。发生这种现象是从物体发出的光线由水面入射到空气时速度增加,使得它们发生了弯曲,改变了你观察这个物体的角度。你可以利用光传播所遵循的斯涅尔定律来解释这个现象。

2. 斯涅尔定律

光纤的工作原理可以利用斯涅尔定律解释:入射角与折射角正弦之比等于光波在这两种介质中的传播速度之比。这个比值等于一个常数,即介质 2 与介质 1 的折射率之比。斯涅尔定律可写为如下公式:

$$\frac{\sin A_1}{\sin A_2} = \frac{v_1}{v_2} = K = \frac{n_2}{n_1} \tag{1}$$

式中,A_1,A_2 分别为入射角和折射角,v_1,v_2 是光波在这两种介质中的传播速度,n_1,n_2 则是两种介质的折射率。

图 1 在几何上解释了这些参数的关系。任一情况下,A_1 为入射角而 A_2 为折射角。介质 1 的折射率 n_1 大于介质 2 的折射率 n_2。这就意味着,光在介质 2 中的传播速度比在介质 1 中大。

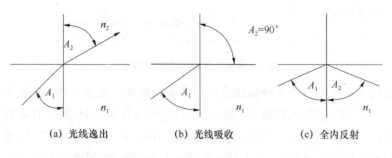

(a) 光线逸出 (b) 光线吸收 (c) 全内反射

图 1 折射率 ($n_1 > n_2$)

图 1(a)说明光线从介质 1 入射到介质 2,如果 A_1 小于临界角,就会通过折射进入介质 2。图 1(b)表示入射角为临界角,A_2 为 90°的情况。光线将沿着两种介质的分界面传播。

如图 1(c)所示，所有以大于图 1(b)中 A_1 角度入射的光线都被反射回介质 1，且 $A_2 = A_1$。满足图 1(c)所示条件是光纤特性之一。

3. 光纤组成

光纤是玻璃或塑料制成的一种绝缘介质波导。它由三部分组成：纤芯、包层和涂覆层。涂覆层用以保护光纤，但不决定光纤的传输能力。

沿着光纤半径方向的不同部分折射率也不同。纤芯折射率 n_c 为一常数或呈平滑降低，包层折射率为另一常数 n。折射率存在差异，可以使进入的光线一直保持在纤芯中传输，即使光纤发生弯曲或者打结。对于可以同时传输多个模式光信号的光纤（称为多模光纤）来说，纤芯直径是所传输光波波长的很多倍。波长指的是同一光波在两个相邻周期间的距离，用纳米（也就是十亿分之一米）来表示。包层的厚度要比纤芯直径大得多。以下是一种多模光纤的典型参数值。

- 工作波长：$0.8\ \mu m$；
- 纤芯折射率 n_c：1.5；
- 包层折射率：1.485（约为 $0.99 n_c$）；
- 纤芯直径：$50/62.5/100\ \mu m$；
- 包层厚度：$37.5\ \mu m$。

光纤包层直径为 $125\ \mu m$，光线如图 2 所示方式传输。

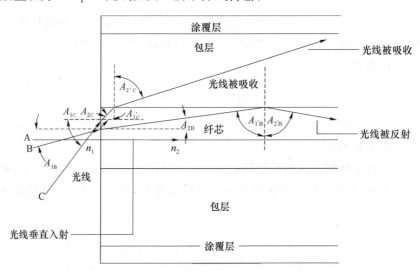

图 2 多模光纤中光线传播路径

光纤发出的光信号相对于光纤轴线呈现很多不同角度。在图 2 中，光线 A 垂直纤芯端面入射，与光纤轴线平行，其入射角 A_1 为 0，因而，它不会发生折射，将一直沿着与光纤轴线平行的方向传播。光线 B 从空气中以 A_{1B} 角度入射，由于 n_2 大于 n_1，将以 A_{2B} 角度折射。当光线遇到纤芯和包层的分界面时，其入射角度 $A_{1'B}$ 大于临界角，因此反射角 $A_{2'B}=A_{1'B}$，光线被反射回纤芯，光线便以这种 Z 字形折线沿着纤芯传输，直至光纤终端。

如果入射角度 A_{1C} 太大了，就像光线 C 那样，当光线遇到纤芯-包层分界面时，将会以小于临界角的 $A_{1'C}$ 入射，光线将有一部分进入包层，在包层中传输或被不透明的涂覆层所吸收。

4. 模式延迟

当光纤直径远大于所传输光波的波长时,光束沿着光纤在芯-包分界面上来回地反射。从光纤的一端传至另一端时,以不同的角度入射的光线发生折射的次数不同。因此,到达远端时其相位关系也与开始时不同。不同的入纤角度称为不同的传输模式(或简称模)。能传输多个模式的光纤就是多模光纤。多模传输导致光线离开光纤终端时既可能干涉相长也可能干涉相消。这种情况叫做模式延迟展宽。

由于大多数光纤通信系统都是以光脉冲这种数字形式传输信息的,所以模式延迟限制了光纤传输可识别脉冲的容量。这是由于图 3 所示的模式延迟在时域展宽了脉冲。

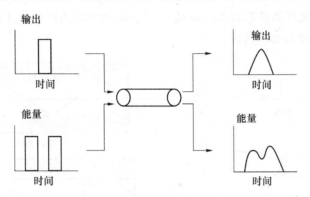

图 3 脉冲展宽

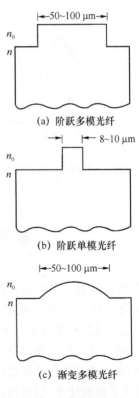

(a) 阶跃多模光纤

(b) 阶跃单模光纤

(c) 渐变多模光纤

图 4 折射率剖面

脉冲展宽的影响在于经过一段距离的传输后光接收机很难或几乎不可能将两个脉冲区分开来。这样,经过一段确定的传输距离后,多模光纤要么会引起误码率的提高,要么使脉冲的可识别能力降低,限制了通信能力。

如果纤芯的直径可与传播光波的波长相比拟(比如说是 3 倍),只有一种模式可以传输,并且在光线之间不会产生干涉相消。这些光纤被称为单模光纤,是大多数传输系统所采用的传输媒介。图 4(a)和图 4(b)给出了折射率沿多模光纤与单模光纤的分布,以及它们的典型直径值。单、多模光纤最重要的一个区别是多模光纤中能量大部分在纤芯中传输,而单模光纤中相当大一部分能量在靠近纤芯的包层中传输。增大波长直至满足单模传输临界点时,约 20%的能量在包层中;将波长继续增大一倍,则超过 50%的能量都在包层中传输。

5. 折射率

光纤也可根据折射率分布不同进行分类。图 5 示例了几种分类,列举如下。

➢阶跃光纤:纤芯折射率均匀分布,在纤芯-包层分界面上有一(折射率)突变。
➢渐变光纤:纤芯折射率随与光纤轴心距离的增加而梯度减小。
➢单模光纤:也叫单色模光纤,折射率均布。这种光纤只允许一种光线通过。
➢渐变多模光纤:折射率沿纤芯直径方向光滑变化,包层折射率为常数,这样的处理使不同的光线传输时有近乎相等的时延,减小了光纤的模式色散。

其他类型折射率剖面用以解决不同的问题,例如减小色度色散。图 5 给出了这些光纤剖面,为了比较,又重复了一次阶跃剖面和渐变剖面。

图 6 比较了阶跃、渐变和单模光纤中光线的传播轨迹。阶跃光纤典型纤芯在 100 μm 到 500 μm 之间,渐变光纤的纤芯为 50 μm 或 62.5 μm,而单模光纤的尺寸在 8~10 μm。阶跃光纤和渐变光纤都支持多模传输。

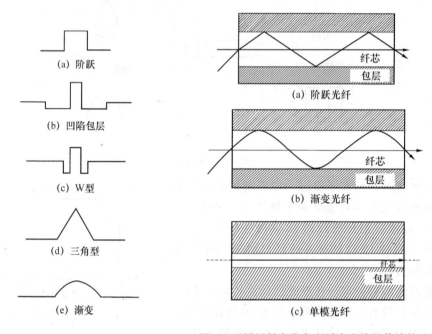

图 5　各种不同折射率剖面　　图 6　不同折射率分布光纤中光线的传输轨迹

第 8 单元　同步数字系列

SDH 即同步数字系列,是用于高速同步光电信网络的国际标准。

1986 年 6 月,国际电话电报顾问委员会(CCITT)第十八研究小组开始了同步数字系列标准的制定。其目标是制定一个同步传输系统的全球标准,该标准可提供给网络运营者以灵活、经济的方式对网络进行管理。

1988 年 11 月,通过了首批同步数字系列标准,它们分别是 G.707,G.708,G.709。这些标准定义了传输速率、信号格式、复用结构,以及用于网络节点接口的支路映射,其中网络节点接口是用于同步数字系列的国际标准接口。

除制定了包括网络节点接口的标准之外,CCITT 还着手制定了决定同步数字系列同步复用运行(如 G.781、G.782、G.783),以及网络管理的一系列标准(如 G.784)。正是由于 SDH 设备在这些方面的标准化,才提供了网络运营者所期待的灵活性,从而能低价高效地应付带宽方面的增长并为今后十年中将出现的新用户业务做好准备。

SDH 标准是基于直接同步复用的原理,这也是其能够灵活、经济地进行网络管理的重要原因。实际上,SDH 可不通过中间级的复用,直接将各支路信号复用至更高速率的 SDH 信号。SDH 网络单元可在现有的网络上直接进行互联,这样既节省设备,又非常经济。

SDH 还具有高级网络管理和维护能力,这样可以有效提高网络管理的灵活性。大约有 5% 的 SDH 信号结构是用以实现高级网络管理的功能。

SDH 信号能够传输当前电信网络的所有信号格式。这意味着相对于现存的用户复用信号的不同类型,SDH 只是一个数据封装标准,而这正是网络运营者所希望提供的功能。

SDH 可用于所有传统电信应用领域。因此,SDH 可完成统一的电信网络架构。SDH 为这统一电信网络所规定的唯一标准有利于各不同厂家生产设备的直接互联。

现在,让我们转向这统一网络的建构单元,以及它们是如何进行配置的。CCITT 已定义了这些网络单元,它们具有复用以及交换的功能。

线路终端复用器(LTM):LTM 能够将大量的支路信号复用至合适的 SDH 光载波,例如 STM-4 或 STM-16。支路信号可以是现存的 PDH 信号,如 2,34 或 140 Mbit/s,或更低速率的 SDH 信号。LTM 提供了由 PDH 信号转化为 SDH 信号的功能。

分插复用器(ADM):一种特殊类型的终端复用单元,它是以"透传"模式运行的。利用 ADM 可实现上下支路信号的功能,如 2,34 或 140 Mbit/s 的信号。

ADM 是 SDH 优于 PDH 的最主要优势之一。因为同样的功能在 PDH 中(实现)需要大量电线连接的背靠背终端设备。

同步数字交叉连接器:这个器件是实现新型 SDH 的基础。对于传输信道而言,它可完成半永久的交换方式,如实现各层次信号从 64 kbit/s 到 STM-1 上的交换。这些器件都有 STM-1 和 STM-4 的接口。DXC 可利用软件快速配置,以提供不同的带宽给数字租用线路或其他服务。

为了表达清楚,STM-1 中的单帧结构可用二维图来表示(如图 1 所示)。这个二维图由 9 行、270 列个模块组成。每个模块表示同步信号中的单个字节,每个字节有 8 个比特。6 个帧定位字节分布在二维图的最左上角。这些成帧字节起着标志的作用,它使帧中的任何字节极易被确定位置。

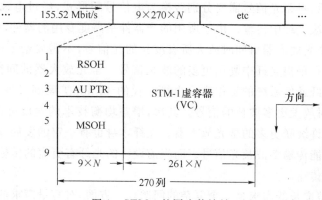

图 1　STM-1 的同步传输帧

信号比特按序从首行依从左到右顺序依次传输。在传输完帧中的最后一个字节后（这个字节位于第 9 行、第 270 列处），随后下一帧的 6 个帧定位字节就又开始发送。

同步传输帧由两个部分组成，它们分别是虚容器部分和段开销部分。虚容器按照用户信息在网络中的传输顺序来组织，而段开销则实现并管理同步网络中虚容器之间相互传输数据的功能，如告警监测、误码率监测和数据传输通道监测。

第 9 单元　波分复用

即使是牛顿、爱因斯坦，或像他们一样在揭示光的本性方面做出极大贡献的伟大科学家，也很难预测到当前光通信网络的巨大发展。光的高速公路穿越全球，眨眼之间传输海量的信息。这相当于数百万电话的通信量通过单根比头发丝还细的光纤进行传输。尽管这些发展令人啧啧称奇，但我们还仅仅处于可能会产生更大成就的开始。

目前全球网络业务的激增充分地表明了我们采用新的通信技术的速度。无线系统和互联网的发展就是一个很好的证明。不管是哪一种产生业务的应用，大多数这种业务将会由统一的光层进行传输。因此，各种应用的增长，如电话（移动或固定）、因特网、视频传输、计算机通信和数据库接入直接导致对光网络通信容量持续增长的需要。将来，光网络极有可能会用以传送大量的视频信息。

近来光网络方面最引人注目的进展就是波分复用领域。这些进展为地面通信系统和海底通信系统都带来了好处，使其通信容量增加了好几个数量级，而相应地降低了成本。

目前，在单根光纤中只能发送单波长或单色的光信号。因此，大量的努力集中于使用单个波长来传输最大量的信息。商用系统很快就实现在单波长上传输 40 Gbit/s 的信息，而在实验室中 320 Gbit/s 的系统也已实验成功。

另一方面，波分复用技术使得利用单根光纤传输很多波长成为可能，这可形象地比喻为传输了一个"彩虹带"的光，而在以前只有一种颜色。今天商用系统可以在一根光纤中实现速率为 400 Gbit/s 的信号传输。这大约等于每秒传输 200 部标准片长的电影。最近，Bell 实验室的一个研究团队展示了在一根光纤中速率高达 3.28 Tbit/s 的长途、无误码信号传输。

全光放大器的问世推动波分复用系统革命性的发展。在光放大器发明之前，当经由光纤传输一定距离后，每路光信号需要分别转换为电信号的形式，经过电放大后，再转换为光信号，随后在下一段光纤中传输。由于所用的光器件是高度专用的器件，因此这种放大方式费用较高。然而全光放大器可同时放大所有波长的光信号，不需要给不同波长分配不同的中继器件，并允许在单根光纤中复用更多的波长信号。全光放大器的问世推动了许多技术的发展。首先，光纤通信系统的工作窗口由第一代的 12 nm 扩展到了现如今的 80 nm。这使光放大器能同时放大更多波长的信号。其次，增益均衡技术的发展可以产生更加平坦的信号响应，这就允许级联更多的全光放大器。光纤本身也有一定的发展，在早期的光纤系统中，敷设的光线不能传输多波长光信号。而当前设计的光纤有更宽的传输窗口，可以优化用于大容量、多波长传输。

对光网络日益增长的需求是一个复杂的问题。一方面，对容量需求的增长非常显著，这本身就是一个需要克服的挑战。然而同时伴随的是不断增长的业务和应用,以及不同业务的更精确的要求。例如,用于传输紧急电话或实况医疗手术的视频直播的信号,相比于不是很紧急的可以几个小时后到达的电子邮件,通信质量需求有很大的不同。

然而,人们希望有光网络结构来支持这种广泛的业务,特别是 IP 业务,正在以指数形式增长。在世界的一些地方,IP 业务有可能在不久的将来构成业务中的大部分。因此,现有网络必须逐步进行优化以满足不同通信业务的需求。在这方面,波分复用系统具有很大优势,就是它可以为不同业务按照需要分配不同的波长。

幸运的是,不久我们就可通过全光网络实现对不同波长的路由功能。随着光子学的发展,在光域实现分插复用和交叉连接的功能已成为可能。我非常乐意介绍这一领域的最新进展。首先,被称为数据封装的技术已进入国际标准化的流程。第二个显著的进展就是全光交叉设备的出现。Bell 实验室现已发布了它们自行研制的全光交叉连接器,该器件被称为波长路由器(Lambda Router)。该路由器采用微电机交换技术,由微反射镜阵列组成,用以改变光信号的传输方向。正是由于采用了这种技术才使得我们能够建构全光网络。随着更多的路由功能在光层实现,就需要更成熟的智能技术来控制和管理全光网络。当前正在研发可管理这些光路由器的控制系统。这种控制系统具有自愈以及 50~100 ms 的快速复位的能力。这些特性就和现如今使用的 SDH 和 SONET 一样。

进一步需要考虑的是接入光网络。大部分用户乐于直接接入到光网络中,以享用其提供的超大流量。但这需要分阶段来实现。多波长光系统已快速地从核心网到终端用户扩展。在人口密集地区和大都市局部地区与城区长途通信有些不同。光纤到家或光纤到桌面的梦想还需要努力去实现,主要是由于这部分网络的费用比较敏感。近期,本地接入可能还是采用铜线,可以使用 ADSL 技术来增加原有传统铜线的容量。然而,对于商业写字楼,可采用光技术将带宽送到终端用户。目前,很多光纤到建筑物网络正在敷设中。这包括 ATM 和 SDH 接入设备。下一步将会利用波分复用来实现这些功能。波分复用将会首先推广应用于工业和校园局域网环境中。

我们正处于通信网络变革的开始,更多的通信容量、更多的业务类型,以及更好的服务质量正在对光网络提出巨大的需求。光网络的革命刚刚开始,正在快速向未来的带宽无限、可靠和低费用的在线世界发展。

第 10 单元 计算机网络简介

20 世纪 50 年代,大多数计算机有一个共同特点,即都有一个主存储器、一个中央处理器和一些外围设备,其中,存储器和中央处理器集中在一块,它们是计算机的核心部分。此后出现的新一代计算机,其计算和数据存储单元不必集中在一处。用户可以从一处获得程序,而在任何一个处理器上运行,并将结果输送至第三方。

将不同设备(如个人计算机、打印机和磁盘驱动器)连接起来就构成了一个网络。通常情况下,网络中的每一个设备可为一个或多个用户提供一种特定的服务。例如,计算机可能会在你的案头,提供你所需要的信息或软件。计算机也可以专用于管理共享文件的磁盘驱动器,我们称之为文件服务器。通常一个网络覆盖一个小的地理区域,如连接单幢建筑或建筑之间的网络设备，这样的网络就称为局域网。而覆盖更大范围的网络，例如一个城市、一个州、一个国家或世界，就被称为广域网。

一般来说，大多数网络可以包括使用多台计算机的多个用户，每个用户都可以访问任何一台打印机或服务器。在这么多人存取信息的情况下，不可避免地会发生冲突。因此，设备必须按照某种方式连接，该方式可使得信息有序地传输。一个很好的比喻就像大城市的街道布局。当只有一个人驾驶时，街道在哪？哪些是单行道？交通信号在哪里？或者如何同步？这些都是无关紧要的。但是在早晨交通高峰期间，当成千上万的汽车驶上大街，一个差劲的街道布局会造成拥挤，从而引起重大堵塞。计算机网络也同样如此。它们必须以一种能让数据在许多用户间几乎没有延时的传播方式进行连接。我们称这种连接方法为网络拓扑。最好的拓扑结构取决于设备的类型和用户的需求。对某用户组工作地很好的网络可能不适用于另外的用户组。

下面将介绍一些基本的网络拓扑结构。

图1表示了一种常用的（简单的）总线结构，该结构连接了如工作站、大型机和文件服务器等设备。它们通过一条总线（一组并行线）进行通信。通常的方法是给每个设备提供一个接口，用于监听总线并侦测其数据通信。若某一接口测定到数据的地址是指定它所服务的设备，它就从总线上读取数据并传送给该设备。同样，如果设备要传输数据，接口电路先检测总线何时空闲，然后再传输数据。这就像交通拥堵时，交通工具等候在高速公路的入口坡道上一样。等到通路时，你是快速地飞奔而过还是强行才能挤过去，这取决于你是驾驶着一辆微型汽车还是一辆大卡车。

有时，两个设备试图同时进行数据传输。每个设备侦测到通道空闲后，还不清楚其他设备的传输情况就开始传输数据，其结果就是信号冲突。当设备在传输信息时仍继续对总线进行侦听，并检测由冲突产生的噪声。当设备检测到信号冲突就停止传输，等待一随机时间后又开始重新传输数据。以上过程称为载波监听多路访问/冲突检出，具体将在稍后讨论。

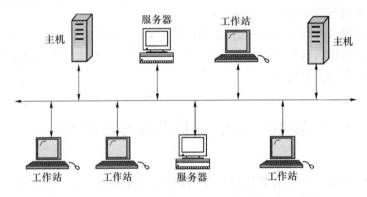

图1 常用总线拓扑

一种很常见的总线网络是以太网，其一般由以太网线缆构成。以太网线缆可以是由铜线、光纤，或两者组合而成的线缆结构。以太网允许终端、个人计算机、磁盘存储系统及办公用计算机相互之间进行通信，其主要优点就是很便利地给网络添加新设备。

另外一种常见的连接形式是星形拓扑结构，如图2所示。该结构使用了可以和网络中其他设备进行通信的中央计算机。控制集中化了，如果设备想要通信，它只能通过中央计算机来完成。再由中央计算机依次将数据发送到目的地。集中化提供了责任中心,这正是星形拓扑结构的优点。而总线结构和星形结构相比具有一些优势,例如,由于不存在中央控制器,不需要考虑其他设备,总线结构就很容易添加新设备。此外,总线网络中某一设备的故障或移除并不会引起整个网络彻底失效。而在星形结构中,中央计算机的故障会导致整个网络的瘫痪。

星形拓扑结构往往包含一个大型计算机,该计算机可以服务于很多终端和次级设备。通过适当的终端仿真软件,个人计算机就能够与主机通信。终端之间或终端与存储设备之间的数据传输只能通过大型计算机完成。

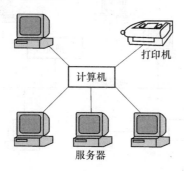

图 2　星形拓扑

在图 3 所示的环形拓扑中,设备连接成环形。每个设备都只能直接与相邻的一方或两方,而不能和其他设备进行通信。如果它想和距离更远的设备通信,它发送的信息就必须通过两者之间每一个设备来接递。

环形网络可以是单向或双向的。单向意味着所有传输在同一方向。因此,每一设备只能和一个相邻设备通信。双向意味着数据可以在两个方向上传输,也就是设备可以和相邻的两个设备进行通信。

环形拓扑,如 IBM 令牌环网,往往将一个办公室或一个部门的计算机连接在一起。一个 PC 上的应用程序可以访问其他机器上的数据,而用不着大型机对通信进行协商。相反,通信的协调是通过在环中所有站点中传递令牌。一个站点只有在它接收到令牌时才能发送数据。

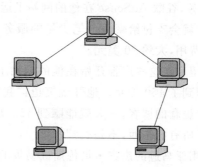

图 3　环形拓扑

环形拓扑的一个缺点是当其中的一站点需要向另一站点发送信息时,两者之间的所有站点都需要参与整个通信过程。因此,和其他拓扑(如总线拓扑)相比,环形拓扑将要花费更多的时间以用于信息的传递。此外,一个站点的故障往往会引起环网的中断,这将会影响到所有站点之间的通信。

许多实际的计算机网络都可由这些简单的网络拓扑结构组合而成。图4给出了一个可行的组合拓扑结构。

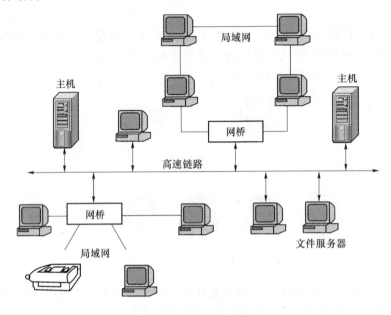

图4　各种拓扑组合

第11单元　分享互联网财富

马特·豪伊白天的工作是一名网络工程师。不过在业余时间,他近乎痴迷于他的硬盘数字录像机。因此,作为一项兴趣爱好,他创建了一个个人网络日志,用来存档视频新闻,并且提供他在网络上发现的小技巧。在2003年7月建立了博客以后,豪伊就签约了一项被称为谷歌 AdSense 的自动化服务,谷歌 AdSense 在他的网站上运行一些小的文本广告。每当他的读者点击一个广告,谷歌就会支付给豪伊一笔少量的服务费。他说:"我最初的目标是能够赚取每个月运营网站的费用,大约20美元。"

事实远远超出豪伊的期望。在这些广告开始在他的网站上运行不久以后,他查询了他的在线报告,发现他一天就赚到了150美元。他开玩笑道:"我曾心想,'如果一个人发现他只需穿着内衣,坐在那里写着愚蠢的博客,一天就能赚到150美元,那么这个世界即将毁灭了。'我的意思是,金钱毁掉了所有的东西,不是么?"

未必如此。我们过去常用亚马逊的杰夫·贝佐斯或易贝的皮埃尔·奥米迪亚取得的巨大成功来衡量互联网所带来的冲击。但那些亿万富翁的故事已不再新奇,它们不过是老故事在新媒体环境下的重新演绎。每一次重要的媒体变革都造就了一批大亨,报纸、收音机、电影、电视机,无不如此。现在,豪伊的150美元表明了另外的一种可能性,将经济上的回报给予那些小人物、非专业人员和业余爱好者。如果你正在寻找一种能够完全地展示这种新媒体能量的趋势,那么你不应该去关注那些刚刚购买了第一架私人飞机的青年才俊,相反地,应去注意那些正在从所经营指环王粉丝网站中赚取租金的年轻人。

我们为什么要关心这些小小的改变呢?因为我们中的大部分人都拥有对于某种事物的激情,无论我们是否承认这一点。也许你是一个充满幻想的天文学家,或你复原了1964—1965年间的轻型护卫舰;也许你是板球运动的狂热爱好者,或你比历史学家更了解安蒂特姆勇士;也许你能够闭着眼睛就能给家庭影院布线。这种智慧对其他人可能确确实实是有用的或者是有趣的,然而除了家人和朋友之外,你也许从未有机会与他人分享。

现在,那些专长有了施展之处。在过去的10年中网络已经逐渐地为个人智慧建立了一个全球性的平台。像AdSense或关注博客的Blogads等其他广告机构提供的服务只是搭建了最后一块木板。现在,你可以足不出户地去创作、设计、发表和推销你的作品,并从中赚钱。一些知名度高的博主,特别是那些专注于政坛政治评论的博主,吸引数十万人浏览他们的个人主页,从AdSense或Blogads上赚够了钱而辞去了白天的工作。自由评论网站"每日科斯"每月的读者量已经超过了像《新共和》、《国家报》这样的正统刊物。但是,在过去几年创建的450万个博客中,大部分都只有几十、上百个访客。这个数字听起来不是很多,但是不要低估这样的期望:经过多年来烦扰朋友和家人之后,你会突然拥有一个可以与500多个爱好者一起讨论内战奥秘的平台。正如技术评论员戴夫·温伯格所指出的:"在网上,每个人都能成为15个人中的名人。"类似于AdSense这样的服务业的崛起预示了这样一个结论:每个人都有可能通过与其他15个人交谈而赚到15美元的外快。

这些新广告系统是如何运作的?AdSense计划的关键技术在于Google能够对网页内容进行分析,并相当准确地分辨出与其内容相符的关键主题。具备这样的能力,Google自然可以在瞬间推送与搜索内容匹配的广告页面。AdSense调整了原有的模式,这项技术不是查找与搜索内容一致的网页,而是查找与广告内容一致的网页。

例如说你是一个广告客户,尝试销售一本节食方面的新书。你首先通过能够吸引消费者的方式创建一段产品的简单描述,同时为你的网站创建一个网址,之后向谷歌购买广告宣传活动。谷歌并不是随随便便地在网页库中的每个网页都运行该书的广告,而是将广告专门放在那些具有语义相关的网页中,例如与食品有关的健康问题的网站,或者是那些叙述某人减肥失败的博客中。这个创意在逻辑上完全可行。那些在网上寻求复杂的碳水化合物信息的人更可能有兴趣去买一本有关节食的书籍。

谷歌在网络中追踪超过40亿个网页。为了论述的需要,假如这些网页中有100万个提到了"饮食",并且它们中的1 000个仅专注于食品问题。谷歌在这1 000个网页中识别出那些与AdSense签约的网页,大约数分钟后,那些特定网页就会为你的新书运行广告。

在那些签约在网页上运行AdSense的人看来,整个系统非常简单。一旦加入了这个计划,你只需在你的网页中插入几行HTML代码,几乎立刻就有广告出现在你的网页上。只要有足够多的人点击这个广告,一两个月后支票便通过邮件发送过来。谷歌并未公开谈及费用,根据广告类别不同,每次点击的报酬在几美分到几美元不等。由于公司利用竞标过程来决定点击价格,因此拥有很多广告商的主题比那些不太受欢迎主题的点击价格要高。那些家庭影音设备的卖家为每次点击支付的费用要比盗版黑格尔的《精神现象学》卖家高一些。

谷歌广告相当智能,它可以根据你个人兴趣的变化而随机应变。如果豪伊突然发了个帖子称赞伯特·巴卡拉克的音乐,广告几乎立刻链接到售卖巴卡拉克唱片的在线音乐网站。这也许就是 AdSense 最神秘之处:像变色龙一样,对张贴在网站上的文章作出迅速的反应,并相应地转换广告。这项服务推出后不久,我曾在我的博客上有过为期几个月的体验。当我对总统大选做出评论时,站内充斥着政治类的广告;而当我在个人电脑上提及编辑家庭电影时,各种数字录像机的广告铺天盖地而来;然后有一天我张贴了一个拉什·林博与镇痛药盐酸羟考酮缓释剂之争的入口,第二天早晨我发现博客里全部是戒瘾中心的广告。

像 AdSense 这样的计划有一个奇怪的副作用,就是商业广告入侵了那些本该极其私人的空间。博主经常以第一人称来叙述他们的生活:他们孩子的故事,他们的罗曼史,他们寻找新工作的奋斗,或者失去爱人。有可能你能搜寻到某个人述说自己苦涩的分手过程,同样也有可能找到有人为自己 TiVo 谱写的情歌。在个人空间中遇到广告是很烦心的,特别是当这个广告与那天事件的主题完全不搭调。就像你打开一封老朋友的信,却从信封里掉出来一些超市的优惠券一样。

当然,没有人去强迫博主们必须在他们的网站上运行广告,许多人选择免受商业信息干扰。而且在长期的运行过程中,独立出版商获得资金回报已经成为网络生态的健康发展。博客广告给政坛博主们带来可观的收入,他们的网站在选举季生意火爆,但是这项服务的创始人亨利·科普兰,却看好几十个月入 200 美元的棒球博主:"我的直觉是,明年运动博客将会像今天的政坛博客一样。"

在线广告的首日火爆很正常,但是马特·豪伊不会每天都再有 150 美元进账,因为对新鲜事物的追逐使得回头客更趋向访问一个新站点,然而他的获利仍然超过预期。这不足以让他辞掉白天的工作,但这只是部分的原因。大部分的博客都不是全职工作。它们是爱好,是消遣,是人们与陌生人分享智慧的地方。在网络时代之前,要找到一个能写作个人喜好的地点几乎是不可能的。现在,你可以向全球的观众发布你的想法,并在此过程中获得收入。豪伊将这些新一代业余网络发行商称为"千元富翁"。他说:"将会有很多人通过撰写他们感兴趣的素材而赚得 1000 美元,这真的棒极了。"

第 12 单元 3G 简介

移动通信的发展经历了 3 个阶段:模拟→数字→多媒体。

迄今为止,已先后出现了三代移动电话,而且一代比一代更可靠、更灵活。你可以很容易地使用模拟蜂窝电话进行语音通话,但通话常常局限于本国内。数字移动电话系统则增加了传真、数据、信息传递功能,还能在众多国家间进行语音电话服务。多媒体服务则使移动设备具有高速数据传递能力,并且允许通过移动电话进行视频、音频及其他新的应用,即可以通过移动终端听音乐、看电视和进入因特网。

利用新一代技术,可配置的服务范围越来越广泛,恐怕有些你都难以想象。我们正进入一个新的 3G 时代。

对第一代(模拟)和第二代(数字)而言,世界不同区域有着不同的移动电话标准,但是基于 CDMA 技术的移动多媒体(称为 3G)则有一个通用的标准。3G 将那些不兼容的标准统一起来。

在模拟和数字之后,接踵而来的第三代移动通信系统即将实施。它能提供带有语音、视频、图像、音频及其他信息的宽带移动通信数字多媒体技术。这种转变过程如下所述:

➢ 20 世纪 80 年代,第一代模拟移动电话,以语音为主,多重标准(如 NMT,TACS 等)。
➢ 20 世纪 90 年代,第二代数字移动电话,以语音为主,多重标准(如 GSM,CDMA,TDMA 等)。
➢ 20 世纪 90 年代末,引入 2.5 代高速数据通信作为第二代和第三代的过渡。其中包括 GPRS 和 EDGE 等服务。
➢ 21 世纪 10 年代,第三代多媒体移动电话,以语音和数据为主,多重模式,单一标准。

1. 3G 的特征

3G 具有如下特征。

(1) 处处分组

采用第三代移动通信技术,信息在发送前被分成若干独立的、但彼此相关的"包",这些"包"在接收端被重新组装。分组交换类似于拼图玩具——玩具拼图从制造工厂出来时被拆分开来,放到塑料袋中;在从工厂到用户的运输过程中,盒中的拼图是随意摆放的。当购买者从袋中拿出所有拼图后,再重新拼成原来的图样。所有的拼图都是相关的,可拼装在一起,但运输和拼装的方式可以变化。

分组交换数据模式比对应的电路交换更通用,基于分组交换的其他例子包括 TCP/IP 协议、X.25 协议、帧中继及 ATM 异步传输模式。在移动通信世界里,CDPD(蜂窝数字分组数据)、PDCD(个人数字蜂窝分组)、GPRS(通用分组无线业务)及无线 X.25 技术(一种国际公共接入分组交换无线数据网的标准)已应用了若干年。

(2) 随处上网

万维网正日益成为主要的通信接口,人们可以在因特网上娱乐、获取信息;在内联网共享公司资讯、联系同事;在外联网上联系客户与供应商。这些都是万维网的衍生物,其目的在于能与不同对象进行联系。现在有一种倾向就是尽量把信息存放在远程的因特网上,而不是以特定软件包的形式把信息存放在 PC 本机上。网络浏览是分组数据的一个非常重要的应用。

(3) 高速传输

3G 的速度可高达 2 Mbit/s,数据传输率取决于所在的呼叫环境——只有在户内和固定环境下才能达到这样的数据传输率。若在高速移动情况下,估计可达到 144 kbit/s 的数据传输率——这大约是现今固定电信调制解调器速度的 3 倍。

(4) 新的、更好的应用

3G 促进了一些新的应用,而这些应用在先前的移动通信网上由于数据传输率的限制不太容易实现。这些应用范围包括从网上浏览、文件传递到家庭自动化——一种能够实现远程进入和控制家用电器设备的能力。由于带宽的增加,这些应用采用 3G 技术实现比用 GPRS 这样的过渡技术更容易。

2. 3G 发展进度表

那么移动多媒体时代什么时候能真正到来呢？现在让你一睹为快，何时何处我们能看到 3G。

无论何时，一项新兴服务正式确立之前都要经过一系列的发展阶段。3G 服务的发展将会包括标准化、基础建设、网络测试、合约定制、网络铺开、终端可用性、应用发展等。

3G 的这些演进如下所示：

里程碑数据

- 1999 年，3G 无线接口标准诞生，首个 3G 实用系统架构和概念终端展示。
- 2000 年，继续进行 3G 网络体系结构的标准化、终端的需求和标准化等方面的工作。
- 2000 年 5 月，国际电联无线通信协会正式批准 IMT-2000 标准。
- 2000 年，欧洲、亚洲政府颁发 3G 牌照。
- 2000 年，世界无线电通信大会确定 3G 第二阶段频谱。
- 2001 年，3G 进行现场试验，日本 NTT 等运营商开通了 3G 商用系统。
- 2001 年夏，3G 商用系统首次在欧洲开通。
- 2002 年初，具备 3G 基本功能的终端批量生产，满足商业用量。
- 2002 年，网络运营商开通并推广 3G 业务，运营商指定的早期用户开始定期使用非语音通信。
- 2002 年 3 月，3G 新应用的开发、网络容量的提高以及高性能终端的出现，进一步拓宽了 3G 的应用市场。
- 2004 年，3G 商用规模化，拥有大量的公司用户和个人用户。
- 2005 年，WRC 2000 决议的 3G 频谱 2 段有望可用。

第 13 单元 GSM 与 CDMA 之比较

CDMA 蜂窝移动通信系统综合采用码分多址和频分复用技术，使其用户可以同时利用同一信道传输信号；而 GSM 系统则利用时分多址（TDMA）和频分复用（FDD）技术来传输和区分其多个用户信号。此外，CDMA 系统还借助码激励线性预测编码 QCELP 算法、RAKE 接收、功率控制、软切换等多种技术的优越性，使其具有比 GSM 更好的系统性能，如更强的抗干扰能力、更大的系统容量、更高的接入成功率、更低的掉线率、低拦截率等。

1. 功率控制和 RAKE 接收

当不同用户向同一基站发送信息时，由于到达基站的传输距离不同，其信号功率大小有所差异，这必然引起信号间的串扰。对于那些远离基站的移动台来说，其信号几乎淹没在基站附近移动台的信号之中，这种干扰尤为严重。

为了解决这一问题，保证系统的高性能，CDMA 系统采用了功率控制技术，可以有效克服这种串扰。作为 CDMA 蜂窝移动通信系统的核心技术之一，功率控制通过调整每个台站的信号功率保证达到基站的所有信号功率相同。

功率控制不仅可以分为开环、闭环控制,还可以分为前向(下行)、后向(上行)控制。开环控制是用户根据测得的误帧率来调整发射功率,而闭环控制则是基站测试接收信号的信噪比,并调整每一移动台的发射功率。

CDMA 系统的后向功率控制可分为以下两种控制技术:仅由移动台站完成的开环后向功率控制和基站与移动台站均可实现的闭环后向功率控制。在另一方面,前向功率控制仅用于减小相邻小区域范围内的干扰。

RAKE 接收技术

移动信道的非理想信道特性使得信号传输时不可避免地产生衰减和畸变,从而使系统性能劣化。RAKE 接收技术的基本原理是通过收集、合并多径信道上的信号,有效地增强接收到的信号功率,从而提高输出信噪比,改善系统的性能。

CDMA 系统在每个手机和基站内分别设置 3、4 个 RAKE 接收机,接收同一信号源发出、经由不同传输路径的各信号分量,对每一信号分量进行单独解调后再将其叠加,即可实现输出信噪比的提升。因此,借助于 RAKE 接收技术,将 CDMA 蜂窝移动通信系统信号多径传输的不利因素变为有利因素。

2. CDMA 的更优性能

(1) 更强的抗干扰能力

由于采用扩频调制方式,用户的信号带宽 B_N 通过分配的唯一伪随机(PN)序列调制后得到极大的展宽,因而调制宽带信号 B_B 具有接近高斯白噪声的谱特性。接收到这种扩展频谱信号之后,所有的 CDMA 接收机都试图利用本地产生的 PN 序列对其进行解调,但是只有那个与接收信号具有相同 PN 序列的接收机才能将这个类噪声的信号转换为可用窄带信号,其他接收机因为没有相同的本地 PN 序列而无法做到(解扩)。因此,除具有相同 PN 序列的接收机外,该宽带调制信号经所有接收机解调后的输出仍然是无意义的宽带噪声信号。

此外,对拥有本地相关 PN 序列的接收机而言,接收信号中因信道传输而叠加的无用窄带信号将受到接收机本地 PN 序列的调制成为宽带信号,使其功率谱密度大大减小。这样,通过窄带滤波器就可滤除其他宽带信号及大部分的带外无用信号,仅留下窄带有用信号及少量的带内窄带无用信号,因而输出信号信噪比大大提高,进而提高了系统的抗干扰能力。

可以证明:B_N/B_B 的比值越大,系统的抗干扰能力就越强。

(2) 系统容量更大,接入成功率更高

与 GSM 移动通信系统的时分多址接入方式不同,CDMA 由于使用码分多址技术,利用每个用户独有的 PN 序列来区分用户信号,可以在频分复用划出的同一子信道频段上同时传输多路用户信号,使每路信号都占用整个频段带宽,调制效率高。在使用相同频率资源的情况下,即相对于相同的信道带宽,CDMA 的系统容量是 GSM 的 4~5 倍。

系统容量大,其接入成功率自然就高。

此外,CDMA 系统采用可变速率的码激励线性编码预测技术,其语音通话的最高传输速率为 9.6 kbit/s,而在通话停顿的瞬间可用最低仅 1.2 kbit/s 的速率传输语音信号。该技术称为语音激活技术,可大大减轻了多个用户同时使用同一信道时对其他用户的干扰,提高了系统容量。而 GSM 系统由于通话停顿时存在一定的时延,所以无法利用语音激活技术。

(3) 语音质量更佳

CDMA 采用了先进的码激励线性编码预测技术,并在每个手机上使用 3 个 RAKE 接收机同时接收不同方向的信号,使声音信号频谱极为丰富且有立体感。此外,CDMA 系统基于 CELP 算法的声码器可以自动调整语音数据传输速率,并选择不同的电平发射功率,降低了噪声的干扰影响。这样,即使在背景噪声较大的情况下,也可以得到较好的通话质量,打电话时几乎没有杂音。

(4) 更低的拦截率

要窃听他人的通话,首先必须要捕获其传输信号,其次则是要能够正确地解码。由于扩频调制,信号进入 CDMA 系统信道传输前的频谱被极大地扩展,功率谱密度大大降低,甚至低于环境噪声,故信号难以被检测到,当然被捕获的几率也极少。

此外,即便是拦截到了 CDMA 信号,由于没有准确的本地伪随机序列,窃听者只能从其接收机上获得毫无意义的宽带噪声。获得解码必需的准确的 PN 序列的概率仅为几万亿分之一!因此,窃听者找出正确的 PN 序列,成功窃听他人几乎是毫无可能。

(5) 更低的掉线率

CDMA 采用软切换技术,即"先连接后断开",克服了 GSM 移动通信系统由于采用硬切换技术导致容易掉线的缺点。

移动通信系统中,基站是通话的保障,当通话中的用户移动到基站覆盖范围的边缘时,基站就应该自动切换以保障通话,否则就会掉线。

CDMA 系统进行切换时的基站覆盖将由"本地区域基站(如 A)单独覆盖"到"相邻两区域基站(A 和 B)同时覆盖"到"下一区域基站(B)单独覆盖",而且手机信号是自动地切换到相邻较为空闲的基站上。也就是说,CDMA 系统只有确认手机已移动到另一基站的单独覆盖区域后,才断开与原先的基站 A 的联系,这样当然不易掉线。

和上述软切换技术不同,GSM 系统采用了与 CDMA 切换处理顺序完全相反的硬切换方式,即"先断开后连接"。这样,当 GSM 用户在通话过程中移动到基站覆盖区域的边缘时,本地基站 A 将首先切断与其的联系,然后移动台站才再次与相邻基站 B 建立新的连接。这一过程中的通话必然先被切断,并由此导致其高离线率。

(6) 频率规划简单

CDMA 系统的用户是按照其使用的不同地址码来区分的,所以相同的 CDMA 载波可以在相邻的小区内使用。故 CDMA 的系统频率规划十分灵活,扩展也很简单。

第 14 单元　分组交换

分组交换是 20 世纪 60 年代末期为数据通信而设计的。数据通信的应用主要是哑终端和共享主机间的交互,这些交互是人类和来自主机响应的控制业务。这些数据的传输是随机发生的,即以随机间隔的突发方式进行的。如果在数据通信中使用电路交换,那么(电路交换)连接的专用资源大部分将是空闲的——(这是)对带宽非常不经济的使用。为了支持突发性的数据通信业务,人们设计了分组交换方式,目的是获得更高的带宽利用率。

分组交换式网络和交换式点对点网络具有同样的体系结构,其中交换机称为分组交换机(如图1所示)。分组交换不像电路交换那样把网络资源静态地分配给某个用户,它是按需把网络资源分配给通信各方——即只有当它们有信息要发送的时候才分配资源,有时也称为按需分配带宽。这样网络资源可以得到很好的共享,尤其是当每个发端业务不多时利用率更为高效。

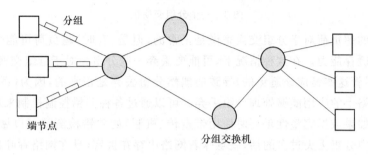

图1 一个分组交换网络

为了较好地共享网络资源,分组交换(技术)把网络资源划分为传输带宽的小单元。带宽请求的单位是给定时刻所传输的数据量,可以通过把用户信息编码为独立的块而完成。数据是以分组的形式进行传输的,每个分组包含了一个头部和作为净负荷的数据块(如图2所示)。每个分组代表了传输的基本单元和分组交换网中通信带宽的量。

图2 一个分组示意图

分组的头部包含了目的节点的地址(加上其他的控制信息)。目的地址被分组交换机用来在分组到目的地的路径上转发分组。确定分组在交换机中输出端口(的过程)称为分组的路由。每个分组交换机都设有一个路由表,路由表可以把目的地址翻译成交换机的输出端口。路由表是通过路由协议建立的,路由协议运行在分组交换机中。分组的传递不需要预先建立连接。作为替代,每个分组的路由是由传输链路上的分组交换机通过该分组的目的地址决定的。分组交换网络主要是在分组的基础上为通信双方提供网络资源,网络不会为空闲的通信双方分配带宽。相反,电路交换网络是在每个连接(或电路)的基础上分配网络资源,并且会持续整个连接时间,即使通信双方是空闲的。

分组交换机中的路由表可以通过路由协议动态改变,比如由于拓扑或负载的变化引起的(路由表)改变。因此,通信双方间的不同分组可能会经过不同的路径到达(目的地)。(在这种情况下)无法保证它们按照传送时的顺序到达目的地。

分组交换机具有4个核心功能:路由、交换、缓存和复用。另外,路由决定了输入分组的理想输出端口。接下来,交换功能把分组从输入端口投递到理想的输出端口。尽管不同来源的分组传输不同步,但是同时到达交换机不同端口的很多分组可能是去往同一个输出端口的。由于每个输出端口只能传送一个分组,其他分组必须缓存。因此,分组交换必须把提供缓存能力作为标准的操作。

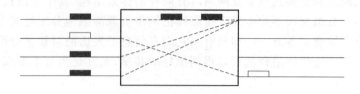

图 3　一个分组交换机

尽管瞬时的超负荷对于分组交换来说是正常的,但是(有时)超负荷可能会严重到超出分组交换机的缓存能力。在这种情况下,可能要丢弃一些分组。对于分组交换网络来说,由于缓存溢出(尽管这些是应该避免的)导致的偶然分组丢弃是正常的,因为(系统默认)运行于分组交换网络上的应用能够处理分组丢弃。可以通过各种差错控制机制来对分组丢弃进行处理,比如,如果数据完整性重要时使用带重传(机制)的差错检测就可以做到。然而,如果一长段时间内分组丢失过多的话,就意味着网络中存在拥塞,且在网络吞吐量和时延性能上显著下降。因此,分组交换网络必须要提供拥塞控制算法,即首先要避免拥塞的发生,并且,当拥塞发生时要去控制它。

分组交换的复用方法是基于统计复用的,这是一种时分复用技术(TDM)的动态形式。分组交换机负责把到达不同输入端口的、并且要去往同一输出端口的、来源不同的分组复用在一起。

分组交换中的 TDM 机制与电路交换中的不一样。在分组交换中,需要每个分组的头部有一个明确的地址(目的地址)把分组和其目的节点联系起来,而分组在时间上的位置与任何信道信息并不对应。实际上,不存在定义位置的帧的概念。没有时隙被预留,任何时隙都可以被到达的任何分组使用(如果多于一个分组到达或被缓存,只有一个分组在当前时隙中传送,而其他分组先缓存,然后再在接下来的时隙中传送)。因而,每个输出链路的传输资源仅仅被分配给活动方,而空闲方不会占用带宽。相反的是,基于时分复用的电路交换的每个时隙属于某个特定的逻辑电路。连接一旦建立了,系统将指定一个逻辑信道给它,此逻辑信道在整个通信建立期间都归其使用。若该连接处于空闲状态,这样会导致空闲时隙的产生,(且)这些空闲时隙不能被其他活动方使用。所以,在支持突发业务方面,分组交换比电路交换要高效很多。

要注意的是:即使对于话音通信来说,电路交换也不是那么高效。原因在于典型的话音交谈中只有 40% 的时间是活动的,其余时间通话双方是沉默的,因而不需要传送任何信息。所以,在过去的二十年里,人们广泛地探索了在分组交换网络中传递话音或分组话音通信。实际上,在互联网上传送话音(业务)比在公众电话网中传送具有内在的(优势)、更高的效率。

除了应用在交换式点对点结构中,分组交换也可应用在广播式共享介质上。广播式共享分组交换网络不需要分组交换机,因为它的交换是分布式方式实现的,这种分布式方式位于端节点中。广播式网络中的分组交换将在本章的后面讨论。

无连接型或面向连接的分组交换

在前面讨论的分组交换的基本形式中,在分组传送之前不需要明确的连接建立过程。事实上,从网络的观点来看,网络中不存在连接的概念。因此,对任何分组传输来说,在带宽、时延或丢包率上没有保障,这意味着服务质量(QoS)没有保障(在任何情况下,连接与带宽之间没有关系)。这种形式的分组交换称为无连接型分组交换。

但是,另外一种形式的分组交换就需要明确的连接建立及拆除命令,这种形式称为面向连接的分组交换。在这种情况下,分组头部包含了一个连接表示符用来表明该分组属于哪个连接。面向连接的分组交换机中设置了一个连接表,(通过)这个表可以把连接表示符翻译成输出端口号。连接建立的目的是预留网络资源。由于每个分组交换机支持的连接数量是有限的,基本网络资源(只能)支持连接自身。原因在于每个连接都需要在连接表中占据一定的内存空间来支持与该连接相关的信息(的传输)。因而,分组交换机中支持的连接数量是内存受限的。除此之外,连接建立(过程)也可以预留其他的网络资源,比如带宽和缓存,这些都是为了保证应用的(传输)性能。

面向连接式分组交换依然保持着非面向连接分组交换式的统计复用性能和支持突发业务相应效率。因此,为了和电路交换网中有专用资源的固定连接区别,分组交换网络中的连接被称为虚连接或VC。虚连接范式允许通过公共数据网中为企业创建虚拟的私有网络。为了模拟私有网络X.25连接和它的后继者帧中继,VC可以在不同企业地点之间建立,X.25和帧中继都是面向连接的分组交换网络的例子,也确实都可以用来建立虚拟的私有网络。

现在,随着基于大型主机的集中式计算范式转变为基于个人电脑和工作站的分布式计算范式,数据通信应用之间产生了很大的差异。但是,由于现在的数据应用(比如文件传输、打印和电子邮件)依然显示着相似的突发行为,所以数据业务也保持着(相似的)突发性质。因而,无论对于局域网(LAN)还是广域网(WAN)数据通信来说,分组交换仍然非常重要。

永久连接

尽管电路交换和面向连接的分组交换都需要在信息传送之前建立连接,但是在端节点或网络中可能没有(设置)这样用来建立连接的协议(称为信令协议)。要想在没有信令支持(的情况)下动态建立连接,网络必须在预定的基础上(永久连接)提供连接,因为网络连接是由网络管理协议在网络提供业务之初建立的。对于电路交换连接(租用线服务)和分组交换连接(X.25、帧中继或ATM中的永久需连接或PV),永久(或非交换式)连接是普遍的,原因在于(设计者)想简化网络设计或者网络中不存在标准的信令协议应用。实际上,一个全连接的点对点网络逻辑上可以通过这些永久连接在电路交换和分组交换网络中构造,就如同它们是点对点连接一样。但是,这种全连接交换式永久连接依然存在着与全连接点对点网络相似的缺点,比如扩展性差等问题。

第15单元 居民宽带

1. 用户环路存在的问题

居民和电话局之间的通信信道是为模拟话音业务设计的,话音业务需要一个适当的带宽,典型的带宽范围为 0.3~3.5 kHz。随着数据业务量越来越多,人们设计出了复杂编码和调制技术的调制解调器,这些编码和调制技术可以使数据以大约 33 kbit/s 或更高速率在用户线上传送。越来越多的居民用户已经过渡到了 V.34 调制解调器时代,其工作速率达到了 28.8 kbit/s。

这种传输速率对于部分应用是足够了,但是仍然不能满足许多其他的应用。举例来说,以 28.8 kbit/s 的速度传输一页的文本文件只需要 1 s 的时间。但是,以 V.34 调制解调器的速率传输单个视频图像文件就需要 120 s 的时间,并且为了后续的回放向下装入未压缩的视频文件以这种速度(工作)的话还需要 840 s 的时间。很明显,用户能从提供比当下使用的调制解调器更高带宽的技术中获益更多。

使用 ISDN 技术并没有对这种情形改善很多,但是缓解了这种(带宽紧张)情况。比如,北美和欧洲的大部分城市地区都(提供)本地环路的 ISDN 业务,这些业务提供了 64 kbit/s 或 128 kbit/s 的带宽。尽管如此,这项技术(ISDN)对于多媒体业务的支持(还是)太有限了,只能提供比 V.34 速率稍微高一点的(带宽)改善。

2. 建议的方法:两个连锁方法,编码/调制和配线

简而言之,本地环路需要更高的带宽。当前,解决这个问题的方法集中在:(a)使用高级的编码/调制技术来更好地利用已有的铜线电缆;(b)使用具有更高带宽的介质取代或扩展铜线(比如使用光纤或同轴电缆来重新铺设部分分配线路)。

为了标准化跨通信链路,达到提高带宽性能的目的,人们发布了许多新的编码和调制技术规范。此外,一些用户环路配线技术也在开发或实现中,其中几个应用了编码和调制机制。图 1 描述了这些机制,图的左边是编码/调制技术,右边是配线方法(用户环路的选择)。为了更好地了解编码/调制机制,本章的主要部分讨论了 HDSL 和 ADSL/VDSL。

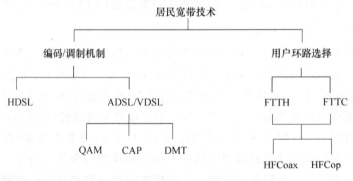

ADSL	=	Asymmetrical digital subscriber line,非对称数字用户线
CAP	=	Carrierless amplitude modulation,无载波幅度调制
DMT	=	Discrete multi-tone modulation,离散双音多频调制
FTTC	=	Fiber to the curb,光纤到路边
FTTH	=	Fiber to the home,光纤到家
HDSL	=	High-bit-rate digital subscriber line,高比特率数字用户线
HFCoax	=	Hybrid fiber coax,混合光纤同轴电缆
HFCop	=	Hybrid fiber copper,混合光纤铜缆
QAM	=	Quadrature amplitude modulation,正交调幅
VADSL	=	Very high ADSL,非常高非对称数字用户线

图 1　用户环路新技术

3. 编码和调制

下面这部分介绍性能最突出的编码和调制技术。用户环路选择将在本章的下一部分进行讨论。

① 高比特率数字用户线(HDSL);
② 非对称数字用户线(ADSL)和非常高 ADSL(VADSL)。

4. HDSL

过去的一些年中,几种值得注意的"新技术"应用在了本地环路中,其中的一种称为"高比特率数字用户线(HDSL)",如图2所示。HDSL 是基于 ISDN(综合业务数字网)的 2B+D 线路编码(2B1Q)的技术。它在 24 规格的铜线上传输距离可达 12 千英尺,在 26 规格的铜线上可达 9 千英尺。这些线缆都是 2 对的全双工线缆,支持 784 kbit/s 的传输速率。

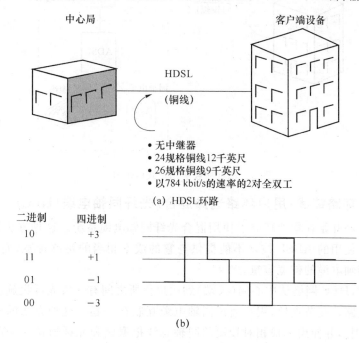

图 2 高比特率数字用户线(HDSL)

HDSL 的支持者认为它是一种简单的、价格不贵的技术,它的(安装)准备快速并且简单。这种技术可使用任何铜线对,不需要特殊对待("特殊对待"指附带条件的)。Bellcore 对这种技术很热心,原因在于它的安装和维护(比较)容易。

虽然这样,但是(由于)它的传输速率局限在千比特每秒之内,所以其他的解决方法也在考虑之内,其中最引人注目的是非对称数字用户线技术(ADSL)。

5. ADSL

另一个较新的技术称为 ADSL(非对称数字用户线),如图3所示。它在本地电话局和用户线间的本地环路上使用改进的编码和调制技术来支持多媒体应用。

ADSL 开始时是作为一种上下行技术来建立的,在这种方式下,下行信号(速率)是 1.5 Mbit/s,而上行信号信道以 16 kbit/s 的速率工作。在同样的线对上也支持常规的电话业务。1994 年,一种速率为 6 Mbit/s 的技术被引入到 ADSL 系统中,这种系统能在 12 千英尺长的铜线上提供 4 个电视信道。

如同刚刚提到的一样,ADSL 在本地环路上的安装不会干扰分配站中的现有电缆,也不需要中断用户电话业务很长时间。这些接口把现有的铜缆划分为多个信道:(a)从中心局到用户方向的信道（下行）；(b) 从用户到中心局方向的信道（上行）。

从用户到中心局的信道频率低于下行信道（从中心局到用户方向）（非对称配置）。因此，相比常规的对称配置方式，非对称方式的串话不是一个很大的问题。并且，这种方法利用了现在许多应用的非对称特性。

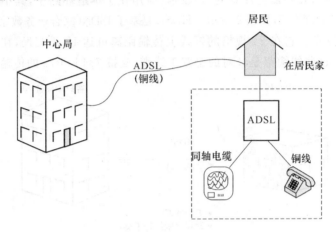

图3 非对称数字用户线（ADSL）

6. 在本地环路铺线：用户环路选择混合/光纤同轴电缆（HFC）

几个国家已经开始在本地环路上使用混合光纤同轴电缆系统。这种方法的支持者认为在常规双绞线上使用的 ADSL 技术不能提供与它的成本相当的足够带宽，而 HFC 技术能够挖掘光纤和同轴电缆的带宽容量。

如图4所示，HFC 网络从中心局（头端）到用户住所之间有一段光纤设施。节点具有前向通路和返回通路。在节点处，用户通过同轴电缆互联在一起。这种方法的思想就是把光纤引入邻里（范围），并使用一根相对较短的同轴总线把家庭和光纤连接在一起。这种方法的设计是平衡光纤和同轴电缆的成本，并且能够为全业务的多媒体流提供足够的带宽。

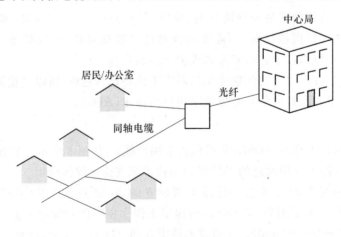

图4 混合光纤同轴电缆（HFC）

HFC 的目的是为支持以下各种业务提供传输技术：(a) 电话业务，(b) 综合业务数字网 ISDN，(c) 广播视频（模拟的），(d) 广播视频（数字的），(e) 交互式视频（数据），(f) 高速全双工数据（数据）。

7. 光纤到路边（FTTC）和光纤到家庭（FTTH）

提升本地环路的另外两种技术是光纤到路边（FTTC）和光纤到家庭（FTTH）。FTTC 使光纤离用户比 HFC 方式做到的更近。光纤线路在中心局到基座之间，可以为 8~16 个家庭提供服务。在最初的计划中，FTTC 提供 96 个话音信道或同样的数据/视频信道，FTTC 的动力是由一条独立的同轴电缆提供的。目前，安装 FTTC 比安装 HFC 的价钱略贵。

FTTH 要求必须在所有进入家庭的通路上铺设光缆，这种技术提供了最大的带宽。在本地环路的进化阶段，它的价格是非常昂贵的。在这种方式中，每个用户必须安装自己的激光器，并且把电视发出的模拟信息转换为光数字信号形式。与 FTTC 和 HFC 相比，人们对 FTTH 的兴趣要小一些。

HFC 的支持者不认为 FTTC 会和 HFC 一样成本低廉。另外一些研究断言：FTTC 技术在使用 CAP 技术的情况下是有能力支持多媒体宽带业务的，这对于 HFC 来说是一个可行的替代方法。

第 16 单元 帧中继和异步传递模式

随着局域网（LAN）的速率和数量的不停增长，为了满足它巨大吞吐量（对网络）的需要，对广域分组交换网的要求也在提高。早期的广域网络中，人们设计了 X.25 协议来完成终端和计算机之间的长距离直接相连。在 64 kbit/s 速率之上，X.25 协议很好的满足了网络需求。随着局域网在局部环境下扮演着越来越重要的角色，由于自身大量的系统开销，X.25 已经不能完全胜任广域互联的工作。幸运的是，一些新生代的广域网高速交换业务（技术）已经迅速从实验室草图标准阶段进入到可商业化的、标准化产品阶段。有很多这样的高速广域网络技术可供人们选择。

确实，为了降低网络容量问题，网络管理者现在面临很多选择。在本文中，我们首先概括不同的广域网连接技术，了解它们的优点和弱点；然后我们集中了解两种最重要的广域网技术：帧中继和异步传递模式。

1. 广域网互联技术

在为商业和其他组织应用考虑广域网技术时，需要分析两个截然不同但有相关性的倾向。一个是为了支持具体应用，满足组织性需求的分布式处理架构，另一个是能够满足这些需求的广域网互联技术。

广域互联提议

为了满足新公司的计算样式需要，业务和设备提供商已经开发了大量的高速业务。这些业务包括了更快速的复用线路机制，比如 T-3 和 SONET/SDH，和更快的网络交换机制，其中就包括了帧中继和异步传递模式。

图 1 列出了来自美国公共电信运营者的几个重要选择，其他国家的选择也是相似的。非交换式的或专线是以固定价格租来的传输链路。这样的链路可以从运营商处租到，用来

互联一个组织中的各个办公室。公认的提议包括：

① 模拟链路：最廉价的方式是租用双绞线模拟链路。需要的专用私人线路调制解调器，数据速率为 4.8~56 kbit/s。

② 数字数据业务：高品质数字线路。需要数字信号单元（而不是调制解调器）更贵些，但是可以获得更高的数据速率。

非交换式（租赁）	速率
模拟	4.8~56 kbit/s
数字数据业务	2.4~56 kbit/s
T-1	1.54 Mbit/s
帧中继	1.54~44.736 Mbit/s
T-3	44.736 Mbit/s
SONET	51.84 Mbit/s~2.488 Gbit/s
交换式（网络式）	Rate
拨号/调制解调器	1.2~56 kbit/s
X.25 分组交换	2.4~56 kbit/s
综合业务数字网	64 kbit/s~1.54 Mbit/s
模拟数字用户线	16 kbit/s~9 Mbit/s
帧中继	1.54~44.736 Mbit/s
SMDS	1.54~44.736 Mbit/s
异步传递模式	25~155 Mbit/s

图 1 美国公共电信运营商的主要技术选择

- T-1,T-3：很多年来，为大业务量话音和数据而最常租用的是 T-1 线路，至今也很常用。T-3 线路是有更大需求的一个普遍选择。
- 帧中继：尽管帧中继是一种交换网技术，但是帧中继也可作为在专用线路上使用的一种便捷、灵活的复用技术。这种方式在用户端需要帧中继设备。
- SONET：速度最快的租用线路，使用 SONET/SDH 可以得到。

公共交换式业务包括以下一些。

- 拨号/调制解调器：连接在公共电话网上的调制解调器提供了一种相对廉价的、能够获得低速数据服务的方式。modem 本身价格不贵，而电话速率在不太长的连接时间内尚能让人接受。对于居民用户来说，这是一种接近普及的接入技术。在组织机构中，许多局域网和私人小交换机都配置了 modem 阵列来提供低成本的、附加的数据传输业务。
- X.25 分组交换：这种较老的备用技术仍然被用来提供数据传送业务。随着图片和多媒体业务的持续增长，以传统数据速率运行的 X.25 正在变得力不从心。典型地，X.25 是基于传送的数据量来收费的。
- 综合业务数字网：综合业务数字网可以在 64 kbit/s 的 B 信道上提供电路交换和 X.25 分组交换业务。它也可提供更高速率的业务。典型地，它的收费是依据呼叫时间来计算的,而与传送的数据量无关。
- 帧中继:它可以提供相当于租用的 T-1 线路速率的交换能力,并且,在一些选择中,速率甚至可以高于 T-1 速率;(另外)它的低开销(优势)使它适合于互联局域网和独立系统。

从这么多不同的租用线路技术和交换技术中做出选择不是一个容易的任务,并且这些技术的变种也增加了选择的困难,而这些变种在其他的国家正在使用。如同人们看到的那样,不同业务的价格结构是不能直接作比较的。这是一个新出现的难题。使问题复杂化的其他问题包括:有组织的、依据广域网需求预测未来业务量的困难以及考虑业务灵活性和用户移动性时预测业务量的困难。

2. 帧中继

帧中继设计用来提供比传统分组交换更高效的传输机制。帧中继的各项标准比 ATM 技术标准制定得更成熟,商业化产品也开发得早一些。因此,帧中继产品拥有坚实的基础。

背景

分组交换的传统方法使用诸如 X.25 之类的用户网络协议。X.25 不但决定了用户网络接口,而且也影响了网络的内部设计。X.25 方法的几个关键特性如下。
- 用来建立和终止虚电路的呼叫控制分组和数据分组在同一个信道和同一个虚电路上传输。事实上,X.25 使用的是带内信令。
- 在第三层进行虚电路的复用。
- 第二层和第三层都具有流量控制和差错控制机制。

X.25 方法导致了大量开销的产生。经过网络的每一跳,数据链路控制协议都涉及了数据帧和应答帧的交换。因此,在每一个中间节点,必须为每一个虚电路维护状态表,这些状态表是为了处理 X.25 协议的呼叫管理和流量控制/拆错控制。当网络中链路上存在错误的可能性相当大时,所有这些开销都是合理的。但对于现代数字通信设备来说,这种方法不是最合适的。今天的网络在高质量、可靠的链路上使用了可靠的数字传输技术,这些链路许多都是光纤。此外,使用光纤和数字传输技术也可获得数据高速传输。在这种环境下,X.25 的开销不但是不必要的,而且还会降低对高速数据速率的有效利用。

(于是),(人们)设计了帧中继用来减少 X.25 协议附加在终端用户系统和分组交换网络上的大部分开销。帧中继和 X.25 分组业务间的主要不同在于:
- 帧中继中,呼叫控制信令由一个单独的逻辑连接来传送。因此,中间节点不需要再在单个连接的基础上维护呼叫控制状态表或处理信息。
- 帧中继中,逻辑链接的复用和交换由第二层而不是第三层完成,撤销了用作处理工作的一个层。
- 在帧中继中,跳与跳之间不存在流量控制和差错控制。端到端的流量控制和差错控制是由高层来负责完成。

因此,用帧中继方式在源端和目的端传递单个用户数据帧,高层产生的应答帧也是以帧的方式进行回应的。在帧中继中,不存在跳与跳之间的数据帧的交换和应答。

我们来考虑这种方式的优点和缺点。相比 X.25 技术,帧中继主要的潜在缺点是失去了逐个链路间的流量控制和差错控制能力(尽管帧中继不提供端到端流量控制和差错控制,但在高层却能容易地提供此项功能)。在 X.25 网络中,单个物理链路承载多个虚电路,链路层协议提供从源主机到分组交换网络以及从分组交换网络到目的主机间的数据可靠传输。除此之外,在网络的每一跳中,链路控制协议可用来保证数据的可靠(传输)。使用帧中继后,这种逐跳间的链路控制消失了。然而,随着传输和交换设备可靠性的提高,这(将)不能算是一个主要的缺点。

帧中继的优点是:可以实现简单高效的通信。(它)简化了用户-网络接口所需的协议功能,对网络内部的处理功能也进行了简化。这样做的(好的)结果是:低层时延和高层吞吐量(性能)的可望提高。研究表明,与 X.25 相比,(通过)使用帧中继,网络吞吐量提高了一个数量级或更多。国际电信联盟的 I.233 建议指出,帧中继将被运用在速率达到 2 Mbit/s 的接入应用中。但是,现在帧中继业务的数据速率可以达到更高。

第 17 单元 程控数字电话交换机介绍

运用数字交换技术的现代程控交换机对世界电信网络产生了重大影响。不管是作为综合数字传输和交换网络的一部分,还是作为模拟交换单元的直接替代产品,程控交换机都带来了许多好处。电信管理部门可以在运营成本和服务特色上从这个系统中得到好处,而用户可以从这个系统中享受到更好的服务质量以及大量的新业务和便利。

1. 数字程控机交换机的发展

当前全电子数字程控交换机显示了电子技术和计算机技术的成功结合。这个结合的成功信号第一次出现在 20 世纪 60 年代早期,然后有二十多年的发展阶段,在这个阶段连续多代的交换系统中都包含了大量的电子设备。在降低成本、提高服务质量、提高机电式电话交换机的可维护性和灵活性的激发下,人们通过利用快速发展的电子和计算机技术研发了这种交换机,而这两种技术都具有已被证明的优势。

电子设备首先应用在了电话交换机的控制部分:存储程序控制。第一部公共程控交换机,No.1 ESS,是由贝尔实验室研发的,1965 年 5 月美国新泽西州的 Succasunna 地区引进了这种设备。这次历史性事件引起了全世界对存储程序控制(交换机)的兴趣。在 19 世纪 70 年代大量的、具有不同程度计算机控制技术的新交换系统被引入(到电话网中)。然而,由于公共电话系统所需要的半导体交换阵列开发过程存在的一些问题,早期的这些系统全部使用了机电式交换设备(比如纵横式和簧片继电器式的)。因此这些混合交换系统都是半电子式的,尽管,为了名声的原因,它们常常被介绍(为电子式的,但事实并不是这样)。

半导体交换机应用到电话(系统)中存在两个障碍。第一个障碍是:具有足够小串话特性的大规模半导体交换矩阵的生产存在困难。如果要消除电路间的干扰,将会对构成交换矩阵的开关断开电阻(性能)要求非常高。(因为)在当时(使用)机电式开关的情况下,半导体开关在模拟模式下不能在传输的线性和近无限的断开电阻(二者)之间达到平衡。第二个障碍是:当时的半导体设备处理不了传统电话所要求的高电压和铃流。

值得一提的是:人们成功开发了一些使用模拟电子开关的小型私人小交换机 PABX(使用了振幅调制/时分复用技术)。它们容量较小,典型地,最多有 200 门电话,这样可以把线间串话控制到足够低,而高电压障碍可以通过使用特殊的话机(克服)达到最低要求。很显然,这种情况在公众电话交换网络(PSTN)中不存在。(因此)半导体设备在公众电话交换中的应用不得不等待数字技术的(成熟)应用。数字技术引入到公众电话网以及半导体集成电路设备的发展影响了(模拟技术)向数字技术的转换和(对这)两个问题的解决。

20世纪60年代后期,许多国家开始把数字传输技术以脉冲编码调制PCM的形式引入到它们的网络中。PCM系统最初被应用在汇接网络中来扩展那时的音频对电缆的容量,(方法是)通过称为"线对增益"的24或30信道的复用(来实现的)。数字传输技术在长途路由上直到70年代后期才开始应用,当时同轴电缆上(已经)运行了24或30个信道群路的复用大容量系统。现在,微波-无线和光纤数字传输系统也已经投入运行。

数字技术在交换机系统的第一个应用是在数字(PCM)汇接路由之间充当汇接交换的角色。这克服了由于数字信号不够敏感带来的串话问题,这样大型半导体交换矩阵才能投入使用。显然,汇接和长途交换机不受第二个障碍的影响,原因在于这里没有用户线牵涉其中,不需要处理高电压或铃流。因此,1968年英国邮政局才可能在伦敦安装实验性的数字汇接交换机,这带来了电话业务很多年蓬蓬勃勃的成功。CIT-Alcatel公司1970年在法国的Lannion地区安装了世界上第一部公众数字汇接局系统,这(对世界电信发展)起了引导作用。在美国,Bell公司从1976年1月开始引入全电子化数字化公众长途和汇接交换机。(当时)使用了4ESS系统。

数字交换的主要优势在于:它取消了对复用设备的使用,这些复用设备通常是和PCM数字传输系统联系在一起并终止于交换机。因此,把数字交换技术引入PSTN的一个主要动机就是在干线(长途)和汇接网中逐渐取消对模数转换设备的使用。把数字交换和传输技术引入到PSTN中形成一个"综合数字网(IDN)",这(也)是调整计划的一个方面。

然而,数字半导体技术在本地交换机系统中的成功运用还要依赖于对第二个障碍问题的解决,即对高电压和用户线相关电流的处理。普遍采用的解决方法是在交换机外围的接口单元处理所有的高电压和用户线直流通路要求。这样,通过对用户线电流的处理,就可以无障碍地开发电子开关设备了。

因此,半导体技术在用户线交换设备的成功运用就对用户线接口设计的经济性提出了要求。(用户线接口)主要的成本部件是模数转换设备。(但是)直到80年代早期,制造数字交换机用户线接口的成本与当时标准的模拟交换机(比如纵横式和簧片继电器式的)相比都没有吸引力(没有价格优势)。所以,每个第一代数字本地交换机(比如E10、System X和AEX10)系统都装备了两种交换系统。一种形式是模拟的笛簧、中继单元,中继单元用来终止用户线,并把用户线的业务汇集到内部高负载中继线上,这些中继线可以把模数转换器经济地连接在一起;第二种形式是一个数字系统,它把内部的数字干线和外部的干线与汇接数字路由连接在一起。这种混合式的模拟-数字体系结构具有的优势在于:可以避免每个用户线都安装昂贵的PCM编码设备;另外,它还可以通过簧片继电器完成用户线支持功能,从而利用其自身内在的直流金属通路。在这种方法之外,北电公司1980年生产出了世界上第一部全数字化本地交换机系统(DMS 100),这个系统为他们的数字PABX系统开发了模数转换器。

20世纪80年代早期,能提供廉价模数转换的通用集成电路设备的出现有效地降低了用户线接口的成本,才使得全数字交换系统能跟模数混合系统得以竞争。因此,当前的程控交换机(本地的、长途的、骨干的和国际的)都装备了存储程序控制和数字电子开关。(但)在用户线接口部分的一些部件中有些例外,(因为)这些交换机只使用了数字技术。

但是,半导体技术的快速发展也给程控数字交换机的设计者们更宽泛的选择。比如,AT&T 的 5ESS 系统就为一些用户研发了使用特别开发的模拟半导体设备的程控交换机。

数字程控交换机为系统的管理者和用户带来了很多好处(参看下一部分)。但是,公平地说,其中一些好处来自于存储程序控制的优点,所以模拟程控交换机也能提供这些好处。此外,所有的优点在数字程控交换机和(周围)环境融合为一个(完全的)数字传输环境以前不能叠加在一起(而完全显现出来)。

2. 存储程序控制的优点

① 灵活性。在程控交换机中,硬件受到存储在电可改写存储器中的程序和数据的控制。这个控制过程以一种方式提供了高度的灵活性:交换机硬件是(按照软件的命令来)定制运作的。灵活性有长期和短期的方面。

首先考虑长期方面。在交换系统的发展过程中,人们开发了大量的程序从而使得基本交换机系统能提供各种各样的能力和灵活性来满足管理的需求。这些特制软件覆盖了网络中本地交换机的通用功能,比如,编号、计费和路由选择规则、呼叫类型提供、管理和用户灵活性等。

程控交换系统提供的长期灵活性的一个重要方面是在不中断业务的情况下对交换机系统进行升级。这使得以前不知道的或未指定的新业务能力和灵活性可以在交换机系统的生命期内纳入到系统中。其中一些这样的改善提高可以仅仅通过纳入新软件来实现,比如,为某一类的用户建立的封闭用户群业务的引入。其他的改进比如数字数据交换的引入也要求增加新的软件。程控交换系统能够仅仅通过改变交换设备的状态来提供短期灵活性。因此,交换机的操作能够很快对网络状况做出快速反应。举例来说,路由算法可(通过软件)被改变,这样在网络中可重新进行路由选择以避免拥塞。程控交换系统的短期灵活性使得系统能够进行广泛的管理操作,并且用户设备的提供(价格)可(更)经济,且容易操作。

② 用户端设备便利。程控交换机能使得大量的用户端设备比非程控交换机更便宜且更易操作。设备由管理部门进行合理的配置。之后,这些设备就可以在呼叫-被呼叫的基础上由用户进行操作了。

③ 管理部门设备便利。程控交换机为管理部门提供了大范围的设备操作便利,否则这些管理操作可能会耗费大量资金或者需要提供密集型的劳动(才能完成)。交换机的大部分日常操作涉及对这些设施的使用以及通过相关的本地或远程操作控制中心计算机终端进行(对程控交换机的)访问。

第 18 单元　蓝　牙

蓝牙无线技术是一种近距离通信技术,目的是取代便携设备和固定设备间的线缆,同时还要保持高度的安全性。蓝牙技术的关键特性是鲁棒性、低功耗和低成本。为了把大范围内的设备连接在一起并进行通信,蓝牙技术规范定义了一个统一的架构。

蓝牙技术得到了全球范围的认可,这样一来,世界上任何地方的、允许使用蓝牙的设备都可以和邻近的蓝牙设备互联在一起。允许使用蓝牙技术的电子设备通过短距离的、称为微微网的无线自组网以无线方式连接在一起。在一个微微网中,每个设备最多可以同时和其他 7 个设备进行通信,每个设备也可同时属于几个不同的微微网。当蓝牙设备进入和离开一定的邻近距离,微微网就可以动态地、自动地建立。

蓝牙无线技术的一个重要的长处是:它能够同时进行数据和话音的传输。这样用户就可以享受到多样的、创新性的解决方案,比如话音服务的免提电话、打印和传真功能、掌上电脑的同步、手提笔记本电脑和移动电话应用等。

1. 核心系统

蓝牙规范将蓝牙核心系统定义为一个通用的服务层协议,这个服务层覆盖了七层协议的下四层,通用接入框架(GAP)定义了服务发现层协议(SDP)和所需要的通用协议子集。一个完整的蓝牙应用需要许多的附加服务和高层协议,这些协议是由蓝牙规范的。

有时,蓝牙协议层的最低三层被划分成为一个子系统,这个子系统称为蓝牙控制器。这是一个通用的划分方式,它涉及蓝牙控制器和系统其他部分之间的标准物理通信接口,这些其他部分包括了 L2CAP、业务层和高层(称为蓝牙主机)。尽管这个接口是任选的、非强制的,但是在体系结构的设计上也考虑到了它的存在及特点。通过定义对等层间协议信息的交换,单个蓝牙设备之间能进行互操作;通过定义蓝牙控制器和蓝牙主机之间的通用接口,蓝牙子系统之间也可进行互操作。

图中显示了大量的功能模块以及它们之间的业务和数据路径。图中的功能模块提供了一定的信息。通常,蓝牙规范不定义应用细节,除非某处有互操作需要。

标准交互定义了所有设备间的操作,在这里,蓝牙设备按照规范交换协议信令。蓝牙核心系统协议包括了射频协议、链路控制协议、链路管理协议、逻辑链路控制适配协议,所有这些协议都定义在蓝牙规范的随后几个部分中。

蓝牙核心系统通过大量的业务接入点提供服务,这些业务接入点在图中以椭圆形表示。这些服务包括了控制蓝牙核心系统的基本原语。这些服务可分为 3 种类型,它们是:设备控制服务、传输控制服务和数据服务。设备控制服务用于改善蓝牙设备的性能和模式,传输控制服务用于创建、修改、释放(信道和链路上的)承载业务,数据服务则为承载业务的传输提交数据。通常认为前面两个属于控制层(服务),最后一个属于用户层(服务)。

人们对到蓝牙控制器子系统的服务接口进行了定义,这样,蓝牙控制器就可以被认为是系统的一个标准部分。在这种配置下,蓝牙控制器运行在下三层上,链路控制适配协议层包含了主机系统蓝牙应用的其他部分。标准接口称为主机到控制器的接口(HCI)。这个标准业务接口的实现是可选的。

随着独立主机和控制器通过 HCI 进行通信的可行性增大,人们定义了蓝牙体系结构,实现了人们的大量设想。相比主机,蓝牙控制器被认为具有有限的数据缓存能力。因此,当系统提交链路控制适配协议数据单元(PDU)给控制器,并要求传输到对等设备时,链路控制适配层被认为可以执行部分简单的资源管理功能。这包括了把 L2CAP 层业务数据单元(SDU)分割为更容易管理的协议数据单元(PDU),然后把协议数据单元分成适合控制缓存器大小的开始和中间数据分组,以及为了保证对有业务质量承诺信道的可用性的控制缓存器的管理。

在蓝牙技术中,基带层提供了基本的请求重传(ARQ)协议。链路控制适配(L2CAP)层可以提供进一步的错误检测和到 L2CAP 协议数据单元的重传功能,这是可选功能。这个特点可以推荐给对用户数据有较低错误概率要求的应用。进一步的 L2CAP 可选特性是基于窗口的流量控制机制,这个机制可以在接收设备端对缓存的分配进行管理。这些可选特性在某些情况下扩展了蓝牙技术的服务质量(QoS)性能。

尽管这些设想对嵌入式蓝牙技术应用(在单个系统中,这些应用包含了所有的层次)来说也许不是必需的,但是在定义总体框架和 QoS 模型时,头脑中必须考虑这些设想。实际上,(最终)定义(结果)为一个通用的、最低级的系统。

有必要对蓝牙核心系统应用进行自动的、一致性测试。这可以通过测试仪经过射频接口和测试控制接口控制应用(部分)来达到目的,射频接口对于蓝牙系统来说是通用的,而测试控制接口则只是在做一致性测试时才需要。

测试仪通过射频接口和测试应用(IUT)进行信息交换,(从而)保证来自远端的设备请求能够得到正确的回复。测试仪通过测试控制接口(TCI)来控制 IUT,使 IUT 通过射频接口发起信息交换,这样设备的一致性就得到了验证。

对每一个体系框架层和协议 TCI 使用不同的命令集合(业务接口)。HCI 指令集的子集被颁布为蓝牙控制器子系统内的每个层和协议的 TCI 业务接口。使用一个单独的接口来测试 L2CAP 层和协议。蓝牙核心规范中没有定义 L2CAP 业务接口,而是单独在 TCI 规范中进行了定义。L2CAP 业务接口实现只需作一致性测试就可以了。

2. 为什么选择蓝牙无线技术?

蓝牙无线技术对于设备间简便的、无线的、短距离通信是一个简单的选择。它是一个全球接受的技术标准,可以无线连接移动电话、手提电脑、汽车、立体声耳机、MP3 播放器等。由于其理念框架的独特性,可使用蓝牙的产品不需要安装驱动软件。现在,人们已经定义了该技术的第四版蓝牙规范。鉴于其与生俱来的特性,诸如尺寸小、低功耗、低成本、高安全性、生命力强、易操作、具备 ad hoc 网络能力等,该技术发展前景广阔。蓝牙无线技术是目前市场上首屈一指的、唯一被证实的短距离无线通信技术;在 2005 年年底,它每星期都在原有的 50 亿个单元的基础上增加五百多万个新单元。

3. 全球可利用

蓝牙无线技术规范对于遍及世界的公司来说都是免费的。来自许多产业的制造商正忙于在他们的产品中实现蓝牙技术,这样可以减少线路的混乱、进行无缝通信连接、汇流立体声音频、进行数据的传输或话音通信的承载。蓝牙技术工作在 2.4 GHz,这是其中一个未注册的工业、科学、医学用无线频段。同样地,蓝牙技术的使用没有成本。你必须向蜂窝网提供者订购使用 GSM 或 CDMA(网络),而除了你的设备的成本外,蓝牙技术在使用(过程)中是没有成本的。

4. 设备的范围

蓝牙技术可以应用在范围空前的应用中,这些应用从移动电话到汽车再到医学设备用户,这些设备被消费者、工业市场、公司和其他更多的应用而使用。功耗低、体积小、成本低的芯片解决方案使得蓝牙技术可以应用在很小很小的设备中。看看蓝牙产品目录中和元件产品清单中列出的、我们成员(公司)们制造的范围广泛的各种产品,(就明白蓝牙技术的设备应用有多广泛了)。

5. 使用简单

蓝牙技术是一种无线自组网技术,它不需要安装固定的设备装置,并且容易安装。设备间不需要使用电缆进行连接。对于新用户来说使用过程是容易的——拿到贴有蓝牙商标的产品,检查设备描述,把它同其他具有相同描述的蓝牙设备连接在一起。接下来的 PIN 码过程容易得就像你在 ATM 取款机上鉴别自己一样。当这些全都完成之后,你就随身携带了你的个人局域网(PAN),并且甚至可以和其他的个人局域网相连。

6. 全球接受的规范

蓝牙无线技术是现代市场上得到最广泛支持的、多功能的、安全的无线标准。全球性的资格认证程序测试成员们的产品,保证它们与技术标准一致。自从 1999 年发布了第一个蓝牙规范,已经有 4000 多个公司成为蓝牙特别兴趣组织(SIG)的成员。同时,市场上蓝牙产品的数量也在飞速的成倍增长。产品数量已经连续四年翻倍了,到 2005 年年底很可能达到 50 亿个单元的安装基数。

7. 安全连接

从一开始,蓝牙技术在设计时就把安全需要牢记在心。因为开放性的 2.4 GHz ISM 频段全球都可使用,所以鲁棒性从一开始就是内置到蓝牙系统中的。它使用自适应跳频技术(AFH)(来减少干扰),信号在不同的频率间跳转,这样就限制了来自其他信号的干扰。更进一步地,蓝牙技术具有内置的安全措施,比如 128 位加密和 PIN 码认证。当蓝牙产品识别到自己的同类时,第一次连接时使用 PIN 码认证。一旦连接成功,则始终(认为)是安全的连接。

第 19 单元　基于事件的半球形成像 RFID 一体化物联网辅助应用

1. 介绍

对大范围远程行为,比如政府设备、公共建筑物或工业环境的实时监控是许多监控应用的先决条件。这些(监控)行为被证实在较小范围空间内(比如家庭和办公室),也是一个辅助性的、有用的补充。现代基于视频的监控系统使用功能强大的实时分析技术,应用广泛。此外,为了提供大范围的监控而使用了多个摄像机,且为了保证监控对象的清晰度而对监控摄像机之间的协作提出了需求,这种协作主要是为了探测感兴趣事件,这些事件增加了系统的复杂度。

射频识别(RFID)技术是对象识别的经过证明的理想方法。它已经被成功地应用在许多地方,比如企业存货的供应链管理和跟踪,当然还有对象识别。经证明,RFID 对普适计算和任何东西的识别也是有用的。RFID 和无线传感器以及纳米技术已经结合在一起形成所谓的物联网。

对几乎每一个普适计算应用来说,另一个必需的要求是实时定位,这来自于对即时可控信息的内在需求。以前,许多系统使用不同的技术解决了自动定位感应问题。本文中我们详细讨论了发展视频监控和 RFID 结合在一起的混合系统的可行性,目的是为了能在视频摄像机的输出端进行自动识别和目标追踪提供一个可靠系统。为了减少对多个摄像机的使用需求讨论了半球形成像摄像机,该摄像机可以使监控系统的覆盖范围最大化,并且明确了影响系统目的的一些因素。

本文的其余部分是这样安排的:第二部分我们概述了 RFID、视频处理技术以及其他的补充性技术;第三部分叙述了利用 RFID 传感器、视频摄像机和二者综合的与监控相关的研究;第四部分描述了必需部件,这些部件是系统必需的硬件和软件,讨论了系统的优点和缺点以及可能的应用问题;第五部分描述了这种综合的可能应用情况。

2. 潜在的技术问题

(1) RFID 概述

普适计算的其中一个关键技术是 RFID 技术。RFID 被划分为宽泛的自动识别技术,它是一个用来描述通过无线形式用无线电波来传送对象识别(以独一无二的序列号的形式)系统的通用词汇。一个典型的 RFID 系统由几部分组成:(a) RFID 标签,包含了一个与它连接的物理对象相关的数字号码;(b) RFID 读卡机(也可称为询问应答机),通常和后端数据库相连。读卡机还安装了天线、转发器和处理器,处理器为了询问标签并读懂内容而广播无线信号。

RFID 系统的最重要的两个特征在某些环境下的范围、数据转发传输上包含不同之处:(a) 能量来源和 RFID 标签的计算能力,(b) 操作频率。按照第一个特征,RFID 标签可分为有源和无源的或二者的结合物。有源标签使用电池且能够在大的作业范围内高质量地自主传递信号,但是价格昂贵且通常体积较大。另一方面,无源标签需要外部能源来激励信号的传输,这个过程需要利用感应耦合或电磁捕获技术,它们利用输入模块和读卡机通信。由于无源标签技术的成本低、体积小以及无限的实际使用寿命,所以它们应用得比有源标签广泛,在很多情况下更受欢迎。此外,RFID 系统可分为四种操作频率:(a) 低频,(b) 高频,(c) 特高频,(d) 超高频(或微波)。随着频率的增加,传输范围和传输速率随之增加,但是对水和物质(比如金属)的穿透力却随之降低。

建立统一的工程标准、方法、过程和定义 RFID 系统特征的实践的需求引发了不同标准(的建立),其中两个标准尤其突出。EPC 全球定义了一个划分标签的复合方法,详细说明了唯一的识别数字(电子产品编码)、频率、耦合方法、电键调制类型、信息存储能力和彼此之间的互操作模式。类似的,ISO(与 IEC 组织联合)开发了识别标准,读卡机和标签之间通信、中间件协议和测试、兼容和安全的标准。

① 识别和 RFID

通常,普适系统的一个十分重要的要求是能够唯一地识别物品和实体,而 RFID 与生俱来的能够满足这种要求。还有几种其他技术能够适合这个目的,每种都有优点和缺点,但是在大多数应用领域都被 RFID 强势取代了。

条形码是光学的、机器可读的、一次写的物品分类表示,它依然是供应链管理中应用最广泛的跟踪产品,也是最便宜的识别方法。条形码技术的最大缺陷是不能提供单个物品的额外信息(但是涉及这个问题的二维象征学)和对条形码物品需在瞄准线以内的要求。

卡片技术是另一类物体识别技术和相应的实体,它包括了磁卡、智能卡和光学卡。这些卡片通常都内嵌有信用卡体积大小的塑料卡片,它们包含了磁条或集成电路,并且具有较大的存储能力。一旦它们包含了微处理器,就具有增强的处理能力,这样这些卡片就可被运用在苛刻的应用中,比如可靠性应用中(但是具有较大的限制)。不过,大部分卡片都要求紧贴或非常靠近读卡器。在应用中,卡的成本也随着卡的特性(的上升)而显著上升。RFID 技术在功效和成本效率之间达到了平衡,同时降低了对瞄准线以内的需求。这就是为什么 RFID 在接入控制、反伪造和跟踪追查应用中能够应用广泛的原因了。

② 实时定位和 RFID

RFID 主要用作识别,过去十年来来的(对 RFID 的)研究成就集中在 RFID 用作实时定位上。还有许多 RFID 的竞争性或补充性的实时定位技术,它们的差别在于:精确度、精密度、复杂度和成本。

用作无线设备互联的 Wi-Fi(也称为 IEEE 802.11)技术大概是配置有 Wi-Fi 标签的定位装置(用来定位)的完美方法,比如膝上型电脑和掌上电脑已经能(使用 Wi-Fi 技术)连接到无线网络中。但是,Wi-Fi 实时定位技术对网络基础设施依赖性较高,它具有严重的扩展性问题,引入了相当的网络负担,容易受到大多数无线技术都能碰到的恶劣环境条件下问题的影响,比如障碍物、温度、湿度。

蓝牙(Bluetooth)是与 Wi-Fi 相似的另一实时定位技术,它是为低功耗和单人范围内网络通信而设计的无线组网标准。蓝牙是标准化的、被广泛采用的、多用途的且相对精确的(定位技术)。然而,蓝牙的接入点范围相当短;并且由于它的询问过程,配置时延相对较长。和 Wi-Fi 一样,蓝牙标签不适合非常小的物体目标。

超宽带(UWB)是另一种可用在低功耗、短距离、高带宽通信环境的无线技术。UWB 系统能够提供小到几个厘米的高精确度,但是 UWB 信号通过金属和液态物质时的干扰一直是常态问题,并且其系统成本至少对小规模应用来说是过分昂贵了。

ZigBee 技术是一种低成本、低功耗的无线网状网组网私有标准。因为它已经标准化过了,所以对来自不同厂商的设备的互操作能力是可以保证的。它在低信噪比环境下也具有优越的性能,且具有容错能力。然而,ZigBee 路由器的工作范围短,信号对墙壁和其他障碍物的穿透力较弱(衰减大)。

至于 RFID,无源和有源标签都可以用作实时定位。无源标签成本非常低,可以安装连接到几乎任何物体上。它们也适合较高的阅读速率(大约为 1 500 个标签/秒)。但是无源标签对恶劣环境的容忍性较差,且为了达到对较宽区域的覆盖它们需要许多个读卡器和天线。另一方面有源标签提高了精确度和容忍能力;但是因为有源标签的使用寿命是有限的,它们对系统维护提出了严重的挑战。当前,没有最好的实时定位感应技术。当应用到真实的环境中时每种技术都有自己独特的性能。(在这之中的)选择显然是在准确度、精确度、系统复杂度和对特定环境的适应能力之间的平衡折中。

(2) 视频监控

闭路电视形式的视频监控已经被广泛应用在使用人类操作员的监控应用中,人在此处估计事件,以此来提供警惕。这些系统主要安装在安全受到主要关注的公共场合。但是,由于人会疲惫或注意力不集中,(所以)监控过程涉及的人的因素极大的影响了监控的有效性。

智能监控(IS)系统已经被开发出来进行目标的自动检测,为了对发生在现场的任何反常行为进行反应,从而跟踪人迹,识别事件。很多文献已经对 IS 系统进行了广泛研究,并为许多应用(尤其是在没法使用人类操作员的情况下)提出了解决办法。最近,这些系统已经被考虑应用在普适应用中,这些应用包括了家庭、电子健康和电子照看系统中。

但是，IS系统仍然有局限性。即使摄像机配备了广角镜头，为了覆盖大的空间范围仍需安装很多摄像机。在这种情况下，由于广泛安装视频监控不能被公众广泛接受，这也限制了它的接受度。尽管在一些情况下安装摄像机证明是有用的，比如在老人的家庭照顾环境下。

因此，这些系统的图像处理模块对复杂环境的变化和对象蔽塞很敏感，对象蔽塞是由跟踪对象隐藏在另一个对象后面引起的。此外，视频相机（通常比静态相机的分辨率低）不能有效监测小的或远的物体。

视频摄像机配备的CCD设备的噪声也影响了目标定位性能。最后，多摄像机环境和对存储能力的要求导致了额外的成本，这些额外成本来自购买高端PC和存储阵列。

第20单元　图像和视频

1. 视频

人类的眼睛有一种特性：当图像在视网膜上闪过时，在从视网膜上消失前能保持几毫秒的时间。如果一系列的图像以每秒50幅或更快的速度在视网膜上闪过时，眼睛注意不到它正在看到的是离散的图像（即眼睛看到的是连续的图像）。所有的视频（比如电视）系统都是利用了这个原理来（使人的眼睛）产生图像是运动的（的感觉）。

为了了解视频系统，最好（的方法）是从简单的、老式的黑白电视机开始。为了把面前的二维图像表示成一维的电压形式（时间的函数），照相机扫描电子束飞快地扫过图像，然后扫描下面的图像，并记录它扫过的光强。在扫描的末端，称为一帧，电子束回扫。作为时间函数的光强是要广播的，接收器重复扫描过程用来重建图像。照相机和接收机使用的扫描方式如图1所示（要补充的是，CCD相机是用来成像的而不作扫描用，但是部分相机和所有的监视器都作扫描用）。

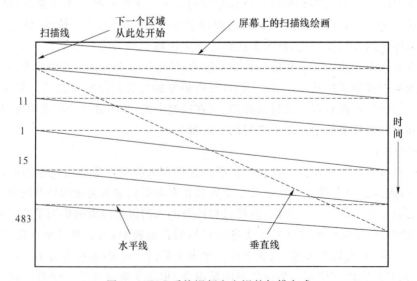

图1　NTSC系统视频和电视的扫描方式

确切的扫描参数各国有一些不同。北美、南美和日本所用的系统是 525 条扫描线的,水平和垂直方向比是 4∶3,每秒 30 帧。欧洲系统使用 625 线,方向比同样是 4∶3,每秒 25 帧。在这两种系统中,最上面和最下面的几条线不显示(在原始的圆形 CRT 中大致是长方形的)。525 NTSC 扫描系统中只有 483 条扫描线可以显示出来(625 PAL/SECAM 系统中有 576 条线可以显示)。在垂直回扫期间电子束是关掉的,所以许多电视台(尤其是欧洲国家的)用这段间隙来广播文电信息(包含了新闻、天气、体育和证券价格等的文本页)。

25 帧/秒的速度捕捉平滑的运动图像已经足够,但是在这个帧速下,许多人尤其是老人可能会感觉到图像在闪烁(因为在新的图像显示之前,旧的图像已经从视网膜上消失)。解决这个问题不需要增加帧速,(因为)增加帧速就要求更多的带宽,而是使用了一种不同的方法,而带宽对于系统来说是稀缺的(资源)。(这种方法是)不是按顺序显示所有行,而是首先显示所有的奇数行,然后显示偶数行,这些半帧称为域。实验表明:尽管人们在 25 帧/秒速度时能察觉到图像的闪烁,但是在 50 域/秒时却感觉不到。这种技术称为交织,不交织的电视或视频成为逐行式的(扫描)。

彩色视频使用的扫描方式和黑白式的一样,除了使用运动的电子束显示图像外,还使用了 3 个一直运动的电子束。一个电子束的作用是显示 3 个加色法基色中的一个颜色。这项技术的工作原理是任何一种颜色都可以表示为红、绿、蓝适当浓度的 3 种颜色的线性组合。然而,为了能在同一信道中进行传输,3 种颜色必须合成为一个单一的复合信号。人们发明彩色电视后,很多种显示色彩的方法从技术上都是可能的,不同的国家做出了不同的选择(注意:这些选择和 VHS 对 Betamax 对 P2000 没有关系,它们是记录方法),这样导致了现有各种系统互不兼容(的情况)。在所有国家,彩色节目能被现有的黑白电视机接收都是一个政治要求。所以,(在这种要求下)最简单的方法(这种方法就是仅仅把 RGB 三色信号单独编码)是不能被接受的,而 RGB 也不是最有效的方法。

第一个彩色系统的标准是由美国国家电视标准委员会制定的,NTSC 标准名字的缩写就是由此而来。几年后,欧洲引进了彩色电视,那时电视技术已经取得了实质性的提高,即具有了较大的噪声免疫能力和更好的色彩。这些(技术)称为 SECAM(顺序传送,彩色与存储),应用在法国和东欧,PAL 逐行倒相制式应用在欧洲的其他国家。NTSC 和 PAL/SECAM 制式色彩质量的差别已经造成了一个工业玩笑,那就是 NTSC 的的确确象征着对同一色彩绝对不会有第二次(扫描的机会)。

尽管这 3 种系统从 RGB 信号得到亮度和色度信号时采用了不同的系数,但为了使黑白接收机能接收到以彩色形式传输的信号,都使用 RGB 信号线性地合成出了一个亮度信号和两个色度信号。有意思的是,人类的眼睛对亮度信号远比对色度信号敏感,所以色度信号不需要传输得那么精确。因此,色度信号可以以和黑白信号一样的频率广播出去,它就能被黑白电视机接收到。两个亮度信号可以在窄带上以较高频率广播出去。为了能单独控制这 3 个信号,一些电视机上设置有控制标签,标记着亮度、色调和饱和度(或亮度、色调和颜色)(等词语)。要想理解视频压缩的工作原理就需要了解色度和亮度(的含义)。

2. 视频点播(VoD)

视频点播常常被比作电子录像租借店。使用者(客户)从大量的视频资料中选择任何一个,然后带回家中观看。只是在视频点播技术中,选择是在家中通过电视遥控器完成的,并且视频可以马上播放,不需要在租借店和家之间往返。不用多说,实现视频点播技术比描述的(言语)有一点复杂。在这部分,我们将对视频点播的情况和实现进行简要的描述。一个真实的实现方法在 Nelson 和 Linton(1995)(的文章)中有描述。有关互动电视的一个更笼统的描述可参考 Hodge1995(的文章)。另外一些相关参考文献是 Chang 等(1994)、Hodge 等(1993)、Little and Venkatesh (1994) (的文章)。

视频点播真的类似租借录像带?或更类似于从 500 或 5 000 个有线电视系统中找到一个电影观看?答案具有重要的技术暗示效果。特别的,录像租借人需要知道(是否)能够停止录像播放,快步到厨房或洗手间去,然后再从录像停止处重新开始。(但是)电视观众却不能期望让节目暂停。

如果视频点播想要在和录像租借店的竞争中获胜,它必须允许用户能任意停止、开始和倒带。要提供用户这个能力几乎就是迫使视频提供者给每个用户一个单独的视频拷贝。

另一方面,如果视频点播被看作是高级电视,而视频提供者播放流行视频,比如,每隔 10 分钟,不停的播放,它的功能足够了。为了等待视频开始,想观看流行视频的用户可能需要等待 10 分钟以上。尽管暂停/重新开始在此处是不可能的,但观众也可以在短暂的间歇之后回到起居室,然后 10 分钟之后转到另一个播放相同视频的频道。其中的一些资料可以重播,但是并没有错过什么(重要的片断)。这种机制称为近视频点播。它具有低成本的潜力,因为(在这种方式下)来自视频服务器的、相同的数据可以同时传送给许多用户。视频点播和近视频点播的差别类似于自己驾驶汽车和乘公交车之间的不同。

一旦宽带网络开通,(近)视频点播只是大量潜在新业务中的一种业务。在系统中心我们看到了一个高带宽(国家或国际的)的广域骨干网。连接到其上的是成千上万个本地分配网络,比如有线电视网或电话公司分配系统。本地分发系统到达(被接入)人们家里,终止于机顶盒。事实上,机顶盒(就)是功能强大的特种个人计算机。

成千上万个信息提供者通过高带宽的光纤连接到骨干网上。其中一些信息提供者提供按次付费视频或按次付费音频 CD 业务。另外一些还将提供特别的服务,比如家庭购物(具有旋转一罐汤并放大来观察成分列表,或观看如何操作草坪汽油动力修剪机的视频素材的能力)、运动、新闻、返回"I Love Lucy",毫无疑问,WWW 接入和数不清的其他服务将成为现实。

本地多任务缓冲处理服务器包括在系统中,它允许视频预先放置在离用户较近的地方,这样可以在峰值负载时间节省带宽。如何把这些部分融合在一起,并且哪个将会赢得胜利在工业界引起了激烈的讨论。下面我们将仔细讨论系统的一个主要部分:视频服务器。

3. 视频服务器

为了实现(近)视频点播,我们需要能同时存储和输出大量视频电影的视频服务器。已经制作出来的电影的总量估计有 65 000 部左右(Minoli1995 年统计)。当被压缩为 MPEG-2 格式时,一部普通的电影大概需要 4 GB 的存储空间,则 65 000 部电影就需要大约 260 TB 空间。再加上以前制作完成的、旧的电视节目、体育节目、新闻影片、购物商品目录等,很明显,存在一个具有工业强度的存储问题。

磁带是存储大量信息最廉价的方法。(使用磁带存储数据最经济)这个事实一直以来都是如此,将来可能也是这样。DAT 磁带可以以 5 美元/吉字节的成本存储 8 GB 数据(两个电影的大小)。大型的机械磁带服务器可容纳上千盒录像带,它的机械手可以取到任意一盒录像带,并把它塞入录像驱动器,现在这种服务器在商业上是可实现的。这些系统存在的问题是：访问时间（尤其是对于磁带上的第 2 部电影），传输速率和磁带驱动器有限性（同时为 n 部电影提供服务，该单元将会需要 n 个驱动器）。

幸运的是，视频租借店、公共图书馆和其他组织的经验表明，不是所有的录像都受到（消费者的）同样的欢迎。从经验上来说，当有 N 部电影可看时，对第 k 个最流行的电影的请求占所有请求的比例为 C/k（Chervenak 1994）。这里 C 被计算为归一化，而总数为 1，即
$$C=1/(1+1/2+1/3+1/4+1/5+\cdots+1/N)$$

因此，最流行的电影被选中的几率是全部 7 个电影中平均几率的 7 倍（假设这里共有 7 部电影）。此结论就是著名的 Zipf's 定律（Zipf, 1949）。

一些电影比另外一些电影更流行的事实暗示了（存储问题）的一个可能的解决方法：存储层次结构的形式，如图 2 所示。在这个图里，（某种机制）所处层次越高，性能也越好。

图 2　视频服务器的存储层次结构

现在我们简单看一下视频服务器的软件。CPU 被用来接收用户请求、定位电影所在位置、在设备之间移动数据、用户收费和其他功能。其中一些功能对时间的要求不高，但是许多功能对时间的要求就很苛刻。因此，一些 CPU（不是所有）就必须运行实时操作系统，比如实时 microkernel 系统。这些系统通常把工作分解成更小的任务，每个任务都有一个明确的最后期限。然后调度器就运行一个算法（安排时间来完成每个任务），比如临近单调算法速度的最接近最后期限算法。

第五部分

附 录

Ⅰ 数学公式的英语读法

1. Logic

$\exists$	there exit
$\forall$	for all
$p \Rightarrow q$	p implies q ; if p , then q
$p \Leftrightarrow q$	p is equivalent to q ; p and q is equivalent

2. Sets

$x \in A$	x belongs to A ; x is an element of A
$x \notin A$	x does not belong to A ; x is not an element of A
$A \subset B$	A is contained in B ; A is a subset of B
$A \supset B$	A contains B ; B is a subset of A
$A \cap B$	A cap B ; A meet B ; A intersection B
$A \cup B$	A cup B ; A join B ; A union B
A/B	A devides by B ; the difference between A and B
$A \times B$	A cross B ; the product of A and B

3. Real numbers

$x+1$	x plus one
$x-1$	x minus one
$x \pm 1$	x plus or minus one
xy	xy ; x , multiplied by y
$(x+1)(x-1)$	x plus one, x minus one
x/y	x over y
$x = 5$	x equals 5; x is equal to 5
$x \neq 5$	x (is) not equal to 5
$x \equiv 5$	x is equivalent to (or identical with) 5
$x > 5$	x is greater than 5

$x \geq 5$	x is greater than or equal to 5
$x < 5$	x is less than 5
$x \leq 5$	x is less than or equal to 5
$0 < x < 1$	zero is less than x is greater than 1
$\|x\|$	mode x ; modulus x
x^2	x squared; x to the power 2
x^3	x cubed; the cube of x ; the third power of x
x^n	the nth power of x ; x to the power of n ; x to the nth
$\sqrt{x}$	the square root of x , root x
$\sqrt[3]{x}$	the cube root of x
$\sqrt[n]{x}$	the nth root of x
$n!$	n factorial
$\bar{x}$	the mean value of x , x bar
x_i	x subscript i ; x suffix i ; x sub i

4. Functions

$f(x)$	fx ; f of x ; the function of x
$x \to y$	x maps to y ; x is sent (or mapped) to y
$f'(x)$	f prime x ; f dash x ; the (first) derivative of f with respect to x
$\frac{\partial f}{\partial x}$	the partial (derivative) of f with respect to x
$\frac{\partial^2 f}{\partial x^2}$	the second partial (derivative) of f with respect to x
$\int_0^\infty$	the integral from zero to infinity
$\lim_{x \to 0}$	the limit as x approaches zero
$\lim_{x \to +0}$	the limit as x approaches zero from above
$\lim_{x \to -0}$	the limit as x approaches zero from below
$\log_e y$ ($\ln y$)	log y to the base e; natural log (of) y

Ⅱ 数的表示与读法

1. 基数的读法(How to Read Cardinal Numbers)

表示数目多少的数字叫基数。如 0 (zero)、1 (one)、19 (nineteen)等。其读法有一些基本规则：

(1) 21～99 的基数，先说"几十"，再说"几"，中间加连字号，如 24(twenty-four)。

(2) 101～999 的基数，先说"几百"，再加 and，再加末位数，如 156 (a/one hundred and fifty-six)；但也有不用 and 的情况，如 850 可读作 eight hundred fifty。

(3) 1 000 以上的数，先从后向前数，每三位加一","。第一个","前为 thousand，第二个","前为 million，第三个","前为 billion(美式)或 thousand million(英式)。如：20 654 693 读作 twenty million six hundred and fifty-four thousand six hundred and ninety-three。

(4) 幂次的读法，如 10^{19} 读作 one followed by nineteen zeros。

(5) 注意：hundred, thousand, million, billion, trillion 等词一般是单数形式。如 two hundred, three million, five billion 等。

2. 序数的读法(How to Read Ordinal Numbers)

表示顺序的数字称为"序数"，如第一、第二等。序数词一般以与之相应的基数词加词尾 th 构成，如 fourth(第四)，但也有特别的地方，主要表现在以下几方面：

(1) one—first; two—second; three—third; five—fifth; eight—eighth; nine—ninth; twelve—twelfth 等。

(2) 以-ty 结尾的词，要先变 y 为 i，再加-eth，如 twenty-twentieth; forty-fortieth 等。

(3) 以 one, two, three, five, eight, nine 收尾的序数词，要按第 1 条方法变，如 thirty-one (thirty-first); eighty-two (eighty-second)。

(4) 序数词有时用缩略形式，如 first (1st); second (2nd); fourth (4th); twenty-third (23rd)。

(5) 序数词表示顺序时，前面常加定冠词，如 The first World War, the third lesson。

3. 分数的读法

分数由分子、分母和分数线组成。在英语中，一般用基数词代表分子，序数词代表分母，除了分子是 1 的情况外，序数词都要用复数，具体如下：

$\dfrac{1}{2}$ one half

$\dfrac{1}{3}$ one third

$\dfrac{3}{5}$ three fifths

$\dfrac{1}{29}$ one twenty-ninth

$\dfrac{3}{178}$ three over one hundred seven-eight

$4\dfrac{2}{7}$ four and two-sevenths

$45\dfrac{23}{89}$ forty-five and twenty-three over eighty-nine

4. 小数的读法

小数由三部分组成，即整数位区、小数位区和小数点。整数部分按照基数读，小数部分的表达需分别读出每个数，小数点读作 point。

（1）整数位区不为零的小数称为"混合小数"。其读法是整数区按照整数的读法，小数点之后的数字按照小数的读法。如 3.576，读作 three point five seven six。又如 2 050.035 7，读作 two thousand and fifty point zero three five seven。

（2）若小数的整数位为零，如 0.45，读作 zero point four five 或 point four five。

（3）若小数是 0.1，0.01，0.001 等，则可读作 one tenth, one hundredth, one thousandth 或 point one, point zero one, point zero zero one。

（4）小数可分为非循环小数和循环小数。如 0.37 读作 zero point thirty-seven；$0.\overset{..}{3}\overset{..}{7}$ 读作 zero point three seven recurring；$0.25\overset{..}{3}\overset{..}{7}$ 读作 zero point two five thirty-seven recurring。

参 考 文 献

[1] 李霞. 电子与通信专业英语. 北京:电子工业出版社,2007.
[2] 翟少成,吴军其. 电子信息工程专业英语导论. 北京:清华大学出版社,2008.
[3] 韩定定,赵菊敏. 信息与通信工程专业英语. 北京:北京大学出版社,2006.
[4] 赵萱,郑仰成. 科技英语翻译. 北京:外语教学与研究出版社,2005.
[5] 刘爱军,王斌. 科技英语综合教程. 北京:外语教学与研究出版社,2007.
[6] 宋宏. 前沿科技英语阅读文选——电子通信篇. 北京:国防工业出版社,2007.
[7] 陶亚雄. 通信技术专业英语. 北京:电子工业出版社,2008.
[8] 丁宁. 电子信息技术专业英语. 北京:机械工业出版社,2008.
[9] 常义林,任志纯. 通信工程专业英语. 西安:西安电子科技大学出版社,2001.
[10] Yasuhiro Koike and Takaaki Ishigure. High-Bandwidth Plastic Optical Fiber for Fiber to the Display. JOURNAL OF LIGHTWAVE TECHNOLOGY, VOL. 24, NO. 12, DECEMBER 2006.
[11] Misha Brodsky, Nicholas J. Frigo, Misha Boroditsky and Moshe Tur. JOURNAL OF LIGHTWAVE TECHNOLOGY, VOL. 24, NO. 12, DECEMBER 2006.
[12] 陈杰美. 通信与信息工程专业英语教程. 北京:电子工业出版社,2006.
[13] William Stallings. Business Data Communications(影印版). 北京:清华大学出版社,2005.
[14] Timothy Kwok, The New Paradigm for Internet-Intranet&Residential Broadband Services&Applications(影印版). 北京:清华大学出版社,2005.
[15] V. Kolias, I. Giannoukos, C. Anagnostopoulos, V. Loumos, E. Kayafas. Integrating RFID on Event-based Hemispheric Imaging for Internet of Things Assistive Applications. PETRA'10, June 23-25, 2010, Samos, Greece.